UNIVERSAL TORAH

Lessons for Humanity from the Weekly Torah Readings

by

Rabbi Avraham Greenbaum

Edited by Nachum Shaw

Promised Land

JERUSALEM LONDON NEW YORK

ISBN 978-09956560-5-5

For further information:

Promised Land Publishers

Apt. 8, 5 Gimmel Alroyi St.

Jerusalem 9210808

ISRAEL

or

Promised Land Publishers

8 Woodville Road

London NW11 9TN

ENGLAND

or

Promised Land Publishers

67 Wood Hollow Lane

New Rochelle

NY 10804

USA

Email: info@promisedlandpublishers.com

www.promisedlandpublishers.com

בס"ד

UNIVERSAL TORAH

Lessons for Humanity

from the

Weekly Torah Readings

Universal Torah is an archive of commentaries on the weekly Torah portion, sharing thoughts and lessons we may draw from the current parshah having universal significance – both for the Children of Israel, the appointed Guardians of G-d's Torah, and for all the families and nations of the earth.

In our troubled times, when the world is facing war, violence, crime, illness and destruction on an unprecedented scale, mankind is in desperate need of the oldest living system of wisdom in the world: G-d's Holy Torah.

For "G-d is not a man that He should lie, nor the son of man that He should change His mind. He spoke - - will He not do it? He pronounced - - will He not fulfill it?" (Numbers 23:19). "For I am G-d, I have not changed." (Malachi 3:6). "Go and let us ascend to the Mountain of G-d, to the House of the G-d of Jacob." (Isaiah 2:3).

BEREISHIT Genesis

SHEMOT Exodus

VAYIKRA Leviticus

*BAMIDA*BAR Numbers

DEVARIM Deuteronomy

בראשית

GENESIS

BEREISHIT

Torah Reading: Gen. 1:1-6.8.

Haftarah: Isaiah 42:5-43:10 (Sephardi ritual) Isaiah 42:5-21

IN THE BEGINNING

*"H*ow fortunate we are that Moses our Teacher showed us the right way. The Torah begins without any philosophical proof, with the simple words, 'In the beginning G-d created the heaven and the earth.' We are commanded to believe in G-d through faith alone, and not to enter into speculation." (Rabbi Nachman of Breslov).

"In the beginning G-d created...": In the three opening words of the Hebrew Torah, G-d "signs" Himself as the G-d of Truth. The last letters of these three words, BereishiT barA ElokiM, are: Tav - Aleph - Mem, forming an anagram of the word EMeT, ***Truth***.

The Rabbis taught that Teshuvah ("coming back to G-d") was created even before the world. This means that the world is not merely random. Everything that exists in the entire universe is part of a vast, unfathomable system serving a purpose that goes way beyond the system itself, a purpose that existed before the system itself in the "mind" and "will" of the One Who created it. The purpose of the system is to bestow good on all G-d's creatures. We can receive this good only when we "return" to G-d -- by seeking out and following the wisdom of G-d's teaching to mankind: the Torah. Teshuvah!

Today the world seems to be on a helter-skelter path to self-destruction. The only way for us to stop it is by "coming back" to G-d.

* * *

THE GLORY OF ADAM -- AND HIS FALL

At the climax of the account of Creation is the story of the creation of Adam. The Hebrew word ***Adam*** cannot simply be understood as "man" or "human being", "homo sapiens" or the like without further elaboration. The fact that there is a resemblance between the physical form of a human being and that of an ape does not mean they are both in the same category or on the same level. The defining qualities of homo sapiens are precisely those that differentiate him from the ape: his uniquely human powers and abilities. Similarly, the fact that two humans resemble each other in physical structure does not mean that they must be equal and identical in all respects. One may be highly intelligent, creative, loving, etc. while the other could be a psychopath, a terrorist or even a demon incarnate in a human body. What makes the two different is the mind, soul or spirit that inhabits each of their bodies. One may have an elevated soul. The other may have a "fallen" soul or the spirit of a demon. Are they both homo sapiens? Are they both Bney Adam, "Children of Adam"?

While the human body is the physical manifestation of ***Adam***, what makes him unique is the soul that animates his body. The soul that G-d breathed into Adam came from His very essence. Adam's soul was created by G-d to be a separate creature, giving him the ability to connect with G-d ***of his own free will***. Adam's destined role in Creation is to lead the entire world to return to G-d. He was appointed ruler over all: "Be fruitful and multiply and fill the world and conquer it and rule over the fish of the sea and the birds of the heavens and over all the living creatures swarming over the earth" (Gen. 1:28). Man has responsibility for the whole world. His task is to attain global peace and ecological balance and harmony, in which all are united in the service of G-d.

Adam was created to attain this exalted destiny of his own free will. As part of G-d's plan, Adam therefore had to be confronted with a choice: to serve G-d by obeying His command, or to follow the "serpent" in his own heart, who tells him he can disobey G-d, do what he wants, and still get away with it. G-d says "If you disobey you will die". But the serpent in the heart lies to us: "Do what you want -- you won't die!" Time after time, man falls for the trick.

Adam was created to rule the entire world, but he cannot even rule over his own heart -- and sins. When a person comes to his senses and understands what he has done by eating the forbidden fruit of evil, he discovers the painful truth. "With the sweat of your brow you will eat bread until you return to the earth, for from it you were taken, for you are dust and to dust you will return" (Gen. 3:19). After Adam's sin, life is a constant struggle, leading only to the grave. Only with death can sin be finally atoned. "To dust you will return". This is because everything must "return"! Everything must come back to G-d! Teshuvah! Man's task is to return to his destiny, which is to conquer the world and join it back to G-d. "Who is mighty? He who conquers his evil inclination" (Avot 4:1).

* * *

THE COMMANDMENTS THAT APPLY TO ALL MANKIND

"And the L-rd G-d commanded the Man saying, 'from all the trees of the garden you may surely eat'" (Gen. 2:16). The Rabbi's taught that G-d's commandment to Adam implies six universal laws which are all allusively contained in the Hebrew words of this verse (as discussed in Midrash Rabbah Bereishit 45:5 and Talmud Sanhedrin 56a; see Rambam Mishneh Torah Laws of Kings 9:1):

1. Idolatry is forbidden.

2. Blasphemy is forbidden.

3. Murder is forbidden.

4. Sexual immorality is forbidden.

5. Robbery is forbidden.

6. Men must govern their affairs under a system of law and justice.

These six laws, together with the prohibition of eating a limb from a living animal (see the following parshah, Gen. 9:4) make up the ***Seven Commandments of the Children of Noah***, also known as the Seven Universal Laws.

* * *

THE PROHIBITION OF MURDER

In the intricate, endlessly profound tapestry of the holy Torah, the Seven Universal Laws are deeply bound up and meshed in with the 613 commandments that apply to the Children of Israel. Thus every portion of the Torah has profound significance for all humanity and each one contains lessons that may deepen our understanding of the Seven Universal Laws.

Of the seven, one that stands out particularly in Parshat Bereishit is the prohibition of murder. The Torah is the "book of the generations of man" (Genesis 5:1): man was commanded to "be fruitful and multiply" -- to breed children and children's children, to cherish and nurture ***life***. The antithesis of life is death. The Rabbis taught that when "G-d saw all that he made and behold it was ***very*** good", The word "very" teaches that even death is beneficial (as it atones for sin). However, death is in the hands of G-d: "See now, for I, I am He, and there is no god with Me; I kill and make alive, I smote and I will heal and there is none to redeem from My hand" (Deut. 32:39). A person who arrogantly takes G-d's prerogative into his own hands and appoints himself as the angel of death to kill another is a shameful, counterfeit ***Adam***, a criminal who should be stoned and then hung ignominiously on a tree before being buried (see Deuteronomy 21:22-3 and Rashi there). Such a man is a "curse of G-d" (ibid). In the words of Rambam (Laws of Murder 1:4): "There is nothing to which the Torah takes greater exception than bloodshed, as it is written (Numbers 35:33): And you shall not pollute the land… for blood -- that is what pollutes the land."

The story of Cain's killing of Abel over the inheritance of the world is the story of human history. Mankind's task is to learn how to settle disputes amicably instead of fighting and killing one another. In our times, it is particularly important to emphasize the criminality of murder because of widespread insensitivity to the seriousness of killing. Many voices can be heard defending killers, and protesting against their execution as prescribed by the Torah. Many in the world even rationalize and justify wholesale murder and violence when committed for the sake of a "cause", and celebrate terrorist attacks against their enemies. This simply illustrates the depths to which "Adam Beliya'al", the Worthless Man, can descend, as in the story of Cain and Abel.

The Torah clearly teaches that murder is an abominable crime which must be requited with death in order to punish the villain and protect human society. Yet at the same time as seeking to impose justice, our societies must also ask themselves why killing, murder and violence are so rampant. These are not inexplicable scourges that have no cause. Our rabbis revealed what causes murder to become rampant: "The sword comes into the world because of the failure to execute justice without delay, because of the perversion of justice and because of those who issue Torah rulings which are not in accordance with the Halachah" (Avot 5:11).

Developing a system of law and government that is just and free of corruption (in fulfilment of the Seventh Universal Law) is the key to cleansing the world of the scourge of murder and violence.

Is it our responsibility to attempt all this? That is the question of Cain: "Am I my brother's keeper?" The lesson of the story is that the answer must be a resounding ***yes***! As brothers and sisters, Children of Adam, Children of Noah, we are and must be our brothers' keepers. We must take responsibility. We must seek the welfare of our brothers and sisters everywhere. How can we best do this? Through studying, practicing and promoting G-d's Torah, which is the master plan for universal peace and harmony.

NOACH

Torah Reading: Gen. 6:9-11:32

Haftarah: Isaiah 54:1-55:5 (Sephardi ritual) Isaiah 54:1-10

Parshat ***Bereishit*** told the story of the first Ten Generations of the Children of Adam, establishing fundamental facts about the world and man's existential situation within it. The parshah of ***Noach*** spans the second Ten Generations, from Noah to Abraham. The parshah teaches profound lessons about "the generations of Noah", the families of the earth -- the Seventy Nations, their fundamental characteristics, how they interact and are destined to interact until the successful conclusion of human history as we know it in accordance with G-d's plan.

"G-d will beautify Yafet, and he will dwell in the tents of Shem." (Genesis 9:27). The genius of human civilization as expressed in Yafet's art and technology will eventually be devoted to the service of G-d in and through the "Tents of Shem", houses of prayer and worship of the One G-d -- especially in the Holy Temple in Jerusalem, the House of Prayer for All Nations.

Human history is that of the rise and fall of civilizations. One after the other, Egypt, Assyria, Babylon, Persia, Greece, Rome. reached the heights of power and arrogance, only to enter into decline -- just as we see contemporary "civilization" in its decline, with the widespread breakdown of security, social order and moral integrity. The parshah of ***Noach*** teaches us about the global, ecological disaster that comes about in the wake of human arrogance, excess and immorality. When man breaks down the boundaries of restraint, the natural order also breaks down in response. This is expressed in the "bursting forth of the springs of the depth and opening of the windows of heaven" that brought the Waters of the Flood upon a corrupt civilization. The breakdown of ecological harmony is caused by the corruption of civilization. [In our times, the breakdown of the natural order in response to chaos in the human social order also finds expression in the widespread incidence of cancer and similar diseases, which are caused when cell growth exceeds the proper boundaries.]

At the core of the disease of "civilization" in the time of Noah were sexual immorality and violent robbery, both flagrant affronts to the dignity of man, ***Adam***, created in the image of G-d. "And the land was corrupted and the land was filled with violent robbery. All flesh corrupted his path on the land" (Genesis 6:11-12). The Midrash teaches that the latter sin was that of the spilling of seed -- sexual immorality. When man abuses his sexual urge for self-gratification alone rather than elevating it to breed future generations who will glorify G-d, the entire earth is corrupted. The violation of the proper boundaries of personal moral conduct leads to a mentality in which everything is permitted, including violent robbery -- ***hamas***.

Noah was one who was fighting against the tide of his entire generation: a lone surviving torch-bearer of the religious truths handed down from Adam: belief in the One G-d, HaShem, the Supreme Power -- and obedience to His law. Noah alone in his generation saw its corruption. However, Noah lacked the power to rectify it -- Noah "went with" G-d, but unlike Abraham, he did not go on ahead "before" Him. Instead, Noah salvaged a remnant: his own family, together with choice representatives of the various species of animals and birds. After the corrupt world was washed clean by the purifying waters of the flood, Noah would build a new world on sound foundations that could endure.

* * *

THE ARK - THE WORD: PRAYER AND MYSTICAL WISDOM

In order to survive the waters of the flood, Noah was commanded to built an ark. The Hebrew word for the "Ark" is ***Teivah*** [not to be confused with ***teva***, which means "nature"]. ***Teivah*** also means a "word": a word is a vessel that sails the airwaves between my mouth and your ear, bearing a cargo of meaning: the message.

Noah was commanded to bring his wife, his children, their spouses, birds, animals, food, fodder -- everything needed to survive -- into his "Ark", the ***Teivah***. This teaches us that to survive the stormy waters of life in this world, we too must bring our lives and all our affairs -- down to the smallest details -- into ***ha-teivah***, "the word", i.e. the words of our prayers. In order to connect our alienated world back to G-d, we have to bring everything into our words of prayer. We should speak to G-d about everything.

The Holy Zohar, repository of the mystical wisdom of the Torah, teaches that the ***Teivah*** of Noah also alludes to the mystical teachings of the Kabbalah, which are a vital lifeboat for those seeking to survive the chaos of the end of time (see RaMChaL, Adir BaMarom). The Kabbalah (which includes Chassidut) reveals the mysteries of the Unity of G-d, teaching us the meaning, purpose and end-goal of the misery-filled, conflict-torn world in which we live. As we navigate the dark, stormy seas of life, the Kabbalah gives guidance, comfort and light: the light of the ***Tsohar*** (=Zohar), the "window" of the Ark (Genesis 6:16).

The theme of words, language and communication is apparent towards the end of the parshah, in the story of the building of the Tower of Babel (Genesis 11:1-9). As the population of the world expanded in the generations after Noah, man set himself a new goal: to unite in rebellion against G-d. "Let us build for ourselves a city and a tower with its head in the heavens and let us make for ourselves a ***name***." (ibid. 4). Man wanted the "name" for himself -- for his own glory -- instead of giving all the glory to G-d. However, G-d confounded man -- by sowing confusion through the very faculty that is uniquely man's: speech. Instead of helping people to communicate with each other, the torrents of words they directed at one another simply led to incomprehension, misunderstanding, hatred and violence.

In order to overcome hatred and war, man must develop a new language and a new way of speaking. This will be a feature of the messianic period in the future. "Then I will turn the language of the nations into a pure language so that all of them will call on the Name of G-d to serve Him with one accord" (Zephaniah 3:9). Then all mankind will unite in prayer to the One G-d in the "House of Prayer for all the Nations" in Jerusalem (Isaiah 56:15). This House of Prayer is the Tent of Shem in which Yafet will dwell.

* * *

NOAH'S SACRIFICE

Underlying the present parshah of Noah and the ensuing parshiyot, which tell the story of the patriarchs, is the quest for the Holy Mountain of G-d, the Temple Mount in Jerusalem. Adam's body had been created from the dust and earth of the Temple Mount. And "to dust you will return!" -- mankind must return to this spot and bring sacrifices in order to attain complete atonement for the "sin of Adam", which is man's intrinsic selfishness.

Noah set off on his quest having no idea where he was going. He was commanded to take seven each of all the pure species of animals into the ark. However, it was only after the flood waters subsided that Noah understood through his own powers of reasoning what G-d wanted him to do with them.

"And Noah built an altar to G-d, and he took from all the pure animals and from all the pure birds and offered elevation offerings on the altar" (Genesis 8:20). G-d in His bountiful mercy gave man command over all of nature, allowing him to take what he wants for his needs and desires. What G-d wants of man is to learn and understand Who is the source of this bounty -- by restraining himself from taking everything, and offering part of the bounty back to G-d, in acknowledgement. "And G-d smelled the sweet savor." (ibid. v. 21).

The essence of the concept of ***korban***, a "sacrifice", is that the offered animal -- symbol of our earthly, animal side -- is "brought near" ***(karov***) and elevated by being brought into the service of G-d in the form of the sacrifice. The sacrifice of a representative of the species elevates the entire species and brings it divine blessing. Noah's offering after the flood established an archetype for the whole of mankind, his descendants. The ultimate fulfilment of what Noah began will be expressed in the sacrifices in the Future Temple in Jerusalem as prophesied by Ezekiel (ch's 40ff.).

When man carries out the will of G-d, the purpose of Creation is fulfilled and G-d maintains and protects the creation in accordance with His Covenant. In response to Noah's willingness to fulfill his mission, G-d established His Covenant with him (Genesis 9: 11). The establishment of the Covenant was accompanied by a "Giving of the Law" to Noah and his children, restating their mission in the world and the laws according to which they must conduct their lives. Prominent among these laws are the prohibition of murder (as discussed in ***Bereishit***) and the prohibition of the consumption of a limb from a living animal. The sign of G-d's Covenant with Noah and his offspring is the rainbow, symbolic of how all the different powers of Creation -- the "colors" -- are actually refractions of the unitary "white light" of G-d.

* * *

MAN'S SIDE OF NATURE

Another of the fundamental laws of G-d's Covenant with Noah is the prohibition of sexual immorality, which was one of the prime causes of the flood. Allusions to the rectification of sexual immorality are found throughout the parshah. In order to correct the excesses of the generation of the flood, it was necessary for Noah and his family to practice complete abstinence during the flood itself (Rashi on Genesis 6:18). This is in accordance with Rambam's teaching (Hilchot De'ot, Laws of Attitudes and Personal Conduct 2:2): "If a person was at a far extreme, he has to distance himself from his previous behavior to the opposite extreme and conduct himself this way for a long time until he can return to the good path, which is the middle way."

"These are the generations of Noah."The names of Noah's three sons are repeated several times in the course of the parshah, indicating that

Noah understood that the true purpose of the sexual urge is to create new life and breed children to glorify the name of G-d.

However, Noah himself was unable to rectify the entire world, and after the flood, he himself fell -- he planted a vineyard, became drunk from the wine, and was uncovered in his tent. The theme of sexual immorality is uppermost in the story of how Ham "saw his father's nakedness". Rashi comments: "Some say he castrated him, some say he had relations with him." Ham is the archetype of the unbridled sexual heat and passion, which brings man to the depths of degradation. Sexuality has its necessary place in the life of man, but its holiness is preserved only when it is appropriately covered with a cloak of modesty and dignity. This is expressed in Shem and Yafet entering backwards into Noah's tent, averting their eyes, and covering his nakedness without looking, earning them Noah's eternal blessing.

* * *

THE TYRANNY OF NIMROD

After the fall of Noah, the ensuing generations again degenerated. The subtle allusions contained within the Biblical text are discussed and elaborated in the Midrash, which provides many details of the world in the period between Noah and Abraham. This was dominated by Nimrod, the archetype of the G-d-denying tyrant. With the world again falling deeper and deeper into chaos, the parshah concludes by tracing the lineage of a new prophet. This was one of Noah's progeny who ***was*** able to accomplish the rectification of the world, albeit not by himself, but with the help of his progeny, Isaac, Jacob and Jacob's children. Abraham did not fall. At the end of Parshat ***Noach*** we see Abraham (or Abram as he then was) setting off on ***his*** journey of destiny -- to the Land of Canaan, and eventually to "the Place", the Mountain of G-d in Jerusalem.

LECH LECHA

Torah Reading: Gen. 12.1-17.27

Haftarah: Isaiah 40:27-41:16

No spiritual seeker can fail to be thrilled by the challenge in G-d's words to Abraham with which this parshah begins: "Go to ***your self***...". G-d's challenge to Abraham is His challenge to every one of us: to go on the journey of destiny in search of the ultimate Source of the self and the soul. For G-d is the source and goal of all things.

All Abraham's descendants, the Children of Israel, and all the proselytes who have taken shelter under the wings of the Shechinah (Divine Presence) are justly proud of the founder of our faith and our nation. Abraham, "father of a multitude of nations", is revered not only in Judaism but also in Christianity and Islam, and evidence of his imprint on the culture and collective consciousness of mankind may be found in the religions of places as far afield as India, Japan and South America.

The Torah teaches us about the attributes of G-d by telling us stories of the outstanding Tzaddikim of all time, who emulated His ways. Study of the parshiyot recounting the lives of the founding fathers and mothers helps us attach ourselves to the very roots of our souls and to inculcate in ourselves the qualities through which we can come to know G-d. The Torah dwells more on the story of Abraham than of any of the earlier Tzaddikim (such as Adam and Noah) because the qualities embodied in Abraham, and particularly his ***Chessed*** (expansive loving-kindness) are the very key to finding G-d.

An originator and creative genius unique in human history, Abraham entered the world in the year 1948 after the creation (1812 B.C.E.), following twenty generations in which mankind had degenerated further and further into decadence. The Children of Adam had strayed far from the glorious role of benevolent kingship envisaged for Adam as ruler over creation and from Noah's New World vision of harmony among his three sons, each in their proper place. The world had fallen under the violent tyranny of Nimrod, son of Kush, firstborn of Ham. Ham was supposed to be the slave ministering to his brothers Shem and Yaphet. But the slave had rebelled: Nimrod had "stolen Adam's clothes" for himself, and was making himself into a world ruler who was determined to impose idolatry by force.

The popular image of Abraham as a placid, smiling white-haired sheik amidst his tents and camels belies much of his very essence. From earliest childhood and throughout his life, Abraham was a revolutionary and a rebel against the complex, sophisticated yet often barbaric culture of the ancient Assyrians, Babylonians, Egyptians and Canaanites among whom he traveled extensively. Priests, mathematicians, astronomers, logicians and philosophers were to be found in plenty, but none of them could satisfy Abraham's unquenchable passion to discover the mystery of G-d's unity. The Midrash states that, without a teacher, Abraham's own kidneys flowed with inspiration and understanding, bringing him to supreme heights of attachment to the ultimate powers of Creation. Abraham was willing to sacrifice his very life to sanctify the Name of G-d. His methods and teachings are inscribed in his Sefer Yetzirah (Book of Creation), the earliest known text of the Kabbalah.

* * *

THE RECTIFICATION OF SLAVERY

Abraham was unable to keep G-d for himself: he had to give Him to the whole world. By the time we meet Abraham when our parshah of ***Lech Lecha*** opens, he is already 75 years old. By the time he received G-d's prophesy to go on his journey of destiny -- which was to bring him eventually to the spot where Adam was formed, the place of the future House of Prayer for all the Nations -- Abraham was already well established. He was travelling with his wife, his orphaned nephew, their possessions, and a company of "souls they had made" during their sojourn in Haran. Who were these souls?

Rabbi Nachman of Breslov tells us that when Abraham would come to a town, he would stand up in the town square and start calling everyone to come and listen to him. He would ask them what was the point of squandering their lives on the pursuit of worldly vanity, telling them to think about the purpose of life in this world -- to find G-d. Abraham set the young people on fire with his revolutionary ideas, and they would come running after him.

The Midrash states that Abraham's chief slave, Eliezer, was none other than the son of Nimrod, who had cast Abraham into the fiery furnace in Ur Kasdim. When Abraham escaped, Eliezer was so overwhelmed by the miracle that he abandoned his defeated father and became Abraham's slave and chief convert. Another prominent figure who was willing to become Abraham's slave for the sake of having a connection with this charismatic man was Hagar, daughter of Pharaoh.

Both Eliezer and Hagar were descended from Ham, the son of Noah, who aroused his father's ire when he saw his nakedness and was cursed to be slave to his brothers. Abraham's journey to the land of Canaan (Ham's son) was in fulfilment of Noah's blessing to Shem that G-d would "dwell in the tents of Shem", who would be served by Canaan. The Canaanite slave had rebelled: the Canaanites were occupying the land destined for the descendants of Shem. Abraham's mission was to return to the source -- the land from whose earth Adam's body was formed -- and to settle in the Land of Canaan.

The society that Abraham's descendants were to build there was to be one in which the concept of slavery was to be transmuted. The details of the Covenant of Sinai begin with the laws regulating slavery (Exodus ch. 21). In the power-crazy world of Nimrod, the slave was the lowest of the low, one held captive in the physical power of others. Historically, slaves have been subjected to every kind of abuse, physical and psychological. In contrast, the Siniatic Covenant gives the slave his dignity. Even the Canaanite slave must keep many of the commandments, including circumcision (as we find at the end of our parshah.) In due course the Canaanite slave may even be freed and become a member of the assembly of the Children of Israel.

Abraham rectified the concept of slavery by turning it into a way of understanding our relationship with G-d. Abraham was the first to call himself "Your servant" (Gen. 18:3). In his humility, Abraham knew that before G-d he was but "dust and ashes". Adam was created to be free and to rule the world, but he abused his freedom and fell slave to his lusts. Man pays the price of his sins by serving -- man has to work. Those who are slaves to other men may pay a bitter price for their sins, but those who are willing to serve G-d become free. The more they serve G-d, the more they are freed from servitude to the cycle of lust, sin and degradation. Through serving G-d, man reaches his greatest heights -- and once again he becomes His beloved son.

By the time we meet Abraham in our parshah, he was already the epitome of humility, and he was therefore capable of becoming a master. Abraham rectified the concept of slavery by having slaves like Eliezer and Hagar, who were capable of serving their master in his mission of bringing G-d to all the world. In this way the power of Ham becomes harnessed in the service of the G-d of Shem. In order to completely rectify the concept of slavery, Abraham's own descendants, the Children of Israel, also had to descend to the level of slaves in Egypt until they were freed by G-d in order to serve Him (see in Parshat Lech Lecha, Genesis 15:13-14).

Very shortly after Abraham entered Canaan, famine forced him to go down to Egypt in the archetypal pattern of descent and ascent that would be repeated by his descendants. Egypt was the land of Ham's second son, and accordingly it was a place of rampant immorality, as exemplified in the story of the capture of Sarah by Pharaoh's officers. Things were only set right again when Sarah was released and Pharaoh's daughter Hagar became her maidservant.

* * *

CONFLICT AND CONFLICT MANAGEMENT

Abraham was childless, and it flew in the face of nature that an old man like him could have children. Yet his mission in Canaan was to take possession of the land that was occupied by the descendants of Ham, who had been cursed, and to settle it with his own descendants, the Children of Shem, who had been blessed. Having no children of his own, Abraham had taken in his orphaned nephew Lot.

As the man of ***Chessed*** -- Kindness -- Abraham displays his love of peace in his dealings with his nephew Lot, as when he suggests that since they are both expanding, they should avoid conflict by going their separate ways. However, Abraham's love of peace does not prevent him from going to war when the necessity arises, as when Lot was captured by the Four Kings and Abraham went out in hot pursuit.

In geopolitical terms, the war of the Four Kings against the Five (Genesis ch. 14) was a war for control over the blessed strip of land on the East Coast of the Mediterranean that is G-d's chosen, Promised Land. "Amraphel King of Shin'ar" is Nimrod -- Ham's grandson and Abraham's implacable adversary. Ham is fighting Shem. What spurs Abraham into action is the capture of Lot -- a mortal threat to Lot's destined progeny, including Ruth the Moabite, grandmother of Mashiach. Abraham rouses his followers -- those he has educated -- namely Eliezer, Nimrod's own son, the rectified slave (Genesis 14:14, see Rashi there), and miraculously rescues Lot. In this way Noah's prophesy is fulfilled and Eliezer, the descendant of Ham, serves Abraham, descendant of Shem, in helping pave the way to Mashiach.

* * *

HAGAR AND YISHMAEL

In many places in the story of Abraham, he is depicted as praying to G-d -- because prayer is one of the main pillars in the path of service of G-d which Abraham established. The simple, direct language of Abraham's prayers are a lesson for all, Israelites and gentiles alike, in how to approach G-d with words.

Faith in the power of prayer is the message of the name that Hagar gave to Abraham's son, Yishmael -- "G-d will hear". Yishmael's service is the service of prayer. It is an historical fact that Yishmael and his descendants brought knowledge of the G-d of Abraham and the service of prayer to many parts of the world, including many of the Children of Ham. As noted earlier, Hagar herself was a descendant of Ham. In this way, the families of the earth are being prepared for the House of Prayer for All Nations, when "Yaphet will dwell in the tents of Shem and Canaan will be servant to them".

* * *

THE COVENANT

"...which G-d created to ***do***" (Genesis 2:3): Man was created incomplete in order that he should acquire merit through ***doing***, serving G-d by completing and perfecting himself. The form of the male ***Adam*** is incomplete as long as the crown of the organ of creation remains covered by the impure ***orlah***, the foreskin, a pleasure-center that keeps those from whom it has not been removed uncontrollably attached to the material. The genitals are vital to the whole body and whole person (cf. Deut. 25:12) and the presence of the ***orlah*** influences the person's mind and outlook, preventing him from becoming a being perfectly attached to G-d.

It is said that Abraham agonized long when he began to understand that circumcision was to be the sign of his bond to G-d and the mark of his slave-like attachment to the Master of the Universe. Abraham feared that by cutting his flesh in this way, he would be setting himself apart from the rest of humanity, making it more difficult to bring them to the knowledge of the True G-d. In the end, however, Abraham accepted G-d's commandment, because the purity which the circumcision bestowed upon him enabled him to serve as Priest of all mankind in bringing man to G-d. The sign of G-d's Covenant with Abraham is inscribed upon the very organ with which we procreate, signifying that the foundation of the Covenant is that we submit our powers of procreation to G-d's service.

The commandment of circumcision is not one of the universal commandments of the Torah, but rather the exclusive mark and sign of the Children of Israel. The descendants of Yishmael consider themselves bound by the commandment of circumcision, but they do not perform the ***p'riyah*** (peeling of the membrane) as practiced by the descendants of Jacob.

Christianity presents itself as a "new stage" in the revelation that began with Abraham, in which the original covenant or "old testament" with Abraham and his biological descendants, marked by the circumcision, was "superseded" by a "new covenant" or "new testament" with all humanity which did not require circumcision. It was the abandonment of circumcision that put the seal on Christianity's break with the Torah of Moses, which states that "an uncircumcised male who will not circumcise the flesh of his foreskin, that soul will be cut off from her people, he has broken My covenant" (Genesis 17:14).

Nothing can change these words, for "G-d is not a man that He should lie or the son of man that He should change His mind. He spoke -- will He not do it? He pronounced -- will He not fulfill it?" (Numbers 23:19). "For I am G-d, I have not changed." (Malachi 3:6). "Go and let us ascend to the Mountain of G-d, to the House of the G-d of Jacob." (Isaiah 2:3).

VAYEIRA

Torah Reading: Gen. 18.1-22.24

Haftarah: II Kings 4:1-37

G-d's Covenant with Abraham, marked by the sign of circumcision, brought Abraham to an entirely new level, making him worthy of fathering Isaac, the descendants of whose son Jacob have been the guardians of G-d's Torah and a "light to the nations" throughout history. While the Covenant is a unique bond between G-d and the Children of Israel, it is of significance for the entire world, and our parshah, which shows Abraham recovering from his circumcision and the ensuing events, is replete with teachings that apply to all humanity.

* * *

HOSPITALITY

The simple, beautiful narrative of Abraham's hospitality to seeming wayfarers with which the parshah begins is in counterpoint with the later accounts of the "hospitality" of the Sodomites and of Avimelech king of Gerar.

Hospitality -- treating strangers and visitors kindly -- is one of the foundations of a civilized world and a defining trait of true Bney Adam. For man's existential situation on this earth is that he himself is but a stranger subject to the mercy of G-d. As Abraham says before G-d, the ***Baal HaBayit*** ("Owner of the House") in our parshah: "I am dust and ashes" (Gen. 18:27). Abraham says to the children of Chet (Gen. 23:4): "I am a stranger and a resident with you." I, with you. We are all in the same situation! Essentially we are all visitors on G-d's earth, and He provides for all of us.

Through the simple human act of showing hospitality to strangers and visitors even under difficult circumstances (Abraham was in the wilderness -- we are not talking about "entertaining" friends for dinner) man imitates his Maker, the Owner of the House. Man himself becomes the "host", providing his guests not only with their physical needs but also with spiritual nourishment. Abraham gave his visitors the waters of spirituality with which to "wash their feet" of false ideas. He brought them in to "rest under the tree" -- the Tree of Life. These are the ways of peace. When we sit down to talk peacefully with visitors and strangers about Torah and the purpose of life, this brings the Divine Presence to dwell with us. Pursuing such ways of peace made Abraham worthy of miracles -- the miracle of the birth of Isaac, a worthy successor.

* * *

THE WAY OF G-D

G-d Himself testifies of Abraham that "he will instruct his sons and his house after him and they will guard the way of HaShem to practice righteousness and justice." (Gen. 18:19). The sign of the covenant is inscribed upon man's organ of procreation in order to teach him that he must elevate his sexual power above the pursuit of selfish gratification. He is to dedicate his strength to the breeding and raising of future generations who will be G-d's torch-bearers in the world, practicing righteousness and justice. The purpose of the commandment to procreate, which was given to Adam, is to fill the world with sons and daughters who are true Bney Adam having ***tzurat Adam***, the "essential form" of Adam not merely physically but spiritually. Only when the world will be filled with people who possess this form will it be possible to say that the world is truly civilized. (Likutey Moharan II:7).

It was because of Abraham's merit that G-d revealed to him the imminent destruction of Sodom, leading to Abraham's bold effort to save the place through prayer. Abraham clearly saw himself as the Baal HaBayit -- "house-owner" -- of the whole of the land he had been promised by G-d. Abraham took responsibility for the land and its problems, including its moral problems (such as the degenerate civilization of Sodom). Abraham hoped there might be enough Tzaddikim to save Sodom. The boldness of his prayers contains a lesson for all of us to be bold and persistent in our prayers. Yet we must also accept that not all our prayers can be answered in the way we might think we want them answered. In the case of Sodom, the Defense (Abraham) could not prevail, and the Accuser went to destroy the place. Yet the Defender's prayers did accomplish something: the salvage of Abraham's nephew Lot and his family from the catastrophe that befell Sodom.

* * *

THE DESTRUCTION OF SODOM

Abraham's virtue as guardian of G-d's Covenant shines out in contrast to the wickedness of his generation in a "civilization" run amok. Those who are familiar with the stark, eerie desert mountain landscape of the Yam HaMelach ("Salt" or "Dead Sea") area with its unique climate and colors may try to imagine it as the setting for one of the most sophisticated "civilizations" that ever was. For prior to the raining down of G-d's anger on Sodom and the neighboring towns in the form of fire and brimstone, that same area was once luxuriantly fertile "like G-d's garden" (Gen. 13:10). The desolate desert areas around the ***Yam HaMelach*** are gaunt, testimony to the fact that unless man repents, sin leads to destruction. Human immorality can destroy not only man himself but the very physical environment around him. (The same lesson is implicit later on in our parshah in the illness that afflicted Avimelech and his household when he kidnapped Sarah.)

The destruction of the civilization of Sodom was an historical and ecological disaster that was deeply etched into the consciousness of antiquity. Numerous passages in the book of Job and elsewhere in the Bible contain allusions to the immorality and subsequent destruction of Sodom. The Midrash is rich in tales of Eliezer's encounters with the inhabitants of Sodom and of their ways. Eliezer as the son of Nimrod was, like the inhabitants of Sodom, descended from Ham, except that Eliezer submitted himself to the slavery decreed upon the children of Ham by attaching himself to Abraham. The inhabitants of Sodom, on the other hand, were so enslaved to human perversity that there was no remedy except to destroy them.

The inhabitants of Sodom enjoyed a fabulous, green watered spa in what is the world's lowest point. They turned "G-d's garden" into a center devoted purely to the worship of self to the exclusion of all others. This finds its ultimate expression in sodomy, which was the sin of Ham when he uncovered his father's nakedness (see Rashi on Gen. 9:22). Sodomy is an extreme violation of the Covenant, which decrees that human sexuality is to be elevated to serve as the bond that brings husband and wife together in procreating and raising holy souls. Instead of this, sodomy degrades and abuses man's highest creative power, his seed, throwing it into the very gutter, the part of the body designed to expel poisonous waste and filth. Sodomy degrades both the passive partner, who is subjugated and used, and the active partner, who is turned into a selfish, lustful animal.

Gang-rape of two apparent visiting strangers was the Sodomites idea of a "gay" evening. ["Gay" sex was also one of the things to which Ishmael later tried to submit Isaac -- see Rashi on Gen. 21:9 -- the other two being idolatry and murder.]

That Lot had chosen to live in a place with such moral standards and that he had, moreover, been appointed by them to be their judge (Rashi, Gen. 19:1) testifies to the weak flaw in the character of this classic waverer dressed up in the guise of liberalism. Lot's father Haran had wavered between Abraham and Nimrod when the latter threw Abraham into the fiery furnace. Only when Abraham emerged unscathed did Haran agree to be thrown in -- and died. The mountain of Abraham's virtue seemed to Lot so high that it appeared unattainable. Lot preferred the less spiritually demanding, more materially indulgent surroundings of Sodom. Yet even in Sodom, a spark of Lot's inherited moral decency remained: even he could not stand it when the locals demanded to rape his very guests -- though he was prepared to throw them his own virgin daughters instead.

The Sodomites typify methodical human nastiness in the guise of rights and laws. ***Middat S'dom*** -- characteristically Sodomite traits -- are typified in many places in the Talmud, such as in the concept of refusing a person some benefit even when one has nothing to lose, or "mine is mine and yours is yours" (Avot 5:10). The Sodomites rebelled against the law of G-d, making up their own merciless laws, rebelling against any effort to reform them, as when they reminded Lot that he was a stranger: "Shall someone come to dwell and make judgements?" (Gen. 19:9). Sodom was the very opposite of the civilization that Abraham sought to create, where residents invite strangers in and sit together to talk peace. In Sodom unwary strangers were grabbed and lynched. There was no remedy for the Sodomites except to overthrow and destroy their entire civilization.

The mystery of the story of Sodom is that out of the wreckage was salvaged Mashiach. For Lot the waverer was made up of two sides: the side that wanted to do good and the side that wavered. Lot's daughters did not waver. When they believed that the entire world was destroyed, they took responsibility to repopulate it even if it meant doing the unspeakable. Out of this holy intention was born the nation of Moab, from whom emerged the holy spark of the soul of one who did not waver for a moment. This was Ruth, who never wavered in her devotion to Naomi and her G-d, and whose great grandson was King David, Melech HaMashiach. Ruth became the archetypal Ger, the "visitor" who takes shelter under the Tree of Life.

* * *

THE KIDNAPPING OF SARAH

Sin need not lead to destruction -- if the sinner repents and makes amends. Like the behavior of the Sodomites, Avimelech's behavior in kidnapping a visiting woman he presumed to be single also fell far short of the standards of hospitality and treatment of strangers G-d wants in the world. There was no fear of G-d in Gerar -- it was a place where if they had thought Abraham was Sarah's husband, they would have killed him to get her. However, unlike the Sodomites, Avimelech was willing to accept rebuke. The story of Avimelech's dream teaches that people of all nations may be worthy of dreams and visions from G-d. As Elijah the Prophet stated: "I testify that anyone, Israelite or gentile, freeman or slave, man or woman can attain holy spirit" (Tanna

Devei Eliyahu). We must be willing to hear and heed the voice of G-d's rebuke, and to see the hand of G-d in the things that afflict us in this world, just as Avimelech learned that the mysterious disease afflicting his entire household was caused by immorality.

Abraham's prayer for Avimelech's healing is the first recorded prayer for healing in the Torah, teaching us the power of altruistic prayer to bring healing and rectification (Likutey Moharan II:1) .

* * *

ISAAC: SUBMISSION

The reward for Abraham's acceptance of the Covenant was the miraculous birth of a son born in purity -- a worthy successor. Abraham's uniqueness lay in his originality: he rebelled against his childhood homeland culture to become a Baal Teshuvah. On the other hand, Isaac's uniqueness, as the second generation, one "born into" the faith, lay in his willingness to submit to a discipline imposed upon him from childhood without rebelling. Only through such submission can the faith survive and be transmitted from generation to generation.

Rashi (Gen. 21:10) tells us that Ishmael contested Isaac's inheritance from Abraham, claiming priority as the firstborn. The descendants of Ishmael dispute Isaac's inheritance until today, claiming that the heritage of Abraham is theirs. Thus the concept of submission, which is central to the faith of Abraham, has a prominent place in Islam. According to the Moslems, Abraham's binding of his son -- the archetypal case of submission to G-d -- was performed on Ishmael on a mountain in Arabia. In this way a tradition that is little more than 1300 years old mirrors a far more ancient tradition that has been preserved faithfully in writing and by word of mouth from generation to generation for over three thousand five hundred years.

The mountain where Abraham and Isaac performed the supreme act of submission, each in his own way, is none other than Mount Moriah, the Temple Mount in Jerusalem. The Torah testifies in our parshah that this is the mountain where G-d will be seen and revealed (Gen. 22:14).

CHAYEY SARAH

Torah Reading: Gen. 23:1-25:18

Haftarah: I Kings 1:1-31

THE LIFE OF SARAH

*T*he parshah opens with ***life*** -- the ***life*** of Sarah -- even though it goes on to speak of her death, and later that of Abraham (Gen. 25:8). This is because it is the very limit that death puts upon life that makes every year of life and every day so precious. "Teach us to count our days" (Psalms 90:12). What gives true value to each day is not the material pleasures enjoyed or the wealth amassed but the eternal goodness attained through the mitzvot one accomplishes each day, each minute.

In the words of Rabbi Nathan of Breslov in his Introduction to Chayey Moharan, the Life of Rabbi Nachman: "There are countless gradations in the life and vitality found in the world. Real life is the life of true wisdom, as it is written: 'Wisdom gives life to those who possess it' (Eccl. 712). And the essence of wisdom is to labor and endeavor to know and acknowledge G-d, who is the Life of life. The closer one comes to God, the more his life is genuine life."

"And the years of the life of Sarah." (Gen. 23:1)

"And these are the days of the years of the life of Abraham that he lived." (ibid. 25:87).

* * *

BURIAL

"And the sons of Chet answered Abraham saying to him. No man among us would withhold his grave from you." (Gen. 23:5-6).

No one in the world is exempt from death. All Adam's children must pay the price of his sin by tasting death. Thus even the Canaanite children of Chet (who were later to prove bitter enemies of Abraham's descendants) were forced to take a share in the mourning for Sarah. ***Ish mimenu*** -- "No man among us." The words imply an awareness that all mankind lives under the shadow of death (Ari).

Burial is one of several possible ways of removing the bodies of our dead from within our midst. Removal of the dead from the midst of the living serves the living, to whom the presence of a decomposing corpse is too offensive and humiliating a reminder of their own mortality. But dead bodies could be burned or disposed of otherwise: Why bury them?

The answer is that burial benefits the dead as well. "For you are dust and to the dust you will return" (Gen. 3:19). Burial brings ***kaparah***, atonement, to the dead person for the sins committed in this world through the body. Being lowered into the earth after a lifetime of proud living above it is the deepest humiliation. The concealment of the person's physical remains beneath the earth, where they decompose and are reabsorbed into the elements, signifies the concealment and atonement of his sins. Eventually everything is merged back into unity and even the sins are turned into merits.

An integral aspect of the honor accorded to the dead through burial is that the atonement is accomplished in a concealed manner, thereby covering and hiding the shame of the dead. "And he shall cover it in the earth" (Leviticus 17:13)

Adam himself was buried in the earth: according to tradition, Adam and Eve were buried in the very Cave of Machpelah in which Abraham buried Sarah (Zohar ***Vayeira*** on the verse "And Abraham ran to the bull" Gen. 18:7). Burial of the dead is an integral part of the heritage of the children of Shem and Japhet -- their reward for the modesty they showed when they concealed their father Noah's nakedness after he became drunk (Gen. 9:21ff.). Rashi comments (ad loc.) that in the merit of this act, Shem earned for his children the modest body covering of the Tallit with its Tzitzit (fringes, Numbers 15:38), while

Japhet earned burial for his descendants, the armies of Gog who are to be buried after falling in the war of Gog and Magog (Ezekiel 39:11). [Since Japhet earned burial for his descendants, how much more so did Shem! Significantly, it is customary to bury Jewish men in their Tallit.]

* * *

ACQUISITION & OWNERSHIP

Abraham found it sufficient to live in tents for his whole life -- he was fully aware that he was but a "visitor and a resident" (Gen. 23:4) on this earth. Only when Sarah died did Abraham find it necessary to acquire permanent accommodation -- a final resting place for the body while the soul goes on to the life eternal. Thus Abraham teaches us that our most important acquisitions in this world are not the material houses on which most people lavish so much money and effort for their temporary stay here. Rather, our truest acquisitions are those that will truly serve us in the eternal life. Buying a burial plot is a ***segulah*** for long life!

Abraham's acquisition of the Field and the cave of Machpelah from Ephron the Hittite is the first case of the acquisition of land in the Torah. [Eve "acquired" a child, Cain, naming him after the acquisition: "I have acquired (***kaniti***) a man with G-d", Gen. 4:1]. Fundamental lessons about ***kinyan***, acquisition or ownership, are derived from the account in our parshah of Abraham's purchase of land from Ephron, the classic example of how business dealings between the Children of Noah are to be characterized by the rule of law and integrity in accordance with the Seventh Universal Law. The negotiations and the transaction were carried out with perfect "transparency". The ears of the Children of Chet heard everything and their eyes saw it all (Gen. 23 vv. 10, 13; 18 etc.) Abraham did not ask for any bargains and he did not receive any. He paid the full price with silver. [Money is soul: people put their very soul into the acquisition of the liquid asset known as ***kesef***. ***Kesef*** is soul, for soul is desire: ***kisufin***.]

Earlier in the story of Abraham, when Malki-tzedek (= Shem) king of Shalem (=Jerusalem) had come out to greet him after he rescued Lot from the Four Kings [Parshat ***Lech Lecha***], Malki-tzedek blessed Abraham in the name of "…the Supreme G-d, ***owner*** of Heaven and Earth" (Gen. 14:19). Abraham swore by the same G-d – "owner of Heaven and Earth" (ibid. 22).

Only when man acknowledges that G-d owns everything can man be said to own anything -- "for if you lack ***Da'at*** (knowledge), what have you acquired?" [***Kinyah*** requires ***Da'at***.] Everything belongs to G-d: "The earth is the Lord's and all its fullness" (Psalms 24:1). When man understands this and blesses G-d before he takes anything from this world, then G-d brings man to his true glory. G-d gives the world to man and allows him to own it: "…And He has given the earth to the children of Adam" (ibid. 115:16).

Although Ephron had been the titular owner of the land, it had meant nothing to him -- it was dark and concealed -- because he did not possess this knowledge. Since Abraham had the knowledge, when he purchased the land it became truly his and associated with his name for ever: "And the field of Ephron stood..." -- ("It had ***tekumah***, an upstanding" -- Rashi) -- "... to Abraham as an ***acquisition***" (Gen. 23:17-18).

* * *

FAMILY PURITY

Everyone knows that G-d rules over the heavens -- even the nearest star is way beyond man's reach. What is concealed from many people is that G-d rules over the earth and over every detail of what happens here. This was what Abraham came into the world to teach.

Rashi tells us (commenting on why Abraham, speaking to Eliezer, invoked "HaShem, the G-d of the heavens" but did not mention "and of earth" -- Gen. 24:7): "Abraham told Eliezer that now He is G-d 'of the heavens ***and*** the earth' because I have made this phrase habitual on people's lips. But when He took me from the house of my father, He was 'G-d of the heavens' but not 'G-d of the earth' because people in the world did not recognize Him and His name was not familiar on the earth".

Abraham's could not allow his work to end with him. It was an integral part of his mission to have a worthy successor who would in turn have a worthy successor to ensure that the knowledge of G-d would never again be hidden from the world.

As a "Prince of G-d" (Gen. 23:6) and of the progeny of Shem, Abraham could not but be discriminating about the family that would provide the appropriate wife for his son and successor. Contrary to the widely held fallacy that people of any and every family and national backgrounds are all "equal", Abraham was unwilling to make a family alliance with any other than his own family back in Padan Aram. This was where they had stayed when Abraham went on his journey of destiny to the Land of Canaan.

Abraham was unwilling to make a family alliance with the Canaanites, for Canaan, son of Ham, was under the curse of Noah. On the other hand, Abraham could not allow his son Isaac to return to Padan Aram even for the sake of being married. This would have undermined the whole purpose of Abraham's departure from that "Old World". Padan Aram (with its high priest, Laban = Bilaam, brain of all the forces of evil, the ***kelipot***) was the old World of Devastation (***Olam HaTohu***, Breaking of the Vessels), whereas Abraham had gone to turn the Land of Canaan in to the Land of ***Israel*** (Yeshurun, Yosher) in order to create ***Olam HaTikun***, the world of repair and healing.

Accordingly Abraham sent his servant Eliezer to Padan Aram to redeem the spark of ***tikun*** -- Rebecca -- from the World of Devastation, Padan Aram, a place characterized by ***deception***.

* * *

ELIEZER'S MISSION

It is significant that Eliezer is the one sent on this mission. Eliezer, son of Nimrod, son of Kush, eldest son of the accursed Ham) was himself an example of a rescued spark. By attaching himself to Abraham, Eliezer himself became "blessed" -- Laban greets him as "Blessed of HaShem" (Gen. 24:31). [Just how blessed this attachment proved to Eliezer's soul is seen in the fact that he was later incarnated as Kalev son of Yephuneh -- who had a particular attachment to Chevron and the patriarchs -- see Rashi on Numbers 13:22, as Benayah ben Yehoyada in the time of King Solomon and as Shemayah and Avtaliyon, leaders in the early rabbinic period and both converts. Ari.]

The Torah devotes much space to the account of Eliezer's journey to Padan Aram because witnessing closely Abraham's devoted servant in action, we learn deep lessons about Abraham and his mission in the world.

Eliezer goes first to the well, because, as "that Damascan" (Gen. 15:2) -- ***Damesek*** -- Eliezer's task was to be "Doleh u-MaSHKeh miTorat Rabo", drawing and giving out to drink from the waters of the Torah of his master: "Ho, everyone that is thirsty, come for water!" (Isaiah 55:1). Deeply embedded in the account of Eliezer's mission is the concept of the ***dli*** ("the bucket = Aquarius) and the drawing of the waters of spirituality into the world for all to drink. [Bney Issaschar, Shevat.]

The first thing Eliezer does at the well is to pray to G-d for help. He asks G-d to make events happen in a way that will enable the kindness of Abraham to be handed down to future generations. Eliezer's request to G-d to make events happen this way is founded upon the belief -- received from Abraham -- that He is "G-d of earth" and not only "G-d in heaven." G-d is in complete control of what "happens" on earth, down to the last detail. It is no "coincidence" that Rebecca steps out to "draw water from the well" just as Eliezer completes his prayer.

The test Eliezer devises for the candidate suited to marry Isaac and bring Abraham's kindness to the world is a test of ***character***. What counts is not what people say (like Ephron, who said a lot but did hardly anything.) What counts is what they actually ***do***.

Rebecca does ***more*** than Eliezer asks her. Not only does she want to give him to drink. She wants to perform kindness, ***Gomel*** Chessed, to the very camels, ***gamalim***. She has the expansive quality of ***Chessed*** characteristic of the true family of Abraham: she was fitted for the role of consort to the new Prince of G-d.

The loss of one member of the family, Sarah, who went into the grave, HaKeVeR, opens the way for the entry of a new member to build the family: RiVKaH. The death of the old generation and their descent into HaKeVeR turns out to be HaBoKeR, a new morning, a new day!

* * *

THE FIELD BLESSED BY G-D

Rebecca's first sight of Isaac was when "Isaac went out to meditate in the field towards the evening" (Gen. 24:63). This was the field of submission, the site where Isaac had been bound on Mount Moriah. Isaac turned his submission into a daily devotion: the devotion of set prayer and meditation.

Prayer is where we make Him "G-d of the earth", involving Him in all our daily affairs and activities and shining His light into the innermost depths of our hearts.

The Talmud tells us that the three founding fathers, Abraham, Isaac and Jacob, were all engaged in laying the foundations for the Temple on this site. Each made his own unique contribution -- and conceived it in a different way: Abraham as a "Mountain"; Isaac as a "Field" and Jacob as a "House". And it is as a "House" that it is destined to be built in Jerusalem in the near future (*Pesachim* 88a)

At first, attachment to G-d is like a high mountain. To scale the mountain, we must discipline ourselves like oxen to plough daily and turn the mountain into a cultivated field. This is the work of Isaac. Finally, we come to the stage where spirituality is part of our lives and comes into our very homes, houses, domestic and family affairs (see Likutey Moharan I:10). This is the work of Jacob, to whom we will be introduced in next week's parshah, and whose garments had the fragrance of the "field that G-d has blessed" (Parshat Toldot, Genesis 27:27).

TOLDOT

Torah Reading: Gen. 25:19-28:9

Haftarah: Malachi 1:1-2:7

"AND THESE ARE THE GENERATONS OF ISAAC"

*I*n the holy structure built by the patriarchs to reveal HaShem to the world, Abraham is the initial thesis: expansive energy, revelation, kindness -- ***Chessed***. Isaac is the antithesis: restriction, control -- ***Gevurah***, while Jacob, who enters the stage in our parshah, is the synthesis: balance, order, beauty -- ***Tiferet***. Jacob, the most "perfect" (***shalem***) of the patriarchs, came to complete the holy House -- the House of Israel, to whom all the nations will turn at the end of history in order to find HaShem: "And many nations will go and say, 'Go, let us ascend to the mountain of HaShem, to the ***House*** of the G-d of Jacob'" (Isaiah 2:3).

As thesis and antithesis, Abraham and Isaac represent two opposite tendencies, each of which has an extreme aspect, an aspect of excess, that must be transmuted and directed to the holy in order for perfect balance and harmony to reign. Thus Abraham and Isaac each had a "first-born" (the aspect of excess) who was rejected from the holy structure. The last section of the previous parshah, ***Chayey Sarah***, completed the story of Abraham's "first-born", Ishmael, the son of Hagar, and his descendants, who embody the "excess" aspect of Abraham: religious fanaticism -- "before all his brothers he fell" (Gen. 25:18, closing words of ***Chayey Sarah***). In introducing Jacob, the perfect patriarch, the parshah of ***Toldot*** also introduces Jacob's challenger, his twin brother Esau, who embodies the excess aspect of Isaac: power and domination used arrogantly for the benefit of self instead of for G-d. The story of Esau is told partly in our parshah, left aside in next week's parshah of ***Vayeitzei***, which focusses exclusively on Jacob, and taken up again in the following parshah of ***Vayishlach***. There the story of Esau and his generations will be concluded with the account of the "Seven kings who ruled in Edom before a king ruled over the children of Israel" (Gen. 36:31). Kabbalistically, the Seven Kings who "ruled and died" represent the World of Devastation (***Tohu***) produced by the "Breaking of the Vessels" for the purpose of bringing evil into the world. From the following parshah, ***Vayeishev***, until the end of Genesis, the Torah concentrates on Jacob and his generations, who represent the World of Rectification (***Tikun***), in which evil is eventually vanquished completely through the House of Israel. The vicissitudes of Joseph and his brothers are paradigmatic of the vicissitudes leading to the eventual revelation of Messiah.

Historically, the descendants of Ishmael and of Abraham's other sons from Keturah brought certain aspects of the monotheism of Abraham to many parts of the world, especially to the east and south, including the Arab lands and many parts of Africa and Asia (the descendants of Noah's son Ham), through Islam. The descendants of Esau brought other aspects of the tradition of Abraham to the north and west -- to Europe, Russia and America (descendants of Japheth) as well as many other parts of the world through Christianity. (See Rambam, Hilchot Melachim 11:4 uncensored version). Although the land given specifically to Esau is Mount Seir, which is south east of the Land of Israel, Esau-Edom is particularly associated with Rome (see Rashi on Gen. 36:43 and also on Gen. 27:39). Rome put its unique stamp upon western culture and its influence is felt until today. (Thus the U.S. Senate is named after the Roman Senate.)

* * *

"AND THE TWINS STRUGGLED WITHIN HER..."

The holy structure to be built by Jacob was to be constructed only through struggle and effort: Jacob's struggle is the struggle to elevate Isaac's power (***Gevurah***) through its use not for the benefit of self, but in order to bring the spirituality of Abraham (***Chessed***) to rule over the fallen ***Gevurot***, the refractory material world of practical action as represented in the figure of Esau (from the Hebrew root ***asa***, "doing"). Only through the struggle to sift and clarify truth and goodness from falsehood and evil ***in the real world*** is the light of truth revealed in all its beauty and perfection.

The history of mankind has indeed been the history of the clash of cultures and civilizations. It may appear cyclical and pointless, but as revealed in our parshah, it has a purpose and an end goal. It is to reveal G-d's unity out of the intergenerational war between good and evil in all shapes and forms. The struggle has been protracted and painful, just as the struggle of the twins in Rebecca's womb was painful to her to the point of desperation. Yet the very pain itself forced Rebecca to "go to search out HaShem" (Gen. 45:22). Similarly, the many pains and troubles later suffered by Jacob (as a result of the hatred and envy of Esau and Laban and family tragedy with Dinah and Jacob) brought him time after time to turn to G-d for help. The way to G-d's truth is indeed often painful and riddled with conflicts -- with others and within our very selves. However, it is possible to give meaning to our pain, struggle and hardship and to actually grow through them when we learn to turn our very pains and trials into a springboard to seek out G-d.

* * *

LENTIL SOUP

The two twins early on showed their different traits. Esau, "man of the field", took after Isaac, who "went out to the field" (Gen. 24:63, last week's parshah). Esau the hunter exemplifies the extreme and unholy distortion of Isaac's holy ***Gevurah***. Esau's is the cunning brute force of the mighty over the weak and unsuspecting. (Esau wears the clothes of Nimrod.) Jacob, on the other hand, "dwelled in tents" -- not one tent but two: the "tents" of learning of his two teachers, the tent of his grandfather Abraham, Man of Kindness (Abraham was still alive until Jacob was 13) and the tent of Jacob's own father Isaac, Man of Power. Jacob's mission was to synthesize the two "tents" and build out of them a "house": to combine the differing paths of the first two patriarchs (Abraham, the paradigm convert and Isaac, the paradigm case of one born into religion) into a unitary tradition capable of constant self-renewal. Jacob, the ***Tam***, possessing the quality of simple honesty, sincerity and the search for truth, was able to do this. Esau was not: he knew only to ensnare -- for he himself was ensnared in the mesh of evil.

According to the Midrash, the episode of Jacob's "purchase" of the birthright from Esau for a cup of soup took place on the day that Abraham died. Jacob cooked the soup as the ***seudat havra'ah***, the "meal of comfort and invigoration" prepared for the immediate mourners after the funeral. As Rashi teaches (on Gen. 25:30), Jacob's lentil soup was intended to convey a profound message to his father Isaac, who was mourning the loss of his father. "The lentil is similar to a wheel, and so too death and mourning are part of the cycle of the world." It is impossible to explain the meaning of death rationally -- the lentil "has no mouth", the mourner has nothing to say. We have no option but to accept death and mourning as an inevitable part of the cycle of destiny.

Jacob's ability to use a material object, the lentil, in order to teach a spiritual lesson, is what gave him power over ***Asiyah*** as represented in ***Esau***. Esau was preoccupied with the material externality of the soup. Esau, the twin brother with whom Jacob was locked in perpetual struggle, was in and of the material world. Esau was exhausted from a day of "hunting". He was hungry. He wanted the tasty, filling soup. He had no time for spiritual meanings. Esau, locked in the time-bound material realm, knew only that he was going to die -- so eat, drink and be merry now! What need did Esau have for a spirituality that brought no immediate gratification? Esau was thus unfitted for the ***bechorah*** the choice first-born portion that was "acquired" by Jacob through his superior wisdom. The superior wisdom of the Torah is itself the choice portion, as indicated in the opening word of the Torah: ***Be-reishit***, "for the sake of the first."

One of the deep mysteries of the Torah is that the natural, apparent first-born are repeatedly rejected in favor of the true, "spiritual" first-born. Cain was rejected while Abel's sacrifice was accepted. Japheth was made subordinate to his younger brother, Shem (Rashi on Gen.10:28) -- Shem and his descendants were the "high priests" who brought knowledge of HaShem to the world. Ishmael and Esau were rejected in favor of Isaac and Jacob respectively. Later on, Jacob's first-born Reuven was rejected in favor of Levi, Judah and Joseph. Ephraim was given precedence over Menasheh. Kehat, the son of Levi, was given precedence over Levi's first-born, Gershon... and Moses attained kingship over the firstborn Aaron, who was three years his senior. Yet through Aaron's humble, joyous submission to his younger brother Moses, whose spokesman he became, Aaron earned the priesthood. Through the balance between the lawgiver and the priest, the transgenerational struggle between brothers that started with Cain and Abel was brought to a satisfactory conclusion: religious service (as represented in Aaron) must be subject to religious law (Moses). Otherwise service turns into excess.

* * *

HISTORY REPEATS ITSELF

History repeats itself because lessons learned by one generation are forgotten by the next and have to be relearned. Just as the generation of Abraham had been afflicted by famine, so too was the generation of Isaac. Just as Abraham had been forced into exile, so was Isaac. Abraham dwelled among the Philistines in Gerar, and so did Isaac.

The popular association of "philistinism" with barbarity is fitting, for the Philistines represent the very opposite of the ***Chessed*** that is the driving force of the religion of Abraham. The numerical value of the Hebrew letters of PhiLiShTYM (Phe 80, Lamed 30, Shin 300, Tav 400, Yud 10, Mem 40) is 860. 86 is the numerical value of the letters of the divine name ELoKiM, alluding to ***Gevurah***, might, power, limitation and concealment. The Philistines (= 10 x 86) represent the forces of limitation and concealment in full array. In each generation their king, ***Avimelech*** (= "I want to rule") wants to steal the Shechinah (represented by Sarah and Rebeccah) for his own selfish pleasure. In each generation the patriarchs had to teach the lesson that the law of G-d must prevail. The kidnapping of a married woman is a crime against the universal law of the children of Noah. Abraham had taught the lesson in his generation, but it had been forgotten, and it had to be taught again in the generation of Isaac. This is because the forces of evil constantly conceal lessons learned by earlier generations. "And all the wells that the servants of his father [Abraham] had dug, the Philistines had stopped up, and they filled them with earth." (Gen. 26:15). The mission of the patriarchs was to uncover the waters of spirituality and bring them to the world, but the Philistines closed up the very sources of the living waters of spirituality with earthliness and gross materialism. Rashi (ad loc.) points out that the Targum of the word "closed up" has the connotation of "closing up the heart" with insensitivity and foolishness. Accordingly, Isaac had to start all over again, re-digging the very wells that Abraham had dug.

Isaac's very success -- which so aroused the ire and envy of the Philistines -- came about because he loyally followed in the ways of charity, generosity and kindness taught by his father Abraham. (Thus, Rashi points out Isaac was careful to assess the lands he sowed with a view to how much they could produce in tithes for charity, see Rashi on Gen. 26:12). Isaac was blessed because he wanted to share his blessings. Faced with the threat of military might from the Philistines, Isaac's response was to call upon the name of G-d. Instead of fighting his enemies, Isaac made peace with them. He practiced the ways of peace: "And he made a feast for them and they ate and drank... and they went from him in peace" (Gen. 26:30-31).

* * *

ISAAC'S BLESSINGS

G-d "made the earth blossom forth every kind of tree pleasant to the eye and good to eat" and bestowed rich blessings upon man to enable him to come to know and attach himself to his Maker. Adam had been tricked by the serpent -- his own pride and arrogance -- into eating of the very tree from which he was forbidden to eat, thereby separating himself from his Maker. Being too clever for his own good, man mixed up good and evil. As a result Adam's descendants were condemned to a multi-generational struggle against that selfsame serpent of pride and arrogance, struggling repeatedly through history to sort out the confusion.

The confusion was so great that the blind Isaac was apparently ready to hand over the power of blessing he had received from G-d (Gen.25:11) to the seeming first-born, Esau, even though Esau was in fact the very incarnation of the serpent (see Targum on Gen. 25:27, where "knowing hunting" is translated as ***nachashirchan***, having the connotation of ***nachash***, serpentine).

The ultimate joke (Yitzchak means "he will laugh") is that Isaac, embodiment of ***Gevurah***, is overpowered and outwitted by his wife, Rebecca, who turns out to be his match in that attribute. Isaac's ***Gevurah*** lay in the fact that he had been "born in" to the religion and brought up to a life of discipline, as symbolized in his being bound to the altar in the ***Akeidah*** that left his eyes blinded by the "tears of the angels" that dropped into them at that supreme moment. Rebecca's ***Gevurah*** lay in the fact that even as a child, she had separated herself from the totally sinful environment in which she had been brought up -- she was the archetypal ***Baalat Teshuvah***. Thus she knew the world better than "blind" Isaac -- and she knew that for the good of the entire world, it was vital that the blessings should go to Jacob. Since the serpent caused Adam's downfall by outwitting him and working on his wife, it was necessary for a woman, Rebecca, to outwit the serpent in order to restore Adam, incarnated in Jacob, to his true greatness. Thus Rebecca took Esau's beautiful clothes -- which he had stolen from Nimrod, who had stolen them from Adam -- and dressed Jacob with them.

"And [Isaac] smelled the scent of his clothes and he blessed him and said: See the scent of my son is as the scent of the field that HaShem has blessed. And G-d will give you of the dew of the heavens and from the fat of the earth and an abundance of grain and wine. The nations will serve you and the peoples will prostrate to you..." (Gen. 27:27-8).

VAYEITZEI

Torah reading: Gen. 28:10-32:3

Haftarah: Hosea 12:13-14:10 (Optional addition Micah 7:18)
(Sephardi ritual) Hosea 11:7-12:12

"AND JACOB WENT OUT FROM BE'ER SHEVA"

The previous parshah, ***Toldot***, completed the story of Isaac, which concluded with Isaac's giving the blessings to Jacob and sending him away from home to find his wife. In our present parshah of ***Vayeitzei***, Jacob, the "perfect" or "complete" patriarch (since he incorporated the best of both Abraham and Isaac) now takes center stage, and the story of his life and that of his twelve sons occupies the remainder of the book of Genesis.

Jacob's departure from his parental home into exile in Padan Aram and his return from there with a complete family and laden with wealth are paradigmatic for the subsequent history of Jacob's descendants, Israel and the Jewish people. Historically the Israelites were repeatedly forced to leave the ancestral Land of Israel, yet always returned in increased numbers, together with the wealth acquired in exile: the souls of the proselytes and actual material wealth.

* * *

"AND HE CAME TO THE PLACE"

While Jacob's journey of exile to Padan Aram is paradigmatic of all later Jewish exile, his detour on the way there to "***the Place***" (Gen. 28:11) -- Mount Moriah, "***the Place*** that G-d said to Abraham" (Gen. 22:9), that same ***field*** where Isaac went to pray -- is paradigmatic of the ***Giving of the Torah***. Thus the numerical value of the Hebrew letters of SuLaM, the "ladder" of Jacob's dream (Samech 60, Lamed 30, Mem 40) = 130 = SINaI, where the Torah was given (Samech 60, Yud 10,

Nun 50, Yud 10). The Torah itself was given "in exile", in the wilderness. The dream of the ladder and Jacob's actions in response to G-d's promise of protection -- his laying the Temple foundation and his vow to tithe all he acquires for G-d -- are Torah. They are the very essence of the Torah, the ***Giving of the Torah*** for all Jacob's descendants. Jacob's eventual return to this ***place*** where he "received the Torah" (see next week's parshah, Gen. ch. 35) is paradigmatic of the return of the Jewish people after exile to build the Holy Temple. The Temple and the Giving of the Torah are one concept.

The ***Place*** that Jacob "hit" (like you hit a target with an arrow or with a prayer) while on his way to Padan Aram was none other than the spot from which Adam was created: the place destined to bring atonement to all the Children of Adam in all generations through the sacrifical altar that is to stand there in the House of Prayer for all the Nations. This was the place where Noah sacrificed after the flood and this was where Abraham bound Isaac on the Altar. This was the field to which Isaac would return to pray. This place is alluded to in the opening word of the Torah, BeRAiSHiYT, the Hebrew letters of which can be rearranged to form the words BAYiT RoSH, "the House that is the Head". As discussed in connection with the parshiyot of the last two weeks, Abraham had conceived of this place as a lofty -- and almost daunting ***mountain*** of spiritual achievement. Isaac had brought the idea nearer to ordinary people by conceiving of it as a ***field*** of regular endeavor. It was the innovation of Jacob, the "perfect patriarch", to bring the idea within reach of everyone (for fields, in which Jacob was expert, are still not accessible to everyone): Jacob conceived of the place as a ***house***. "This is none other than the ***House*** of God" (Genesis 28:17; see Likutey Moharan I, 10).

In the words of the Talmud (Pesachim 88a): Said Rabbi Elazar: What does Isaiah mean when he says, "And many peoples will go and say, 'Come let us go up to the Mountain of G-d to the ***House*** of the G-d of Jacob!'"? Why the G-d of Jacob and not the G-d of Abraham and Isaac? The answer is: Not like Abraham, who saw it as a Mountain ("as it is said this day, On the Mountain HaVaYaH is seen" -- Genesis 22:14). And not like Isaac, for whom it was a Field ("And Isaac went out to meditate in the Field" -- Genesis 24:63). But like Jacob, who called it a House: "And he called the name of that place Beit El, the House of G-d" (Genesis 28:19).

This passage comes to teach that at the consummation of human history, when "many peoples will go" in search of G-d's truth, the idea through which G-d will be understood by the peoples will be Jacob's idea: the idea of the House -- the Holy Temple. The conception of the Temple as a House brings the idea of devotion to G-d right into the house and home. The Temple is the epitome of all houses. Thus it has a kitchen (the ***Azarah*** or central courtyard) and oven (the Altar), a "living room" (the Sanctuary), with its "lamp" (the Menorah) and table (the Showbread Table), and a "bedroom", the Holy of Holies, place of the ***zivug*** of the Holy One and the Shechinah (Divine Presence).

The Temple is the universal paradigm of what all of our homes should be, a place for the dwelling of the Divine Presence. At the very center of the Temple vision is the "ladder" that has angels "ascending and descending" on it. This is the ladder of devotion. Our prayers, blessings and simple, everyday "homely" mitzvot and acts of devotion send "angels" ***ascending*** upwards to realms that are beyond our comprehension. The ascending angels in turn elicit angels of blessing who ***descend*** into this world and into our very lives (such as the angels who accompany us from the synagogue to the home on Shabbat night and who, on seeing that we have made everything ready for Shabbat, bless our table, which is like the Temple altar.) The vow Jacob made upon inaugurating the House of G-d is the paradigm of all the different "vows" or commitments we make involving some kind of self-restraint and sacrifice in order to elevate ourselves spiritually and elicit G-d's protection. These acts of self-sacrifice send up ascending angels, drawing down descending angels of blessing. The foundation of devotion is our ***commitment*** (but without actual vows).

* * *

ENCOUNTER WITH THE WORLD OF OLD

Given that Jacob conceived of divine service using the metaphor of the ***house***, it is fitting that the central focus of the story of his life is on how he built his house, namely the household of wives and children who made up the House of Jacob, and how he faced all their subsequent domestic problems -- the kidnap of Dinah, the quarrels and hatred among the twelve brothers, the sale of Joseph and all that followed from it.

The building of Jacob's House could be accomplished only through struggles of many kinds -- for truth, Jacob's quality, is born out of struggle on all levels, material and spiritual. In order to build his House, Jacob had to struggle with two major antagonists: Esau and Laban. Esau embodies the threat to the Holy House from the forces of excess and evil in the material world, ***Asiyah***. The encounter with Esau is a central theme in next week's parshah: ***Vayishlach***. In this week's parshah of ***Vayeitzei*** the focus is on Jacob's encounter with Laban, whose threat to the Holy House is from the forces of excess in the spiritual worlds. Thus while Esau is portrayed as a ***hunter-warrior***, Laban is portrayed as a ***priest*** (Rashi on Gen. 24:21, Gen. 31:30ff).

To build his House, Jacob had to rescue the sparks of holiness that were still to be found in the land of the Sons of the East (Gen. 29:19), literally the "Sons of ***old***". These sparks of holiness were embodied in Rachel and Leah and their handmaidens, who were to mother the Souls of Israel. In order to rescue them, Jacob had to struggle with Laban, the High Priest of the "Old World", the unrectified World of ***Tohu*** (confusion) created by G-d to spawn the realm of evil with which man has to struggle in order to attain his destiny. Laban was the father of Be'or who was the father of Bilaam, also called Bela. Bela the son of Be'or is the first of the Seven Kings of Edom who ruled "before there was a king in Israel" (Gen. 36:31 ff.). These "Seven Kings" allude to the seven sefirot in their "fallen" manifestation as a result of the "breaking of the vessels". Kabbalistically, Bela corresponds to ***Da'at*** of the ***Sitra Achra***, the evil consciousness that is the opposite of G-dly knowledge and awareness, the root of all the other Sefirot. The Ari states that Bilaam-Bela was the incarnation of Laban, who is the very brain of the realm of evil, as indicated by his name, which consists of the letters Lamed (30) Beit (2) corresponding to the 32 Pathways of Wisdom, and Nun (50), corresponding to the 50 Gates of Understanding. Jacob's conflict with Laban continued in Moses fight against Bilaam and his pernicious spiritual influence.

Laban is the arch swindler and deceiver, symbolizing the force in creation that conceals G-dliness through our quirks of false-consciousness that make evil seem like good and good seem like evil. Laban ***translates*** one thing into another (we find an example of Laban as a translator in Gen. 31:47), distorting the entire meaning in the process. Time and time again, it turns out that Laban actually means something entirely different from what he appears on the surface to be saying. White-appearing Laban (Lavan in Hebrew = "white") is actually filthy black.

Since the devotions of Jacob (the Children of Israel) are accomplished by using the homely objects of this world to create the House of G-d through which the Divine Presence may dwell in the world, it is essential to cleanse the world of the mental distortions (the deceptions of idolatrous Laban) that could undermine the entire message of the Holy House.

Each one of us has the personal work of using Jacob's honesty to cleanse ourselves of the inner Labans that have us working for years chasing after phantoms, only to find ourselves sadly deceived...

* * *

THE WORK ETHIC

Jacob followed the example of Abraham's servant Eliezer (Gen. 24:11) in going to the ***well*** in order to find his ***zivug*** (soul-mate). As father of the people who were to bring the spiritual waters of Torah to all mankind, Jacob expected to find the appropriate soul-mate at the place of the "water-drawers". There Jacob saw his first love, Rachel, whose beauty was visible also on the exterior, as opposed to Leah, whose spiritual greatness was more concealed. The swindle by which Laban motivated Jacob to work for seven years for Rachel but actually gave him Leah, forcing him to work another seven years to get Rachel too, was a harsh lesson in how life may give us what we didn't bank on.

The implicit message in Jacob's deals with Laban, whereby Jacob worked for everything he gained -- his wives, his children and his flocks -- is that honest work is good, even when swindlers lurk. The heavens and earth were made "to do" (Gen. 2:3). "For six days, work shall be done..." (Exodus 35:2): Work is a good thing! Jacob had received rich blessings from Isaac, but that did not mean he had what he gained through sitting back and doing nothing. It was his very conscientiousness in working to earn the promised good that made him deserve the blessings.

The repeated seven-fold cycles in our parshah (seven years of work for Rachel and Leah, the seven days of the marriage celebrations) are bound up with the underlying six-day/Shabbat cycle of creation which comes to rectify the seven fallen Sefirot of the world of ***Tohu*** spawned by Bilaam-Laban. The holy sparks rescued by Jacob through his "work" -- Rachel, Leah, the handmaidens, their children, and the "flocks", namely the holy souls -- are all reordered in the world of ***Tikun*** (Rectification, the Sefirot in their holy manifestation) in the House of Jacob. Here Jacob (corresponding to Zeir Anpin, the unity of G-d) is joined and unified with his wives, Rachel (the revealed world) and Leah (the concealed world).

Jacob's main work and that of his wives was that of ***breeding*** -- the breeding of children and the breeding of "flocks". This comes to emphasize the centrality of family, education and good breeding in true civilization. The House about which Jacob's Temple comes to teach is not a far-off concept. It is the actual house and home in which we live, where our work must be to educate ourselves and our children to see and manifest G-d in our mundane, everyday activities.

Jacob is the archetype of the faithful employee. He starts off with nothing (according to the Midrash, Jacob was stripped of all his possessions by Esau's son Eliphaz as he set off for Padan Aram). He works conscientiously to benefit and enrich his employer, with scrupulous honesty and devotedness (as expressed in Jacob's eloquent self-defense, Gen. 31:38 ff.). Jacob is pitted against a slick liar who keeps on changing the terms of agreements, who sells his own daughters, who watches his nephew work for his wives, children and flocks for 20 years and still says, "They are all mine...."

The practical teaching about the work ethic that emerges from this section of our parshah telling of Jacob's way of working applies to all mankind. It is an important aspect of the universal law against stealing:

"Just as the employer is cautioned not to steal or withhold the wages of the poor man, so the poor man (the employee) is cautioned not to steal the work of the employer by wasting a little time here and a little there so that he spends the entire day cheating his employer. The worker is obliged to be strict with himself in the time he devotes to his employer's work... and he is obliged to work with all his strength. For the righteous Jacob said 'For ***with all my strength*** I worked for your father...' And therefore he took the reward for this even in this world..." (Rambam, Laws of Hiring 13:7)

Those who are inclined to pass the working hours drinking tea and coffee, chatting, making irrelevant phone calls, etc. should take note.

VAYISHLACH

Torah reading: Gen. 32.4-36.43

Haftarah: Hosea 11:7-12:12 (Sephardi ritual) Obadiah 1:1-21

THE ENCOUNTER WITH ESAU

*A*t the end of the previous parshah, ***Vayeitzei***, we saw Jacob at ***Mount*** Gil'ad in his final encounter with Laban, who represents the evil husk in its spiritual manifestation, fake ***Chessed***-kindness. At Mount Gil'ad, Jacob made a "treaty" with Laban demarcating the boundaries which they and their descendants were to observe: these are the boundaries that neither good nor evil may overstep in the unfolding drama of human history. In prevailing over Laban, Jacob demonstrated that he had made a complete acquisition of Abraham's quality of ***Chessed***. As discussed in connection with previous parshahs, it was Abraham who went to the ***Mountain***, and thus Jacob's "treaty" with Laban was struck at ***Mount*** Gil'ad.

In the present parshah, ***Vayishlach***, we see Jacob struggling with the evil husk in its material manifestation, the "fallen" ***Gevurot***, worldly power and strength, as embodied in Esau, man of the ***field***. Thus at the beginning of the parshah, Jacob, who is about to enter the Promised Land, sends emissaries ahead to his brother Esau in the land of Seir, the ***field*** of Edom (Gen. 32:4).

Esau was called the "man of the field" (Gen. 25:27), having received the trait of ***Gevurah***, power and strength, from Isaac, who, as the embodiment of holy ***Gevurah***, self-discipline, "went out to the field" (Gen. 24:63). However, the aspect of ***Gevurah*** which Esau received from Isaac was the excess, unholy aspect: Esau's "field" was the wild outdoors. Thus later on, the Torah writes: "And if ***in the field*** the man finds the engaged girl and the man takes hold of her and lies with her, that man that lay with her shall die, he alone... for as a man rises up against his neighbor and murders him, so is this matter" (Deut. 22:25).

This ***field*** of rape and murder is the field of idolatrous slaughter: "the sacrifices that they slaughter on the face of the ***field***... their sacrifices to the ***goat***-demons (***se'irim***) that they lust after them..." (Leviticus 17:5-7). According to the Rabbis, on the day when Esau came in "from the field" (Gen. 25:29) and sold his birth-right to Jacob, Esau was "tired" from the three cardinal sins of idolatry, sexual immorality and murder.

In order for Jacob to complete his acquisition of the birth-right and enter and acquire the Promised Land, he had to demonstrate that together with the ***Chessed*** he had inherited from his grandfather Abraham, he had also made a complete acquisition of the trait of holy ***Gevurah*** embodied in his father Isaac. Jacob demonstrated this in his struggle with Esau, where he prevailed through applying his consummate wisdom and humility. Thus we find in our parshah that Jacob also made a treaty of boundaries and separation with Esau. This boundary will prevail "... until I will come to my lord to Seir" (Gen. 33:14) -- "And when will he go? In the days of Mashiach, as it says, 'And saviors will go up on Mount Zion to judge the house of Esau'" (Obadiah 1:21, in our Haftarah, see Rashi on Gen. 33:14). A substantial portion of our parshah is devoted to Esau, including the concluding section, which traces all the generations of Esau, including Amalek (Gen. 36:12) the historical counterfeit of Israel, and Rome (Gen. 36:43, "Magdiel", see Rashi ad loc.).

Jacob was first characterized as "a dweller of tents" (Gen. 25:27) -- the "tent" of Abraham (***Chessed***) and the "tent" of Isaac (***Gevurah***). "Planting" tents in a field turns the ***field*** into a place of residence. Jacob's mission was to join and synthesize the holy traits of his fathers and teachers, ***Chessed*** and ***Gevurah***, in order to build ***Tiferet***, truth, beauty and balance. This is the ***house***, the House of Jacob -- the ***House***, family and people of Israel, and also the archetypal, model physical ***House*** that is to serve to guide all mankind to return to G-d, the "House of Prayer for all the Nations", the "***home***" of G-d: the ***Holy Temple***. In the course of our parshah, we see Jacob busy building houses. He travels to Succot, "***tabernacles***" -- temporary homes. There Jacob built himself a ***house*** while making booths for his livestock.

Jacob then came "***complete***" to SheCheM (Gen. 33:18). The Hebrew word for "complete" is ShaLeM -- made up of the letters Shin, signifying fire, ***Gevurot***, Mem signifying water, ***Chassadim***, and the transcendent center-column Lamed, that shoots upwards exactly like the Vav on top of the Kaf from which the Lamed is formed. SheKheM signifies ***shafel***, the lowly material world, ***kochavim***, the stars and constellations that direct what happens here, and the ***malakhim***, the angels or the spiritual forces which "drive" the stars and planets (Likutey Moharan I:9). In Shechem, Jacob "acquired the lot of the ***field*** in which he ***planted his tent***..." (Gen. 33:17-19). Finally, at the climax of our parshah, "And Jacob said to his ***house*** and to all that were with him, remove the strange gods that are in you and purify yourselves and change your garments. And let us arise and go up to the ***House*** of G-d..." (Gen. 35:2-3). And then the House of Jacob was complete: "And the sons of Jacob were twelve" (Gen. 35:22).

Jacob could only succeed in building this ***house***, the House of Israel and its center ***House***, the Holy Temple, after having won a complete victory over Esau, representing ***Asiyah***, the world of material action, with its many traps and dangers. When the Temple stands, order prevails, and atonement is brought to Israel and the world through sending the ***seir***-goat of atonement away to die in the wilderness (Lev. 16:21-22).

* * *

A GIFT, A PRAYER... AND/OR WAR

Esau came against Jacob with the implacable envy and enmity of the serpent towards Adam, for "he will stamp on you on the head and you will bite him at the heel (***akev***)" (Gen. 3:15). Even when Esau kissed, he really came to bite (see Baal HaTurim on "and he kissed him" Gen. 33:4 -- "in gematria, 'and he came to bite him'"). Jacob, Ya***akov***, was so named because he "gripped the heel (***akev***)" of Esau (Gen. 25:26). This was how Jacob reclaimed Adam's greatness, the ***reishit***, "head" or "birth-right", thereby stamping on and crushing the serpent's head.

Esau came with 400 men, the legions of death. 400 corresponds to the Hebrew letter Tav, last letter of the Aleph Beit, the ultimate in multiplicity. 400 signifies a complete array of numbers -- 10 x 10 -- on all four sides: number, measurement and limitation everywhere. This multiplicity stands counter to G-d's unity, represented by Jacob and his twelve sons (the twelve constellations and twelve hours, time and space), arranged in order in a square (= perfect balance) around the House, the Sanctuary, the ***BaYiT*** (from BereishYT), which ends in the letter ***Tav***. The House of Jacob comes to overcome death, ***mavet***, which also ends with the letter ***Tav***. For "her feet go down to death" (Proverbs 5:5) -- plurality, the worship of many gods.

Esau's ***Gevurah*** was ***brawn***, the power of physical force. ("I have abundance" Gen. 33:9). But Jacob overcame Esau's brawn through ***brain, rosh***, the wisdom gained from Jacob's synthesis: this is the ***Tiferet – Da'at*** center-column, the faculty of "putting things together" (***Chochmah*** and ***Binah***, ***Chessed*** and ***Gevurah***). This is achieved through ***give and take***. Thus, Jacob is the ultimate in humility: "I am too ***small*** for all Your kindnesses" (Gen. 32:11). "Say they belong to ***your servant*** Jacob, a gift sent to ***my lord*** Esau" (ibid. v. 19). "And he ***prostrated*** to the ground seven times until he approached his brother..." (33:3).

For Jacob is Ya-***akov***, the one who grasps the heel, and "the ***heel*** (***akev***) of humility is ***fear of G-d***" (Proverbs 22:4) -- "how ***awesome*** is this Place" (Gen. 28:17). The fear of G-d is the "beginning" of wisdom, the ***reishit***, the birth-right (the Hebrew letters of the word ***reishit*** include the letters of the word ***ya-re***, "he is in awe"). For "the ***beginning*** of wisdom, ***Chochmah***, is ***Fear of G-d***" (Psalms 111:10) and "what wisdom made her crown, humility made the sandal on her heel (***akev***)" (Midrash).

Jacob knows that this world is but the heel of an entire system of worlds, and this is what gives him his mastery over this world. He is able to use this world to serve G-d by configuring and ordering the world properly. Jacob understands that there has to be give and take with Esau. He understands that Esau has chosen This World. Jacob thus "bribes" Esau with the "goat for Azazel", the gift of material wealth, which Jacob, as the source of all blessings, has the power to draw down and channel to the world.

The abundant gifts of livestock that Jacob sends to Esau contain a message. Rashi on Gen. 32:15 brings a midrash showing how the varying ratio of males to females among the different kinds of livestock alludes to the appropriate ***onah*** or time of conjugal union for people in different walks of life (see Rashi there). In other words, the same Jacob who sent messages to Isaac in the "lentil soup" is now teaching the sexually wild Esau a lesson in how to tame and direct animal lust for the sake of good breeding. In this way, Jacob's material "gift" to Esau brings order and rectification to the world of ***Asiyah***.

Jacob offers peace and gifts (***Chessed***), but he is prepared for war to the very end (***Gevurah***). Yet in his humility, Jacob knows that all the gifts and all the might of ***Asiyah*** will not prevail against Esau without the help of G-d. "He prepared himself for three things: for a gift, for ***prayer*** and for war" (Rashi on Gen. 32:9). Prayer is at the center, in between ***Chessed*** (gifts) and ***Chessed*** (war). "And Jacob said: G-d of my father Abraham and G-d of my father Isaac...." (Gen. 32:10).

Jacob struggled with Esau's root -- his ***Sar*** ("guardian angel") -- and it was his success against the angel that enabled him to prevail over Esau himself. Jacob's success was ***win/win***, for even Esau gained what he really wanted: the material glory of this world. While Esau takes the material wealth, Jacob struggles to find the inner "face", the roots and inner meaning of the wealth and glory of this world. Thus Jacob calls the place of his struggle with the angel ***Peni-el***, "for I saw G-d ***face to face***" (Gen. 32:31). Yet in order for the world to continue to exist after we uncover the inner face, there has to be give and take. Jacob gets injured "in the leg" -- ***Hod***. In this world, ***kulo omer kavod***, "everything cries out glory". In the very outcry of worldly glory, G-d's glory becomes concealed! As a result, Jacob's children -- "the legs" -- "do not eat from the slipped tendon" (***gid hanasheh***). The Children of Israel are unable to eat all the material blessings of this world because of the blemished glory. In this world the glory is taken by Esau, for if Jacob's glory, the glory of Israel, were fully revealed, there would be no free will.

* * *

THE SIN OF THE MEN OF SHECHEM

The integrity of the House -- the family -- of Jacob depends upon family ***purity***, observance of the laws of sexual decency and restraint. "Shall our sister be treated like a prostitute?" (Gen. 34:31). Moral purity is the very foundation of the Covenant of Abraham, which is sealed in the flesh of the male Children of Israel on the organ of procreation, indicating the need to restrain animal lust and elevate it in the service of G-d in order to breed righteous children to "guard the way of HaShem" (Gen. 18:19).

The rape of Dinah was a violation of this integrity by Shechem the son of Hamor (= donkey, physical animality) the Chivi (Chivia in Aramaic is "serpent" see Targum on Gen. 3:1). Shechem is the opposite of Joseph "the Tzaddik", the archetype of sexual discipline, who restrains himself with Potiphar's wife and eventually receives SheKheM (the three worlds, the lowly world, that of the stars and that of the angels, as discussed above) as well as -- according to the midrash -- marrying Dinah's daughter = Asnat.

Dinah's urge to go out and about "to see the daughters of the land" (a trait unbefitting the daughter of Jacob) exposed her to danger in a world that was still untamed. Abraham and Isaac had both faced trials because of the fallen morality of the Egyptians and the Philistines. Now Jacob's own daughter is raped by Shechem the Hittite, descendant of the accursed Canaan, son of Ham.

According to Torah law, Dinah, as a ***penuyah***, "unmarried", was not forbidden to Shechem. What was forbidden was the manner in which he "saw her... and he ***took*** her and lay with her": Shechem kidnapped Dinah. His crime was the violation of the Noachide Law against stealing, which prohibits the unlawful taking not only of goods but of people. The crime of the men of Shechem who were sitting "in the gate of their city" (Gen. 34:20) -- i.e. they were the judges of the city -- was that they watched this violation of Noachide law and did nothing.

In the words of Rambam (Maimonides) Laws of Kings 9:14: "In what way are they (the Children of Noah) commanded with regard to the rule of law? They are obliged to establish judges and magistrates in every region to judge cases relating to the other six commandments, and to warn the population. And any of the Children of Noah who violates one of these seven commandments is to be killed by the sword. ***And for this reason the rulers of Shechem were liable to execution***, for Shechem ***stole*** and they saw and they knew and they did not bring him to justice..."

The zeal of Levi and Shimon in perpetrating justice did not escape Jacob's censure, both in our parshah (Gen. 34:30) and in his blessings to his sons before his death (Gen. 49:5, "Shimon and Levi are brothers, weapons of might are their swords... Accursed is their anger... I will divide them among Jacob and scatter them among Israel...") Zeal is necessary yet dangerous. It is controlled when the zealots are divided and scattered. Levi was "scattered" by having to go around to all the farms to collect the Levitical tithes. This honorable scattering was the reward for the zeal showed by the tribe later on, at the time of the sin of the Golden Calf. However, Shimon's zeal was not so pure, and led to excess, as when the Zimri, Prince of the tribe of Shimon, took Kozbi the Midianite and challenged Moses. (Zimri was killed by Pinchas, son of Aaron from the tribe of Levi, exemplar of Holy Zeal). To rectify the challenge to Moses by the Prince of the House of Shimon, members of the tribe of Shimon were "scattered" by having to become scribes and teachers of Moses' Torah (see Rashi on Gen. 49:7).

* * *

LET US GO UP TO THE HOUSE OF G-D

The significance of the section of the parshah describing Jacob's "pilgrimage" with his family to Beit El, the ***House*** of G-d, has been discussed above. At Beit El, Jacob's acquisition of the birthright and the Promised Land was sealed, and he attained his name of greatness -- Israel -- from the mouth of G-d.

The House of Jacob was completed by the birth of Benjamin, who was the only one of Jacob's twelve sons to be born in the Land of Israel and who founded the tribe that was to contribute the first king of Israel, Saul, who was "head and shoulders above all the men of Israel" in his outstanding modesty and righteousness. Shammai, the Mishnaic Tanna and Av Beit Din ("father of the court") in the time of Hillel the Elder, was a descendant of King Saul, while Hillel, who was the Nasi or Prince (and as such, the highest in rank) was a descendant of King David. Thus the ***machloket*** (controversy) throughout the ***Shas*** (6 orders of Mishnah), between ***Beit Shammai*** and ***Beit Hillel*** is bound up with the struggle between Judah (son of Leah) and Benjamin (son of Rachel). This struggle is resolved through the process of clarifying the halachah, which practically always follows the opinion of Beit Hillel.

Conflict and its resolution is the theme of all the remaining parshiyot in the book of Genesis from next week (***Vayeishev***) until the end of Genesis (***Vayechi***). This is the story of the rectification of the world, which comes about through Mashiach son of David (who is from the tribe of Judah, son of Leah) and Mashiach son of Joseph (son of Rachel). In order to clear the way for the story of rectification, namely the story of Joseph and his brothers (in which the bond between Judah and Benjamin plays a central part), the Torah concludes our parshah of ***Vayishlach*** with an account of the generations of Esau. The theme of sexual immorality recurs in this account, for several of Esau's children and grandchildren were ***mamzerim*** (bastards -- see Rashi on Gen. 36:2 and 36:12 etc.)

This account ends with the account of the Seven Kings who ruled over Edom -- and died -- before there was a king in Israel. It is well known that these Seven Kings allude to the seven "fallen" Sefirot of the World of ***Tohu*** (devastation), while the last-mentioned king -- the eighth, of whom it does not say "and he died" -- is Hadar = Abraham, father of the World of Rectification.

This throws light on the meaning of Rashi's first comment on next week's parshah (on Gen. 37:1): "After the Torah writes for you the dwellings of Esau and his generations in brief, since they were not sufficiently important to tell in detail... the Torah now comes to the dwellings of Jacob and his generations at length and all the cycles (***gilgulim***) of causes, for they are important before G-d... It can be compared to a jewel that fell in the sand. A person feels through and sieves all the sand until he finds the jewel. And when he finds the jewel, he throws away the pebbles and takes the jewel."

VAYEISHEV

Torah Reading: Genesis. 37:1-40:23

Haftarah: Amos 2:6-3:8

"FROM THE DEPTH OF HEBRON": JACOB AND HIS CHILDREN

"These are the generations of Jacob. These are their dwellings and rollings (***gilgulim***) until they came to a state of habitation (***yishuv***). The first cause was that 'Joseph was seventeen years old.'

" 'And Jacob dwelled...': Jacob wanted to dwell in tranquility, but the storm of Joseph sprang upon him. The tzaddikim want to dwell in tranquility, but the Holy One, blessed be He, says, 'Is it not enough for the tzaddikim that the World to Come is prepared for them, but they want to dwell in tranquility in this world?' " (Rashi on Gen. 37:2).

Now that the Torah has completed the stories of Abraham and Isaac and that part of the story of Jacob in which he is the chief actor, we now turn to the story of Jacob's children: "These are the generations of Jacob". Their "dwellings and rollings" -- as recounted in the remaining four parshiyot of Genesis, allude to all their future history, in the Land of Israel and in exile, until we will finally come to a "state of habitation" (***yishuv***) in the Land of Israel, with Melech HaMashiach: a state of ***yishuv hada'at***, "a settled mind" -- expanded consciousness. Jacob sought immediate tranquility in the Land of Israel, but this tranquillity could only be attained in the Future World, after many "rollings" -- (***gilgulim***) incarnations and generations.

The Children of Israel are destined to be a Light to the Nations. As such, they must be at peace with each other, for how can they shine to the nations when they are at war with one another? But in our parshah of ***Vayeishev***, the Children of Israel were unable to make inner peace: "...And they could not speak to him [Joseph] peaceably" (Gen. 37:4).

Joseph exemplified the true leader -- "and he was pasturing his brothers" (v. 2) -- but as yet his brothers could not accept him. He was too saintly. The brothers were still out for themselves: "...They went only to pasture ***themselves***" (Rashi on Gen. 37:12). Their in-fighting turned into a hypocritical religious war: "They said, 'Let us go to Dotan'" (from the root ***dat***, "religious law"; Gen. 37:17). They went "to seek out religious contrivances" (***nichley datot***) in order to kill the true leader (see Rashi on this verse).

Yet Jacob sent Joseph into the middle of all this "from the depth (***emek***, valley) of Hebron" (Gen. 37:14). -- "But surely Hebron is on a ***mountain***, as it says, 'And they ***ascended*** from the south and he came to Hebron' (Numbers 13:22)??? But what it means is ***from the deep plan*** of that tzaddik who is buried in Hebron, i.e. Abraham, to fulfil what was said to him at the Covenant Between the Pieces, 'for your seed will be a stranger' (Gen. 16:13)" (Rashi ad loc.).

In other words, the "deep plan" necessitated the sale of Joseph into slavery in Egypt, which would eventually cause all his brothers and Jacob himself to go down to Egypt, in order to bring about the exile of the Children of Egypt there in preparation for their eventual Exodus. The paradigm of Exile / Redemption recurs repeatedly in Jewish history in the exiles of Babylon, Persia, Greece and Rome (Edom-Yishmael).

All the "rollings" and incarnations of the Children of Israel from generation to generation refine and purify their souls in preparation for the eventual state of ***yishuv***, "habitation", which depends on peace among the Twelve Tribes. In the coming parshiyot, we will see how the wise leader exemplified in Joseph skillfully manipulates everything to bring his "exiled" brothers to repent of their fractiousness and enmity and make peace with one another. Repentance is a recurrent theme of this and all the remaining parshiyot in Genesis. Reuven repented his "sin" (Gen 35:22; Rashi on 37:29); Judah repented, confessing: "she was more righteous than me" (Gen. 38:26); Joseph's brothers repented: "but we are guilty" (Gen. 42:21).

The essential fissures among the Children of Israel in their later history were between Benjamin vs. the other tribes (Judges Ch. 19ff), and the House of Judah (representing fidelity to the Oral Torah) vs. the House of Israel, the Ten Tribes, who rebelled under the leadership of Jeraboam son of Nevat of the tribe of Ephraim = Joseph (representing worldly success). (This is also the clash today between the "religious" and "secular".) In the coming parshiyot we will see how Judah (from the Children of Leah) becomes a "guarantor" (Gen. 44:30) for Benjamin (from the sons of Rachel), and how the state of near war between Judah and Joseph (Gen. 44:18) is transformed into a state of reconciliation between Joseph and all his brothers (Ch. 45). Judah's repentance and taking responsibility make him worthy of being the religious leader. "And he [Jacob] sent ***Judah*** before him to Joseph to ***rule***." (Gen. 46:28).

The bond forged between Judah and Benjamin exemplifies the concept that "all Israel are guarantors for one another" (Shevuot 39a). This bond is embodied in the fact that the territories of the two tribes of Judah and Benjamin are contiguous, meeting in Jerusalem, Yeru***shalayim***, City of Peace, at the site of the Holy Altar in the Temple on Mount Moriah. The bond between Judah and Benjamin is also embodied in the figure of Mordechai, who although from the tribe of Benjamin is nevertheless called ***ish Yehudi***, a man of Judah (Esther 2:5). The Code of Jewish Law also represents peace between Judah and Benjamin, in the sense that the stringent House of Shammai (Benjamin) receives honor and is always mentioned first, yet the legal decision in almost all cases follows the opinion of the compassionate House of Hillel (Judah).

The transformation of the war between Joseph and Judah into a state of reconciliation and peace is paradigmatic of the future reconciliation of the Jews (= Jude, Judah) and the lost Ten Tribes, and also the reconciliation between the "religious" and the "secular". All this comes about through Mashiach son of Joseph (Rachel) and Mashiach son of Judah (Leah).

However, in our parshiyot, all these hints of future history are contained in allusion only, for prior to attaining the future state of

yishuv and ***mochin d'gadlut*** -- "settled" and "expanded consciousness" -- the world is in a state of ***bilbul*** and ***mochin d'katnut***, "confusion" and "limited consciousness". Thus our parshah deals with negative feelings and emotions: the hatred of the brothers for Joseph; their deception of Jacob with the blood of the slaughtered goat; the deception of Judah by Tamar; the attack on Joseph by Potiphar's wife, etc. etc.

The state of ***mochin d'katnut*** is the state of exile. Thus in our parshah, the scene changes from the Land of Israel to Egypt, ***Mitzraim*** = ***meitzar***, the "narrow" or "constricted" place. While Israel is the "face" (the ***pnimiut***, the hidden "interiority"), Egypt represents the revealed exterior, the "back-side". Thus the King of Egypt is Pharaoh, the Hebrew letters of whose name when rearranged spell out ***ha-oreph***, "the ***back*** of the neck", opposite of "the ***face***". In this state of exile, there is no more prophecy, only dreams. Joseph dreams. The Butler and the Baker dream. Pharaoh dreams. G-d appears to Jacob "in the appearances of the night" (Gen. 46:2). Constricted consciousness!

* * *

"AND JUDAH WENT DOWN." THE LIGHT OF MASHIACH

"The tribes were busy with the sale of Joseph; Joseph was busy with his sack-cloth and fasting; Reuven was busy with his sack-cloth and fasting; Jacob was busy with his sack-cloth and fasting; Judah was busy getting himself a wife. And the Holy One, blessed be He, was busy creating the light of the King Mashiach. -- 'And at that time Judah ***went down*** (Gen. 38:1). Even before the first oppressor [Pharaoh] was born, the final redeemer was born" (Midrash Rabbah, Bereishit 85:1).

Immediately after the story of the sale of Joseph to Egypt (the beginning of the exile) the Torah immediately tells us the story of Judah and Tamar, which culminates with the birth of Peretz (Gen. 38:29) who was the ancestor of King David, the Messianic King (Ruth 4:18-22).

The story of Judah and Tamar is one of sexual sin and its rectification. Of the three cardinal sins, Abraham rectified that of Idolatry (fallen ***Chessed***) while Isaac rectified the sin of Bloodshed (fallen ***Gevurot***. The mission of Jacob and his sons was to rectify the sin of ***gilui arayot***, Sexual Immorality (fallen ***Tiferet***-Beauty), which is why the preceding parshiyot were preoccupied with how Jacob built his House, with his Four Wives and the Twelve Tribes arranged around his pure "bed", the Holy Sanctuary. Sexual immorality was the main theme in the story of Dinah, recounted in last week's parshah of ***Vayishlach***. The theme continues in our parshah. Thus Joseph was "a lad" -- "he was engaged in puerile behavior, he arranged his hair carefully and smoothed his eyes in order to look beautiful" (Rashi on Gen. 37:2 and see Rashi on Gen. 39:6). Judah came in to "the harlot" (Gen. 38:15ff); Potiphar lusted for the beautiful Joseph and his wife attempted to seduce him...

Sexual immorality was an essential element in the original sin of Adam, which the rabbis conceptualized as ***keri***, an "impure emission" of seed. Adam had been commanded to "be fruitful and multiply and fill the earth and conquer it and rule." (Gen. 1:28). But in "eating the forbidden fruit" of the Tree of Knowledge of good and evil, Adam fell into material lust. His seed, intended to produce future generations that would know G-d, "fell" and became prey to the forces of unholy lust. Thus the holy sparks became trapped in exile. This had to be rectified by Adam's descendants, the Children of Israel, whose mission -- as mentioned above -- was to rectify sexual immorality [see Kavanot of the Ari, Pesach]. However, Er, the firstborn of Judah, failed the test and spilled his seed in order that his wife Tamar should not conceive and lose her worldly beauty (see Rashi on Gen. 38:7), and as a result G-d killed him.

According to the law of Levirate marriage (***yibum***), Er's surviving brother Onan should have "raised up seed" in the name of his dead brother (i.e. the dead brother would be reincarnated in order to rectify his sin in a new life), but Onan was also selfish, and spilled his seed (Gen. 38:7).

Only through the resourcefulness of Tamar (who was the daughter of Shem = Malki-Tzedek, the "Priest", symbol of moral purity, see Gen.

9:23) was the sin rectified through the mystery of Judah's encounter with the "harlot", which led to the birth of Peretz and eventually of David, King Mashiach.

Rabbi Nachman of Breslov stated that the main task of Mashiach is to rectify the spilling of seed.

* * *

"AND HE WAS A SUCCESSFUL MAN"

The reason why Joseph was "a successful man" (Gen. 39:2) was precisely because "HaShem was with Joseph" (ibid.) -- "the name of Heaven was regularly on his mouth" (Rashi ad loc.). Joseph had the power to see and find G-d even in Egypt, the place of ***mochin d'katnut***, "constricted consciousness", the "back-side". This was the key to his "success". Joseph was the very essence of Jacob, as Rashi goes to some lengths to prove (see Rashi on Gen. 37:2).

As the key figure in the "generations of Jacob", Joseph had the same mission as his father: the building of the archetypal holy ***house***, as discussed in connection with the preceding parshiyot. At first, Joseph dreams of being in the ***field***, where all his brother's sheaves prostrate to him. Later Joseph strays in the ***field*** (Gen. 37:15). Yet at length his dream comes true in Egypt. There his brothers prostrate before Joseph, who orders them to be brought to his ***house*** (Gen. 43:16ff.), where they eat and drink.

The Children of Israel are not disembodied souls. They are ***in*** the material world, their task being to elevate and spiritualize it. This is done through turning the mundane material house into a ***home***, a Sanctuary of G-d -- "and I will dwell within them" (Exodus 25:8).

It is the moral integrity of Joseph -- who succeeds in finding G-d even in Egypt, constriction, the "back-side" -- that is the key to this house-making. As we will see in next week's parshah of ***Miketz***, Joseph knows the secret of material, economic success (as exemplified in his successful management of the Egyptian economy even in times of famine). Through the story of Joseph, the Torah teaches us that the foundation of genuine long-term material success is moral purity and integrity. Even when Joseph was faced with the supreme moral test -- alone in the house with his master's wife tempting him day after day -- he set the unchangeable Law of G-d before him: adultery is forbidden. "How could I do this great evil and sin against G-d?" (Gen. 39:9).

Joseph observed G-d's law despite the fact that this led to his incarceration in the king's prison and his disgrace in the eyes of sophisticated Egypt. Joseph is the archetype of "the tzaddik who has it bad" (Berachot 7a). Yet even in this adverse situation, "HaShem was with Joseph" (Gen. 39:21). As before (ibid. v. 2), this teaches that "the name of Heaven was regularly on his mouth". That was the very key to Joseph's "success". Joseph knew that G-d speaks to us through the happenings of this world, and that we can find divine messages and meaning everywhere and in everything. Thus Joseph (***Da'at-Yesod***, Knowledge-Foundation, the Center Column) could "interpret dreams", even those of the Butler (fallen ***Chochmah***-Wisdom) and the Baker (fallen ***Binah***-Understanding). These two, together with the Captain of the Guard (fallen ***Da'at***-Knowledge) in whose ***house*** Joseph was a slave and captive, were the Chief Officers of Pharoah, the very embodiment of the "Back-Side", where holiness is initially concealed. It was through Joseph's incorruptible moral integrity (***Shemirat Ha-Brit***, Observance of the Covenant) that he was able to turn everything around and find divine meaning and messages even in darkness and dreams of the night. This is what brings Mashiach.

And so may our Chanukah Lights light up the darkness of night, heralding ***Geulah Shleimah***, complete redemption with Ben David Melech HaMashiach quickly in our times. Amen!

MIKETZ

Torah Reading: Genesis. 41:1-44:17

Haftarah: I Kings 3:15-4:1

"AND PHARAOH WAS DREAMING."

*T*he exile of the Children of Israel in Egypt and their subsequent redemption and exodus are the paradigm of all exile and redemption, physical and spiritual. The chief oppressor is Pharaoh, King of Egypt, a figure first introduced in the Torah several parshiyot earlier, in ***Lech Lecha*** (ch. 12, v. 10ff). Famine had forced Abraham to go down to Egypt, the "nakedness of the earth" (just as in our parshah, famine forces his descendants down to the same place). Egypt is the stronghold of ***Mitzraim***, second son of the accursed Ham, who had "uncovered" his father Noah's nakedness. In the same tradition of sexual immorality, Pharaoh, representing the evil, self-seeking aspect of earthly power, kidnapped Sarah, embodiment of the Indwelling Presence of G-d, until a divine plague forced him to release her. According to tradition, Sarah was released on the night of the 15th of Nissan, the date of the later Exodus of her descendants from Egypt.

Our parshah of ***Miketz*** traces the successive stages in which the snare was laid to force Jacob and his Twelve Sons to follow Joseph down into exile in Egypt in preparation for the ultimate redemption of the Children of Israel years later on that same date. The net is artfully prepared by Joseph, who alone of all the sons of Jacob had the power to stand in the House of Pharaoh. Joseph is the archetype of the Tzaddik who enables us to survive in This World. Having been drawn down to Egypt by Joseph, the Children of Israel are eventually redeemed by Moses, who, having been brought up in the House of Pharaoh, had the power to stand there. Moses is integrally linked with Joseph, and thus Moses "took the bones [= the essence] of Joseph with him" up out of Egypt. Moses is the Tzaddik who teaches us the path leading through the wilderness of This World to the Land of the Living -- the Land of Israel.

This World is but a dream. Pharaoh is dreaming. Pharaoh is the "back-side" (PHaRAO = ORePH, the back of the neck) -- the external appearance of This World as opposed to its inner "face", the inner spirituality and meaning. The outward appearance is frightening: plump prosperity turning into wizened waste.

Pharaoh is the worldly ego. "So says the Lord G-d, Here I am against you, Pharaoh king of Egypt, the great crocodile [= primordial serpent] lying down in his rivers, who says: 'The river is mine, and I made myself' (Ezekiel 29: 3, from the haftarah of Parshat ***Va'eira*** which recounts the plagues sent against Egypt). Pharaoh thinks he is all-powerful -- "I made myself" -- but in the end he is humiliated by G-d's plagues, which show him his limitations. As yet his downfall is still far-off -- a distant vision, a bad dream. Yet already Pharaoh is being humiliated. The dream is terrifying. Pharaoh's own magicians and wise men are helpless: they cannot give meaning to his dream. The only one who can help Pharaoh is "a man who has the spirit of G-d in him" (Gen. 41:38), the truly righteous Tzaddik: Joseph.

* * *

THE VIRTUE OF THRIFT

Temporal leaders may imagine they are pulling the strings, but the underlying forces that drive human history are great global cycles of success and decline ("Seven years of plenty" / "Seven years of famine") that are in the power of G-d alone. Likewise, G-d alone has the power to send truly wise leaders to guide us through these cycles to a better end.

While Pharaoh is the archetype of the self-seeker, Joseph is the archetype of self-discipline. The latter is the virtue needed to get through This World successfully. Pharaoh knows how to consume to gratify the self here and now -- to live the dream of This World. This may work as long as the river keeps flowing. But Pharaoh does not know what to do when the flow stops. He is unprepared, because Pharaoh is ***paru'ah***, undisciplined. He does not know how to conserve and save for lean times.

Pharaoh's self-seeking is rooted in the fundamental flaw of Adam: ***keri***, spilling the seed in vain -- waste. Thus it is said that the sparks in the seed spilled by Adam fell to Egypt, where they had to be rectified in the generation of Joseph and in the generation of Moses. The rectification in the generation of Joseph was accomplished by the ***discipline*** which Joseph brought to the country. Joseph used the Seven Years of Plenty to teach the Egyptians to put limits on ***immediate consumption and gratification*** in order to ***save*** for the ***future***. (Similarly in the generation of the Exodus, the Children of Israel, incarnation of Adam's spilled seed, were rectified through the building of Pharaoh's "store-cities".) We must all learn how to set limits to the physical gratification we receive from this world in order to make the best use of our time here to acquire and "save" Mitzvot and good deeds. These are our ***tzeidah la-derekh***, the "sustenance for the way" that leads to the Land of the Living, the Future World.

The world today is suffering from the catastrophic effects of ***immediate consumption*** on the global ecology in the form of reckless depletion of resources, pollution etc. and on the moral fabric of contemporary society. The model of happiness entertained by most of the world – ***conspicuous consumption*** -- is unsustainable and destructive, and must be replaced with Joseph's model: that we must "circumcise" ourselves and learn self-discipline. Only by thriftily "saving" Torah and good deeds can we attain true happiness. Thus Joseph told the "Egyptians" to "circumcise" themselves (see Rashi on Gen. 41:55).

* * *

CHASTISEMENTS OF LOVE

"It is good when manifest reproof stems from hidden love" (Proverbs 27:5).

The essence of good leadership is to teach people to lead themselves -- to take themselves in hand and use self-discipline to attain the good that is available in this world.

Had Joseph revealed himself to his brothers immediately on their first arrival in Egypt, he would have elicited little more from them than superficial expressions of contrition for a sin whose seriousness they still did not understand. "Do not stand idly by the blood of your neighbor" (Leviticus 19:16) -- don't "sit down to eat bread" when your brother is screaming in the pit (Gen. 37:25).

Joseph used his consummate wisdom to engineer events that would put his brothers in the same situation in which they had placed him. As the compassionate leader, Joseph sought to make his brothers draw their own conclusions, knowing that the lessons we learn on our own flesh are more deeply inscribed and instilled than those we simply hear from others.

Joseph engineered events that would force his brothers to "read" and "interpret" for themselves the message of reproof the events implied. So it had been from the beginning. When Joseph dreamed of the sheaves bowing down to him, it was the brothers who interpreted the message for themselves. "Will you surely rule over us?" (Gen. 37:8).

Years later, the brothers bowed before the Egyptian Viceroy ***Tzaphnat Pa'aneach*** ("Interpreter of that which is Hidden", as Joseph had been named by Pharaoh, Master of the Dream).

"And Joseph saw his brothers and he recognized them, ***and he made himself strange*** [vayit***nacher***] to them" (Gen. 42:7).

In order to chastise his brothers and bring them to genuine contrition, Joseph acted not like a ***brother*** but like a ***nachri***, a ***stranger***. He clothed himself in the garb of a stranger with a heart of stone, deaf to all appeals.

Joseph's way of teaching and educating his brothers can help us understand how G-d may sometimes have to beat down the walls of people's insensitive hearts by chastising them with enemies that appear strange and incomprehensible to them.

"G-d will bring up a people against you from afar from the end of the earth, like the eagle swoops, a people whose language you will not understand, a people of fierce countenance who will not show respect to the old or compassion for the youth." (Deuteronomy 28: 49).

But like Joseph's indirect, roundabout reproof to his brothers, G-d's reproof has but one purpose: "And they will confess their sin and the sin of their fathers and the treachery that they have committed against Me, that they went contrary [with ***keri***] against Me; So I will go with them contrary [with ***keri***, apparently chance events] and I will bring them in the land of their enemies, and then their uncircumcised heart will be humbled and then they will make appeasement for their sin. And I will remember My ***covenant***." (Leviticus 26:40-42).

With consummate skill, Joseph brought a series of "troubles" upon his brothers that would bring them to successive levels of self-understanding and genuine contrition. Joseph's first step was to separate one brother (Shimon) from the others and hold him in detention. The brothers read the message: "And one said to the other, But we are guilty over our brother, the pain of whose soul we saw when he pleaded with us and we did not hear: that is why this trouble has come upon us" (Gen. 42:21).

The final stage was when Joseph engineered the framing of Benjamin with Joseph's "stolen" divining goblet (Gen. ch. 44). Still appearing to his brothers as the Egyptian Viceroy Sorcerer, Joseph's choice of scenario was one that had special meaning for the brothers, as they had all (with the exception of Benjamin) witnessed their ***diviner*** grandfather Laban (Gen.31:33) searching the tent of Rachel, for his stolen ***terafim*** (idols).

At last the brothers grasped the complete message. They had stolen their brother and sold him as a slave. "And Judah said, 'What shall we say to my lord, what shall we speak and how can we justify ourselves? G-d has found your servants' sin.'"

In next week's parshah we will continue with the beautiful story of how Judah steps forward to ***take responsibility for his brother***. This was the goal of all Joseph's "reproof".

The above-quoted words of Judah are woven into our ***Tachanun*** (supplicatory) and ***Selichot*** (penitential) prayers:

"What shall we say? What shall we speak? How can we justify ourselves? Let us search out and investigate our ways and return to You. For Your right arm is stretched out to receive those who return. Please G-d, save us."

VAYIGASH

Torah Reading: Genesis 44:18-47:27

Haftarah: Ezekiel 37:15-28

"AND JUDAH STEPPED FORWARD."

*T*he key to the dramatic encounter between Judah and Joseph with which our parshah of ***Vayigash*** begins is to be found in the haftarah our sages attached to this parshah: Ezekiel's vision of the joining of the two sticks. One stick the prophet was to inscribe with the names of Judah and the Children of Israel his friends -- the kingdom of Torah Law and spirituality under David. The other stick he was to inscribe "to Joseph Tree of Ephraim and all the House of Israel his friends" -- secular, assimilated Israelite might: economic, political, military, involvement in the material world. The prophet was to join the two sticks and make them one, signifying that they will become --

"One nation in the earth in the mountains of Israel, and one king will be over all of them as King, and they will no longer be two nations and they will no longer be split into two kingdoms. And my servant David will be king over them and one shepherd will be for them all [King Mashiach]. And they will go in My laws and guard My statutes and do them. And they will dwell in the land that I have given to My servant Jacob in which your fathers dwelled, and they and their children and children's children will dwell upon it forever, and David My servant will be Prince to them forever. And I will cut for them a Covenant of Peace, an eternal Covenant will be for them. And I will give them and multiply them and I will put My Holy Temple within them forever. And My Dwelling will be upon them and I will be G-d for them, and they will be My People. And the Nations will know that I am HaShem who sanctifies Israel that My Sanctuary should be among them forever" (Ezekiel 37:28).

The encounter in our parshah between Judah and Joseph is the paradigm of this necessary joining between the two aspects of Israelite being in the world, spiritual and material. For its own existence, the Torah "kingdom" depends upon the successful material presence of Israel in the world, be it in the Land of Israel or in "Goshen". ("Goshen" would include all historical and present-day centers of Jewish sojourn in exile and dispersal east or west.) For "if there is no flour [bread to eat], there is no Torah". Likewise, material Israel cannot survive without true Torah leadership -- Melech HaMashiach. Jacob saw this, which is why "he sent Judah ahead of him to Joseph to rule before him to Goshen" (Gen. 46:28). It is the Torah leader who must rule over Israel, and Torah leadership must direct Israeli worldly power to the nation's prophetic mission of being worthy of building the Temple in the Land of Israel from which the Law will go forth to all the Nations.

* * *

THE POWER OF WORDS

Judah's heart-rending appeal to Joseph (standing there before him as a hard-hearted Egyptian tyrant) is the prototype of the Tzaddik (which may be any one of us) facing ***middat ha-din*** (the aspect of G-d's harsh judgment) and using prayer to turn it into ***Rachamim*** (Compassion). Judah appealed to Joseph's heart and to a fundamental sense of ***fairness*** that exists everywhere in the world including among the Gentiles (see "Rabbi Nachman's Wisdom" #78 for a profoundly insightful discussion of this subject.) At some point there is a universal loathing for blatant unfairness

This is because even the Seventy Nations are at root vitalized by a spark of G-dliness deriving from ***Keter***, the "Crown" of G-d's will, which gives life and sustenance to the side of evil, as represented in Egypt. For the duration of history, this vitalizing root is contained in the Seven "Crowns", the seven Commandments of the Sons of Noah, which come to rectify the Seventy Nations as exemplified in Egypt (Ham) under the rule of Joseph (Shem).

Judah's appeal to Joseph is a heart-to-heart appeal, man to man. Judah is willing to sacrifice his entire life and submit himself to slavery in order to save his younger brother Benjamin. Judah is the true ***areiv*** ("guarantor") for his brother - the ultimate in loving your fellow as yourself.

From the way we appeal to the heart of a fellow human, we are to learn how we should appeal to G-d in prayer. This must be "face to face", as to a friend, even if all seems clothed in ***middat ha-din***, the power of strict judgment. From Judah's appeal to Joseph we are to learn how in prayer we are to plead and offer to sacrifice our very selves in servitude to G-d, in order to turn G-d's ***Din***, strict judgment, into ***Rachamim***, mercy.

Judah's eloquent appeal to Joseph's sense of fairness can serve as an exemplar to all of us in the art of prayer and entreaty, particularly in times of stress and danger. Eloquence in prayer is a good trait for all of us to cultivate -- it comes by speaking from heart to heart. We need to be bold and speak out our complaints and requests to G-d from our hearts.

* * *

"NOT YOU SENT ME HERE BUT G-D"

After revealing himself to his brothers, Joseph provides them with a peace-making way of re-perceiving the past, even where negative, as part of a divinely-prepared plan -- in this case to draw the Children of Israel down into Egypt. "Not you sent me here but G-d" (Gen. 45:8) -- "for sustenance G-d sent me before you" (ibid. v. 5).

In all circumstances, understanding that all the various humans who surround us are in reality agents of G-d, Who is behind and within all phenomena, is one of the main keys to understanding our personal situation in the world.

As expressed by the great early-20th century Polish Breslover Chassid, Rabbi Yitzhak Breiter (in his "Seven Pillars of Faith"):

“Other people are also free agents, yet everything they do is ultimately controlled by God. If someone insults you or in some way harms you, know that this has been sent by God as a way to cleanse your soul. If things go against you, be patient. When you accept everything as God's will, this causes the veil of concealment to be removed, thus manifesting God's control over all creation”.

“...Everything we experience is actually a communication from God. This includes our inner thoughts and feelings. Even negative thoughts and feelings - heaviness, lack of enthusiasm, depression and the like - are from God. Everything you hear, see, or experience in life, whether from people you know or from complete strangers, is a call to you from God. Even unclear or contradictory messages are sent with a purpose: to give us choice and free will in order to test us. The way to sort out which messages we should follow and which we should ignore is by evaluating everything in the light of Torah teaching” (Pillars #4 and #6).

* * *

FORCED BY THE MOUTH OF THE WORD

“Forced by the ***word of the mouth*** of G-d”– “***anoos al pi-ha-dibbur***” -- is a phrase from the Haggadah explaining why Jacob and his sons went into exile. Historically, exile was forced on the Jews as a kind of "rape" of the Shechinah, the Jewish Soul, by the material world, making it necessary to go out to "slavery" in the "Egypt" of the Seventy Nations for sheer survival. Again and again in Jewish history, economic needs ("famine") caused Jews to migrate.

G-d's plan in sending Joseph down to Egypt to prepare for the subsequent Israelite slavery and ultimate redemption may be seen unfolding repeatedly in the later history of Jewish exiles. For example, the Jews who spread wide in Poland and what was once its empire, the very centers of Ashkenazic Jewry, (Ukraine, Belorussia, Lithuania, Galicia, etc.) were originally enticed there in the 11th Century and thereafter from Germany by Polish kings (Pharaohs) who wanted to enrich themselves with industrious Jewish managers (Joseph). The Jews of Germany had themselves been enticed there in better days from France, the original "Ashkenaz".

For centuries, the Jews of the "Four Lands" of the Polish empire were practically an independent Torah kingdom within the kingdom, even after the dispersal of another Torah kingdom, the Jewry of "Sepharad" -- Spain, remnants of whom reached Israel. For Polish Jewry, the tide changed from the times of the Chmielnitzki Massacres of 1648-9 and thereafter, when Jewish worldly influence and actual Torah practice among the Jews of Russia, Poland and its former empire declined to the point of near extinction under communism. Meanwhile the Jewry of Europe was rapidly assimilating. For generations from the 1800's onwards, Jews were looking westwards, especially to America. The culminating points were the Pogroms, the Russian Revolution and the Holocaust, which annihilated European Jewry spiritually and physically. After the Second World War most of Sephardic and Oriental Jewry migrated to Israel or to the west. Thus the main world Jewish centers shifted to Israel and America, both of which contain an uneasy balance of "Judah" and "Joseph" Jews -- Torah observant and secular.

Israel was built up by the returnees to the Land from the East and from the West and is today the key to ultimate Jewish survival and victory -- Israel is ***land***: it is ***the*** Land. The holocaust appears to have been the "price" for the birth of the State of Israel, which today is confronted by an existential struggle for survival, under attack, directly or in disguise, by all of the Seventy Nations.

The key to Jewish survival today is the bond between "Israel" under the leadership of Judah -- Torah, Melech HaMashiach -- and "Joseph", "Ephraim", the main body of Jewry in Israel and throughout the world.

* * *

CONNECTION TO THE LAND

The concluding section of our parshah of ***Vayigash***, recounts how in the years of famine in Egypt, Joseph "purchased" the Egyptians' land, their livestock and their very bodies for Pharaoh (Genesis 13-27).

One point found in the commentators is of special note in ***Universal Torah***, which focuses on aspects of Torah that apply to all humanity. It is that Joseph worked assiduously for the benefit of Pharaoh and did not seek to use his position as Viceroy for personal enrichment. He could have sent sacks of silver back to store for himself in Canaan, but he did not. He worked diligently for his employer and was an exemplar of service.

The "purchase" by Joseph of the land and the very bodies of the Egyptians for an annual tax of 20% -- one fifth of all income -- institutes fundamental principles of the modern state. Military power is controlled by the "king" or government, who is expected to protect the population and alleviate "famine", providing everything necessary for general wellbeing ("health of the economy").

One of the features of modern history has been great migrations of people of all nations from country to country and continent to continent. This has tended to separate the population from connection to the land in the form of land-ownership, while urbanization has separated over 50 per cent of the world's population from direct connection with nature.

The only people on earth who have a continuous historical link with one and the same country going back thousands of years is the People of Israel and the Jews. Israel is the only country on earth that belongs to the Jews.

The twenty percent tax Joseph instituted for Egypt alludes to the 20% of net income that a person should ideally separate for Tzedakah (just as Jacob said, ***asor*** (10%) ***a'asrenah*** (10%) "I will surely tithe" --

Genesis 28:22, Ma'aser Rishon ("the first tithe") and Ma'aser Sheini ("the second tithe").

"And Zion will be redeemed through justice and her returnees through charity" (Isaiah 1:27)

VAYECHI

Torah Reading: Genesis 47:28-50:26

Haftarah: I Kings 2:1-12

AND JACOB LIVED.

"*A*nd Jacob lived in the land of Egypt seventeen years" (Gen. 47:28). These were "good" years (17 is the gematria of ***tov*** = "good") as opposed to the first one hundred and thirty years of Jacob's 147-year life. The first hundred and thirty years were riddled with suffering. Through the suffering Jacob endured while struggling to build his family, the House of Israel, he rectified Adam's 130 years of separation from Eve (see Rashi on Genesis 4:25), during which Adam wasted his seed and created demons, instead of peopling the world with Bney Adam.

G-d's first command to Adam was "Be fruitful and multiply and fill the earth and conquer it" (Gen. 1:28). As explained by Rabbi Nachman (Likutey Moharan II:7), this commandment is fulfilled not by producing anthropoid monsters but by giving birth to, raising and educating true Children of Adam, who bear the ***tzurah*** ("form") of ***Adam***, who was made "in the image of G-d".

Ever since Adam and Eve ate the fruit of the Tree of Knowledge of Good and Evil, their generations were flawed. Cain killed Abel, Canaan sodomized Noah, the Sodomites wanted to sodomize the angels, the kings of Egypt and of the Philistines and the crown prince of Shechem kidnapped women, Ishmael lived by the sword, Esau was a rapist.

Only Jacob was ***shalem***, "Whole" or "Perfect" (Gen. 32:18): Jacob bore the true ***tzurah*** of ***Adam***, of whom it is said: "And upon the likeness of the throne was a likeness having the appearance of ***Adam*** upon it from above" (Ezekiel 1:26). When man perfects himself, G-d shines through him and is thus revealed in the world.

Jacob is sometimes called Yaakov, sometimes Yisrael. Yaakov is "small" ("Yaakov her ***small*** son" Gen. 27:15; "How will Yaakov rise, for he is ***small***" Amos 7:5). In his "small" aspect -- his time of struggle and suffering (***mochin d'katnut***, "constricted consciousness") -- Jacob signifies that the revelation of G-d is as yet incomplete and is still proceeding in stages. But Yisrael, Israel, is Jacob's name of greatness -- "for you have struggled with G-d and with men and you have prevailed" (Gen. 32:29). In his "great" aspect (***mochin d'gadlut***, "expanded consciousness") Jacob -- Israel -- signifies that G-d's greatness is revealed and manifest in the world.

This was the case at the time of the Exodus from Egypt and the Giving of the Torah, when the entire world shook with G-d's self-revelation. It was the case during the reigns of King David and his son Solomon, who built the Holy Temple in Jerusalem. And it will be the case again in the near future, when G-d's House of Prayer for All the Nations will stand in the center of the world on Mount Moriah in the Holy City of Jerusalem. [The intensity of the hatred in much of the world today for all that goes by the name of Israel signifies how far the world is from HaShem. But "the people that go in darkness will see great light and those who dwell in the land of the shadow of death, light has shone upon them" (Isaiah 9:11).]

Our parshah of ***Vayechi*** puts the seal on the first of the Five Books of Moses, the book of Genesis (Bereishit), portraying Jacob, the rectified Adam, in his "good" years at the end of his life. They are good years, because Jacob is now reunited with Joseph, who is in his place of true glory ruling over Egypt. Jacob's main love was essentially for Rachel. It was for her that he served Laban, and it was because Joseph was Rachel's firstborn that "Israel loved Joseph out of all his sons" (Gen. 37:3). While Leah signifies the "hidden realm", Rachel signifies G-d's glory revealed in and through this world. This comes about when Jacob-Israel (= ***Adam***, the Soul complete with its Nefesh, Ru'ach and Neshamah levels) conquers Esau (= the Serpent, ***Asiyah***, the realm of material activity), using this world to build a sanctuary for G-d.

Our parshah of ***Vayechi*** also contains a number of specific allusions to the Temple in Jerusalem, as in Jacob's blessing to Judah (Gen. 49:11) and especially his blessing to Benjamin (ibid. v. 27). The Temple Altar stood in the territory of Benjamin, son of Rachel. Thus in Jacob's funeral procession, his twelve sons carried him up to the Land of Israel in the same positions in which their descendants the twelve tribes encamped around the Sanctuary in the Wilderness. Jacob and his sons, the House of Israel, are the Sanctuary in which G-d dwells in the world. "And I will dwell within them" (Exodus 25:8).

* * *

HEAR O ISRAEL!

Jacob spent the final "good" years of his life fulfilling the commandment to be spiritually fruitful -- by educating the young, especially his grandson Ephraim (see Rashi on Gen. 48:1: "Ephraim was habitually with Jacob learning"). Jacob's final blessings, will and testament to his sons, with their harsh chastisements, were also intended to be educational.

According to tradition, "At the time when Jacob our father assembled his sons in Egypt at the hour of his death, he commanded and spurred them on in the unification of the name of G-d and that they should follow the path of HaShem that Abraham and Isaac his father walked. He asked them and said, 'My sons, maybe someone among you is flawed and does not stand with me in the Unification of the Name?' They all answered and said, 'Hear Israel HaShem our G-d HaShem is One' -- that is, 'Hear from us, our father Israel, HaShem our G-d HaShem is one'. The old man answered, 'Blessed be the Name of the Glory of His Kingship for ever and ever!' And this is why all Israel has the custom of repeating the expression of the praise used by Israel when he was an old man after this verse". (Rambam, Laws of Recital of Shema Ch. 1:4).

* * *

JACOB'S BLESSINGS

Jacob's death-bed blessings to his sons contain some of the most beautiful flights of Biblical poetry. It is noteworthy that Onkelos, author of the best-known Aramaic Targum (= "translation") of the Five Books of Moses, departs here from his usual practice of giving the simplest, clearest ***p'shat*** (= "simple meaning") of the Biblical text except where ***drush***, Midrash, "searching out" beneath the surface is absolutely indispensable. However here, as in the case of some other highly poetic passages (the Song at the Sea, Bilaam's blessings, the Song of Moses – ***Ha'azinu*** -- and his final blessings), Onkelos felt obliged to introduce ***Midrash*** into his Targum in order to bring out the essential meaning of the text, which contains allusions to all historical periods and especially the time of Mashiach.

Thus it is Onkelos who informs us that ***Shilo*** (Gen. 49:10) is Mashiach. The Tribes are compared to various animals. Judah is a lion, Issachar is a wide-boned donkey, Dan is a serpent, Naftali a gracious hind, Benjamin a preying fox. In the case of Jacob's children, the animal qualities are elevated in order to destroy the wicked and give the victory to G-d. Thus Onkelos translates Gen. 49:14-15 as: "Yissachar will be wealthy in possessions and his inheritance is between the boundaries. And he saw that his share is good and that the land produces fruits. And he conquered the territories of the nations and destroyed their inhabitants and those who remain of them will serve him and pay him taxes." Onkelos translates the blessing of Benjamin (Gen. 49:27: "Benjamin is a preying fox, in the morning he devours the prey, in the evening he divides the prey") as: "In the land of Benjamin the Shechinah will dwell (= ***Tishrei***) and in his inheritance the Holy Temple will be built, in the morning and in the afternoon the priests will offer sacrifices and in the evening they will divide the rest of their portions from the other offerings".

Onkelos himself was a ***ger tzedek*** ("righteous convert"). He was the son of the sister of the Roman Emperor Titus." It is said that before Onkelos converted, he raised the spirits of Titus, Bilaam, and Yeshu from hell in order to find out the truth. All three confirmed that the nation of Israel is held in the highest repute in the world to come

(Gittin 56b, 57a). Onkelos learned Torah from Rabbi Eliezer ben Hyrcanus ("Rabbi Eliezer the Great") and Rabbi Yehoshua, who were outstanding students of Rabban Yochanan ben Zakkai and were also the teacher-partners of Rabbi Akiva. Onkelos' Targum is the first and most authoritative "commentary" on the Torah.

* * *

AND THE DWELLER OF THE LAND OF THE CANAANITE SAW.

When Joseph went up with his brothers to bury Jacob, "they came to the threshing floor of Atad (= bramble)" (Gen. 50:10). According to Rashi, "It was surrounded by brambles. All the kings of Canaan and princes of Ishmael came to war, but when they saw the crown of Joseph hung on Jacob's ***aron*** (= Ark), they all stood and hung their crowns and surrounded him with crowns from the threshing-floor which was surrounded by a fence of brambles.

The kings and Canaan and princes of Ishmael were confounded by the ***aron***, the holy ark of Jacob, crowned with the crown of Joseph.

According to tradition, this took place during Chanukah-time. Jacob's ***histalkut*** (ascent) was on the 15th of Tishri, the first night of Succot. The Egyptians wept for him seventy days, upon which Joseph and his brothers went up to Israel to bury him. The seventieth day after the 15th of Tishri is the 25th of Kislev, the first day of Chanukah. The initial letters of the four Hebrew words in the verse "and the dweller of the land of the Canaanite saw" (Gen. 50:11) are the permutation of the name of HaShem that holds sway in the month of Kislev (see Kavanot of Rosh Chodesh Musaf prayers).

There is an integral conceptual connection between Jacob's funeral procession and Chanukah, which is the time of the inauguration of the Temple. Jacob's twelve sons, the holy House of Israel, under the leadership of Joseph the Tzaddik, were taking Jacob -- the archetypal House-Builder -- to his final, eternal house and home in the Cave of

Machpelah, the resting place of Adam and Eve as well as the patriarchs and matriarchs.

The funeral procession was a "rehearsal" for the formation in which the twelve tribes would bring the Ark of the Covenant up from the wilderness and into the Holy Land. This is paradigmatic of the building of the Holy Temple, the House of G-d on the spot where Jacob had his dream of the ladder: "This is none other than the House of G-d and this is the Gate of Heaven" (Gen. 28:17). That place is alluded to in the opening word of the Torah, ***Bereishit***, the letters of which, when re-arranged, spell out ***Bayit Rosh***, the House that is Head (= Tefilin shel Rosh). It was to that place that Joseph promised his brothers that they would return from Egypt: "G-d will surely redeem you and bring you up from this land to the Land which He swore to Abraham, to Isaac and to Jacob" (Gen. 50:24).

CHAZAK! CHAZAK! VE-NIT'CHAZEK!

"Be strong! Be strong -- and we will be strong!"

שמות

EXODUS

SHEMOT

Torah Reading: Exodus 1:1-6:1

Haftarah: Isaiah 27:6-28:13; 29:22-23
(Sephardi ritual) Jeremiah 1:1-2:3

"AND THESE ARE THE NAMES OF THE CHILDREN OF ISRAEL": ISRAEL ON THE WORLD STAGE

*W*ith the beginning of the book of ***Shemot***, "Exodus", Israel enters the world stage as a people. Pharaoh himself, their oppressor, recognizes them as "the ***people*** of the Children of Israel, many and mighty." (Ex. 1:9). Their servitude in Egypt is in fulfillment of the promise given to their founding father, Abraham: "Surely ***know*** that your seed will be strangers in a land that is not theirs and they will serve them and they will oppress them. And also the people that they will serve I will judge, and afterwards they will go forth with great wealth" (Gen. 15:13-14).

The Exodus of the People of Israel from Egypt is the pivotal event in the history of mankind, paradigm of all true freedom and liberation, the eternal proof that G-d is not only the Creator of the natural world but also directs and controls all aspects of human affairs with ***hashgachah pratit*** - "providence in every detail" - for good.

For the sake of G-d's self-revelation to the world, it is not sufficient that He should be known privately to a select few. The climax of G-d's revelation is when "the earth will be full of the ***knowledge*** of G-d like the waters cover the seas" (Isaiah 11:9). Even those who are turned away from G-d, even those who resist knowing Him, must be forced to admit -- even against their will -- that G-d is King of the whole world.

Thus when Moses first calls on Pharaoh in the name of G-d to release His People, "...and Pharaoh said, 'Who is HaShem that I should listen to His voice. I do not ***know*** HaShem." (Ex. 5:2). But in the end Pharaoh himself was forced to send them away: "Go, serve HaShem as

you said" (12:31); "And Egypt said, let me flee from Israel, for HaShem is fighting for them against Egypt" (14:25).

In Egypt the Children of Israel, G-d's emissaries, were in an upside-down world. "There is an evil that I have seen beneath the sun like a mistake that went forth from before the Ruler: folly is put in many high places while the wealthy [= Israel, Rashi] sit in the low place. I have seen slaves on horses while princes walk like slaves on the ground" (Kohelet 10:5-7). Noah cursed the nations of Ham to be "a servant of servants to his brothers" (Gen. 10:25). But now Ham's second-born, ***Mitzraim*** (Gen. 10:6) -- Egypt -- were lording it over the choicest of the line of Shem. It looked as though Pharaoh was the "first-born". G-d's revelation to the world depended upon showing that "My son, My first-born is Israel" (Ex. 4:22). Even the Egyptians saw this when G-d smote all their first-born while saving all the Israelite first-born.

Even the Egyptians had to come to ***know***. Even Jethro -- who tried every religion in the world -- had to admit in the end: "Now I ***know*** that HaShem is greater than all the gods." (Ex. 18:11). More than anyone, the Israelites -- who in slavery fell into the false consciousness imposed on them by their oppressors -- had to learn the lesson on their own flesh. The Exodus from Egypt is the pivotal event in the history of the People of Israel, the very birth of the nation. The climax was to come at Mount Sinai, when the entire nation, together and in unity, witnessed G-d's revelation. The revelation at Sinai was a "mass conversion": the Rabbis point out that the three acts associated with conversion -- circumcision, immersion in the Mikveh [the Torah root of "baptism"] and [in Temple times,] a sacrificial offering, were all observed at Sinai.

After introducing us to the "upside-down" world of Egypt in the first chapter of Exodus, our parshah of ***Shemot*** immediately moves to the concepts of revelation and conversion. When Moses was born, "the whole house was filled with light" (Rashi on Ex. 2:2 "and she saw him ***that he was good***" corresponding to "and G-d saw the light ***that it was good***" Gen. 1:4). Immediately afterwards, "And Pharaoh's daughter went down to wash by the river" -- "she changed her religion and went to convert" (Baal HaTurim ibid.) In the merit of Batya's compassion for the baby Moses and her act of saving him, she was worthy of being one of the greatest ever converts. Batya's predecessor, Hagar, daughter of the Pharaoh of Abraham's days and mother of Ishmael, "went astray" (Gen. 21:14). But Batya married into the princely tribe of Judah (Sanhedrin 19b on I Chronicles 4:18). The other prominent convert introduced in our parshah is Jethro.

* * *

THE CONSTRICTION OF THE THROAT

In the upside-down world of Egypt it looks as though not G-d is running the world but Pharaoh. As discussed in the commentaries on Genesis, PhaRaOh is the embodiment of the OrePh, the "back of the neck" of the Creation as opposed to its inner face. Pharaoh is the epitome of worldly power and control, "the great crocodile squatting in his rivers who says 'the river is mine and I made myself' " (Ezekiel 29:3, haftarah of next week's parshah when not Rosh Chodesh).

Pharaoh "does not know" HaShem: he resists knowing. Thus ***Mitzraim*** is related to the root ***meitzar***, the "narrow strait", a place of constriction. In kabbalistic literature, Pharaoh is called "the constriction of the throat" (***meitzar ha- garon***). Through the neck run three narrow channels that are vital to survival: the windpipe, the gullet and the jugular veins (corresponding to Pharaoh's three "officers", the Butler, the Baker and the Captain of the Guard). Life depends upon the free flow of gases, fluids and solids through these channels from the head down into the body, while all our functioning is governed through the most heavily protected channel of all: the spinal column, which extends down from the brainstem into the body via the neck.

The book of Genesis is the "head" of the Torah: ***Bereishit***, "at the head". The first word and first verse of Genesis contain the entire creation "in a nutshell" (King Solomon's "garden of nuts"). The first book of the Torah is the head and brain in the sense that it introduces us to all the fundamentals of true religion. The rest of the Torah is the "body". Exodus is the "arms" ("for with a mighty ***hand*** G-d took you out of Egypt" Ex. 13:9). Leviticus is the middle and heart of the Torah: "You shall be holy, for I HaShem your G-d am holy" -- "and love your neighbor as yourself" (Leviticus ch. 19 v. 2 and v. 18). The Book of Numbers is the "legs": the Children of Israel are on the move through the wilderness -- "these are the journeys of the Children of Israel" (Numbers 33:1). Finally Deuteronomy is the "feet" -- Malchut, the lowest level: "the ***end*** of the matter, when all has been heard: fear G-d and observe His commandments, for that is the Whole Man" (Kohelet 12:13).

With the opening of the book of Exodus, we are at the beginning of the transition from "the head", Genesis, to the "body", the rest of the Torah. We are at the "neck". This is why we must now encounter Pharaoh, the "back of the neck" -- the real Pharaoh, no longer Joseph's "friendly" patron but a wicked tyrant who, to perpetuate his own rule, is hell-bent on keeping the world from ***knowing G-d***.

Pharaoh's scheme is to constrict the passage of ***Da'at*** from the head and brain down into the body. Whereas the nervous system connects the body with the brain, bringing sensation, awareness and consciousness to all parts, Pharaoh's officers work to constrict the flow of awareness. The Butler and the Baker make us want to eat and involve ourselves in the material world, but our material involvements, although vital for our survival, often tend to distract and separate us from the life of the spirit. We fall into false consciousness, and the battle for physical survival and material gratification becomes paramount. We spend our lives building "store cities for Pharaoh" (Ex. 1:11).

The role of Moses is to bring ***Da'at***, spiritual knowledge and awareness from the "head" down into the "body". It is not enough to know that there is a G-d in our minds. We have to bring that knowledge down into our actual lives and daily activities. "And you shall ***know today*** and ***bring down into your heart*** that HaShem is G-d in the heaven above and on the earth below, there is none other" (Deut. 4:39).

* * *

THE KEY IS SHABBAT

Adam was created for the highest mission, to "fill the earth and conquer it and rule over the fish of the sea and the birds of the heavens and every living being swarming on the earth" (Gen. 1:28). But Adam fell from his mission, and instead of "tending and guarding" the Garden of Eden (Gen. 2:15), he was driven out to become slave to the earth: "With the sweat of your brow you will eat bread." (Gen. 3:19).

The only way for the Children of Adam to escape this servitude is through the Shabbat, which each week releases man from slavery to the material world and the battle for survival, lifting him above it to the world of ***Da'at***, the knowledge and awareness of G-d.

Thus when Moses first went into Pharaoh, his initial request was that the Children of Israel should have a holiday from their slavery: "Let us please go for a journey of three days into the wilderness, and there we will sacrifice to HaShem our G-d" (Ex. 5:3).

Pharaoh's immediate reaction was to resist the idea: "Why are you disturbing the people from their labors, go back to your tasks. You are causing them to cease from their tasks" (Ex. 5:5). The Hebrew for "you are disturbing" is ta***Ph***h***R***iy***OO***, containing the word ***Pharoah*** -- as if Moses and Aaron are the tyrants. The Hebrew for "You are causing them to cease" is ve-hi***SHBAT***em, containing the word ***Shabbat***. Pharaoh's scheme for preventing ***Da'at*** spreading from the head, Moses, to the Children of Israel, the body, was to make the Children of Israel so busy with this-worldliness that they would not have ***time*** to be aware of G-d. And indeed the Children of Israel became so wearied by their intensified servitude on the threshold of redemption that "they did not listen to Moses because of shortness of spirit and hard work" (Gen. 6:9).

Moses had to legislate the Shabbat because there is a wicked force in man -- Pharaoh -- that will not allow him to rest from the world until he must by law! Shabbat was the first commandment given to the Children of Israel directly after their entry into the wilderness following the crossing of the Red Sea (Rashi on Ex. 15:25). Shabbat – ***sh'vita***, the willful cessation of and resting from ***melachah***, deliberate, manipulative labor -- is the very key to man's freedom from the tyranny of this world.

* * *

THE RIGHTEOUS WOMEN

"In the merit of the righteous women that were in that generation, Israel were redeemed from Egypt" (Sotah 11b).

The Midrashim give many examples of the heroism and self-sacrifice of the women of the period of exile and slavery in Egypt in lifting their husbands' spirits and breeding new generations for a better future.

While our parshah introduces the Savior of Israel -- Moses -- who was a man, it is striking that the most decisive roles are played by women. In Genesis we saw a succession of great women turning and shaping history on their own initiative, such as Sarah, Rebecca, Rachel, Leah and Tamar. In our parshah this is a recurring phenomenon: four outstanding women take decisive action on their own initiative to bring about redemption: Jochebed, Miriam, Batya and Tziporah.

Thus when Pharaoh wanted to kill the Israelite boys, it was the two midwives, "Shifra" and "Pu'ah" (= Jochebed and Miriam) who cleverly frustrated his plans. When Amram "took the daughter of Levi (= Jochebed)" (Ex. 2:1) from whom he had separated because he did not want to breed children who would be killed, it was on the initiative of Miriam that he relented (see Rashi ad loc.). By drawing Moses out of the water, Batya saved the entire world. The dauntless Miriam went straight up to the king's daughter offering to bring someone to take care of the rescued baby. Batya had the good sense to understood the crucial importance of good nurturing. Jethro's daughters were perhaps too modest to invite Moses home until their father told them -- after all, they thought he was an Egyptian (Ex. 2:19-20). However, Tziporah showed no hesitation when she saw an angel consuming her husband

Moses for failing to circumcise Eliezer: she took a flint and performed the bloody circumcision herself, showing that as a true righteous convert, her heart was circumcised to G-d.

In all these cases and examples, the heroism and initiative of these women are bound up with breeding and rearing future generations to know and serve G-d.

VA'EIRA

Torah Reading: Exodus 6:2-9:35

Haftarah: Ezekiel 28:25-29:21

"WITH MY NAME YKVK I WAS NOT KNOWN TO THEM"

*A*t the end of the previous parshah of ***Shemot***, we saw how, precisely when Moses started the process of Geulah (redemption) by asking Pharaoh to send away the Children of Israel, the latter responded by intensifying their oppression and servitude. This caused even Moses to question his mission: "Lord, why have You done evil to this people? Why have You sent me?" (Ex. 5:22).

Our parshah of ***Va'eira*** opens with G-d's answer to Moses. It contains a profound teaching about faith. G-d promises, and it is up to G-d to deliver! He can be relied upon absolutely to do so -- in His own good time. Even in the thickest darkness, we must have faith that G-d will redeem us. We must understand that the darkness is most intense just before the morning.

In G-d's answer to Moses, He says that He appeared to the patriarchs Abraham, Isaac and Jacob as "the Eternal G-d" but "***by My name YKVK I was not known to them***" (Ex. 6:3). What does this mean? It is a fact that the essential name of HaShem, YKVK -- expressing the perfect unity of G-d within and beyond all phenomena -- was indeed known to the patriarchs, as we see many times in Genesis. However, as pointed out by Rashi here, the Hebrew text (***nodati***) does not mean, "I did not make it known to them". Rather, it implies: "I was not known and ***recognised*** for my quality of truthfulness... as HaShem Who am faithful in proving the truth of My words. For I promised them but as yet I have not fulfilled the promise" (see Rashi).

An integral part of faith in G-d is to have faith that He will bring about everything He has promised through His prophets, even if we cannot see how this can possibly come about. The Exodus from Egypt is the proof of this faith, for G-d had promised the patriarchs what He was going to do: "And also the people that they will serve I will judge, and afterwards they will go forth with great wealth" (Gen. 15:13-14). At the height of Egyptian power and arrogance, it seemed impossible that this could come about. But in this and the coming parshiyot telling the story of the Ten Plagues and the Exodus, we see that G-d indeed brought it about.

No less essential a part of the promise than the redemption from Egypt was that G-d will "bring you to the Land that I swore to give it to Abraham, to Isaac and to Jacob, and ***I will give it to you as an inheritance – I am HaShem***" (Ex. 6:8). It is not sufficient for the Children of Israel "go out from Egypt", even in the spiritual sense of being released from the chains of servitude to the evanescent material world. G-d's plan for a perfect world will be fulfilled only when the Children of Israel dwell securely in their own Promised Land, fulfilling all the commandments that are bound up with the Land. We must have complete faith that G-d will bring this about.

* * *

KAL VA-CHOMER - "LIGHT AND STRINGENT"

When the Children of Israel could not hear Moses' message of redemption because of "shortness of spirit and hard work" (Ex. 6:9), Moses wondered: "If the Children of Israel did not listen to me, how will Pharaoh listen to me?" (ibid. v. 12).

Moses' argument is based on making an inference from a "light" case -- the Children of Israel -- to a "stringent" case: Pharaoh. In Hebrew, such an inference is known as ***kal va-chomer***, "light-and-stringent". In the written text of the Five Books of Moses there are ten cases of arguments using ***kal va-chomer*** (Rashi ad loc.) The ten cases are listed in the Tannaitic commentary on Exodus, "Mechilta". The argument of ***kal va-chomer*** is one of the most important of the hermeneutical methods by which the sages derived teachings by inference even though they are not written explicitly in the Torah text. ***Kal va-chomer*** is the first of "thirteen rules of Torah interpretation" set down by the tannaitic sage, Rabbi Ishmael. These have become part of the daily order of prayer, being recited at the conclusion of the sacrificial portions prior to ***Pesukey D'Zimra***, the verses and psalms of the morning service. Besides Rabbi Ishmael's thirteen, there are other hermeneutical rules, such as the Thirty-Two rules of Midrash collected by Rabbi Eliezer son of Rabbi Yosi HaGlili (printed in the ***klalim***, "rules" of the Talmud, after Tractate Berachot).

As in the case of Moses' argument by ***kal va-chomer*** that Pharaoh would not listen, all the other rules of interpretation are themselves contained in the biblical text. It is through the application of these rules that extensive parts of the Oral Torah were developed by the early sages and rabbis. When rules like ***kal va-chomer*** are applied to the text, it is possible to infer new teachings that are not explicitly written in the text but are logically implied. The legitimacy of this method of argument is sanctioned by its use in the Biblical text itself, as here. This shows the essential unity of the Oral and Written Torah.

* * *

THE TEN PLAGUES

In the event, G-d took on the "harder" task of bringing down Pharaoh and breaking his stony heart. This was what would make the Children of Israel listen! This was accomplished through the Ten Plagues. The gripping account of the first seven plagues occupies the greater part of this week's parshah of ***Va'eira***, while next week's parshah of ***Bo*** bring us to the climax with the last three plagues and the Exodus itself.

Many have sought to explain the sequence of plagues according to some rationale. One of the most celebrated explanations is that mentioned by Rashi on Ex. 8:17, quoting from Midrash Tanchuma Parshat ***Bo*** #4, a Tannaitic source:

"Our Rabbis of blessed memory said: The Holy One blessed be He brought the plagues upon them using the tactics of worldly kings. When a region rebels against a king of flesh and blood, he sends his legions to surround it. The first thing he does is to shut off their water supply. If they relent, all the better! If not, he brings against them criers with loud voices...then arrows...barbarian hordes. He hurls heavy weights at them...shoots burning oil... fires cannon...rouses multitudinous armies against them. imprisons them...kills their great ones. In the same way, the Holy One blessed be He came against the Egyptians with the tactics of kings. With the plague of blood, He stopped up their water supply. The "criers" were the frogs with their loud croaking. His "arrows" were the fleas. His "barbarian hordes" were the wild animals. The "heavy weights" were the "heavy pestilence" that killed their livestock. The "burning oil" was the boils. The cannon shots were the hail. The "multitudinous armies" were the locusts. The Egyptians were "imprisoned" through the plague of darkness. Finally, He killed their great ones in the plague of the first born.

A kabbalistic explanation of the sequence and rationale of the plagues is provided in the writings of the ***Ari*** in Sha'ar HaPesukim (the Gate of the Verses) Parshat Va'eira. The Ten Plagues correspond to the Ten Sefirot, ascending from the bottom of the "ladder" to the top. Thus the seven plagues recounted in this week's parshah of ***Va'eira*** correspond to the seven "lower" Sefirot, from Malchut-Kingship up to Chessed-Kindness, while the three plagues recounted in next week's parshah of ***Bo*** correspond to the top trio: Binah-Understanding, Chochmah-Wisdom and finally Keter-Crown. According to this explanation, the Ten Plagues came as successive manifestations of the 10 different aspects or "attributes" of G-d's kingly power over all the world (the ten Sefirot of ***Malchut*** -- or "***Nukva***" -- of ***Atzilut***). In this way, the arrogant supremacy of worldly power, the "Evil ***Malchut***" -- the force that conceals G-dliness -- was broken. Behind the nightmare to which Egypt was subjected -- apparently the very opposite of ***seder***, "order" -- lies the supreme order of the Sefirot.

* * *

THE PHARAOH WITHIN US

"Do not rejoice when your enemy falls, and when he stumbles, let not your heart exult. Lest G-d will see and it will be bad in His eyes" (Proverbs 24:17).

We may not laugh over Pharaoh's downfall, because there is a Pharaoh in each one of us. This is the stubborn ***melech*** (king) who rules in our hearts, in our ego, our vanity and pride. I, me!

Writ large in the drama of Moses coming against Pharaoh in the name of G-d is the story of our inner lives, our daily conflicts and struggles in the test of free will to which we are all subjected. One side of us -- Moses, "conscience" -- knows what we should do. But another side -- Pharaoh, "the evil urge", the king riding the chariot -- resists. There are constant ups and downs in the trial of free will. Today one "wants to" -- Pharaoh relents. Tomorrow, he hardens his heart again and resists.

Does it need plagues to beat this Pharaoh down? Or can we find better ways to get free and to take our destiny into our hands?

BO

Torah Reading: Exodus 10:1-13:16

Haftarah: Jeremiah 46:13-28

G-D ALWAYS HAS THE UPPER HAND

"Who then is able to stand before me?
Who has given Me anything beforehand, that I should repay him?
Whatever is under the whole heaven is Mine" (Job 41:2-3).

*I*n the story of the Exodus, it is obvious who is the villain: obstinate Pharaoh, who will not bow to G-d until his very first-born and those of all his people are smitten. But who is the hero of the story? Can we say it is the Children of Israel? They certainly responded with faith when they heard the good news of their imminent deliverance (Ex. 4:31). They were willing to hear, listen and obey. "And the Children of Israel went and did as HaShem commanded Moses and Aaron, so they did" (Ex. 12:28). But otherwise, the role of the Children of Israel's was mainly passive in the unfolding drama in which Pharaoh's power over them was broken. They were the slaves, and they were released: not the most heroic of roles. They were almost devoid of all merits. The very memory of it should induce humility.

Then is Moses the "hero"? It is true that "also the man Moses was very great in the land of Egypt in the eyes of Pharaoh's servants and in the eyes of the people" (Ex. 11:3).

With the unflinching courage that his true prophecy conferred upon him, Moses, with his brother Aaron, played the central role in heralding the awesome and terrible signs through which the redemption came about. Yet it was not Moses who "liberated" or "saved" the Children of Israel. Moses was the greatest of all prophets, but he was still "the ***man*** Moses". Moses could say that the first-born would be smitten "***about*** Midnight" (Ex. 11:4). But G-d alone could make the plague actually happen "***at*** midnight" (Ex. 12:29) -- at the exact moment.

G-d alone is the "hero" of the Exodus. "And I shall pass through [Targum = I shall be revealed in] the land of Egypt on this night" (Ex. 12:12) -- "I and not an Angel; I and not a Saraf; I and not a messenger." (from the Seder Night Haggadah, commenting on "And I shall pass through / be revealed").

The whole purpose of the Exodus was not to glorify a man or a nation, but to reveal G-d's absolute power over all creation. As Moses reminded the people forty years later, at the end of his ministry:

"For you are a holy nation to HaShem your G-d; HaShem your G-d chose you to be His treasured nation out of all the nations that are on the face of the earth. Not because you were more numerous than all the nations did HaShem desire you and choose you, for you are the smallest of all the nations. But because of HaShem's love for you and through His guarding of the oath that He swore to your fathers, HaShem took you out with a mighty hand and redeemed you from the house of slaves, from the hand of Pharaoh king of Egypt. Know that HaShem, your G-d -- He is the G-d, the Power, who is faithful and guards the covenant and shows kindness to those who love him and who guard His commandments for a thousand generations. And He pays those who hate him in their face, to destroy them; He shall not delay to the one who hates him, He will repay him to his face." (Deuteronomy 7:6-10).

* * *

THE REAL START OF THE TORAH

In Rashi's opening comment on the Torah (Gen. 1:1), he indicates that the real "beginning" of the Torah is in our present parshah of ***Bo***. "Rabbi Yitzchak said: the Torah should have started from 'This month will be for you the head of the months' (Ex. 12:2) since this is the first commandment that the Children of Israel were commanded." [See

Rashi on Gen. 1:1, where he explains that the account of the Creation and the ensuing history recounted in Genesis are proof of the Children of Israel's G-d-given right to the Land of Israel.]

In other words, the "real" start of the Torah is when we read it first and foremost as a message about our obligations rather than one about our rights. Having been passively freed by G-d from servitude to man, we have obligations to the "hero", the only true Savior. If anyone lays claim to any lien on us, G-d's lien always has priority.

The first mitzvah of the Torah to the Children of Israel is that of "sanctifying the month" (***Kiddush Ha-Chodesh***). This involves counting the months of the year from Nissan, the month of redemption, and, when the Sanhedrin sits in the Land of Israel, taking testimony from witnesses who have sighted the new moon in order to declare the start of the new month. Marking time from the point at which the moon, having briefly disappeared from sight, begins to wax and grow, is a sign of constant regeneration and vitality. The sign of the crescent was taken over by Islam, but the unique power of the crescent of the new moon as a symbol of renewal is known only to the Children of Israel, who observe the commandment of Sanctifying the Month. Alone among the nations, the Children of Israel possess the Secret of ***Ibbur*** (literally "pregnancy"). This involves the method of reconciling the Lunar year (of 354 days) with the Solar year (of 365 days) through the insertion of an extra month in certain "leap" years (= ***shanah me-uberet)***, a "pregnant" year of 13 instead of only 12 months). It is to this and the related astronomical and mystical wisdom of the Children of Israel that Moses alluded when he said: "For this is your wisdom and your understanding in the eyes of the nations" (Deut. 4:6, see Shabbat 75a).

The month of Nissan is governed by the astrological sign of Aries (***T'leh***, the Ram), called the "head" or first of the constellations, since this is when the annual "regeneration" of the world begins in springtime. The Egyptians, who were masters of astronomy and astrology, worshipped sheep (see Gen. 46:34 and Rashi there). The commandment to the Children of Israel to take young sheep, ritually slaughter and eat them, was indicative of the destruction of the

Egyptian religion through the Exodus and its replacement with a completely new and revolutionary way of coming to know G-d.

This commandment applied to those who went out of Egypt (***Pesach Mitzraim***) and it applied in later generations, when festival pilgrims would bring the Paschal lamb sacrifice to the Holy Temple (***Pesach Dorot***, "Pesach offering of the generations"). After its slaughter and the offering of its blood and fat on the altar on the afternoon of the 14th of Nissan, the lamb would be taken by the pilgrims to their lodgings in Jerusalem, roasted and ceremonially eaten with Matzah (unleavened bread) and bitter herbs as the centerpiece of the Seder Night commemorating the Exodus. Our present parshah of ***Bo*** contains the laws of both ***Pesach Mitzraim*** and ***Pesach Dorot*** (Ex. Ch. 12 verses 3-28 and 43-49).

"And you shall say, 'This is the ***Pesach*** sacrifice for HaShem, who jumped over (= ***pasach***) the houses of the Children of Israel in Egypt when He smote the Egyptians and He saved our houses'" (Ex. 12:27). Rashi (on Ex. 12:23) states that the Hebrew root ***pasach*** in this passage carries the twin connotations of "had mercy" (as translated in the Targum here) and "leapt over". In other words, G-d's mercy for the Children of Israel was expressed in the fact that He "leapt over" and spared their houses while striking at the Egyptians.

The Torah contains numerous negative prohibitions (such as the incest prohibitions) whose infringement carries the penalty of ***karet*** (physical and spiritual excision). However, there are only two positive commandments in the entire Torah whose willful neglect carries this penalty. These are the commandment of circumcision of all males and that of participating in the Pesach sacrifice (in Temple times). The two commandments are interrelated, for males may eat the Pesach sacrifice only if they are circumcised.

Fulfillment of the two commandments of circumcision and the Pesach sacrifice is integral to membership of the Community of Souls constituted by the Children of Israel, while for the penalty for infringing them is ***karet***, excision from that community.

Significantly, the laws of the Pesach lamb require that it be eaten in the company of a Chavurah, a group of friends and fellows, in a house. The significance of the house and the use of "domestic" functions such as communal eating as a focus for religious devotion has been discussed in relation to the story of Abraham, Isaac and Jacob "the House-builder" (see ***Vayeitzei***).

An indication of the centrality of the Pesach sacrifice in the true Torah tradition may be seen in the fact that the image of the Paschal lamb (like many other aspects of the Torah) was taken over and transmuted by the early developers of Christianity, as if their savior, who by all accounts was executed on the 14th of Nissan (see Sanhedrin 43a uncensored version), somehow became the paschal lamb. They introduced a new rite of "communion" in which the consumption of the sacrificial lamb was replaced with the eating of the founder's transubstantiated "flesh" (wafers of "bread" = Matzah) and the drinking of his "blood" (wine = "cup of redemption"). This rite could be performed in places of worship anywhere and was, within a generation, opened up to anyone, including the uncircumcised. The purpose was to try to displace the Children of Israel, G-d's true circumcised, from their role in Creation, and to displace the Temple in Jerusalem and its sacrificial system, as laid down in the Torah, from their central position in the atonement of man's sins.

None of this can change what is written in the Torah about how man draws close to G-d through sacrifice (see Leviticus 1:1). For "G-d is not a man that He should lie or the son of man that He should change His mind. He spoke -- will He not do it? He pronounced -- will He not fulfill it?" (Numbers 23:19). "For I am G-d, I have not changed." (Malachi 3:6). Long before Christianity was established, G-d already told us through His true prophets that in the end of days, "Many peoples will go and they will say, Go and let us ascend to the Mountain of G-d, to the House of the G-d of Jacob, and He will teach us of His ways and we will go in His paths, for the Torah will go forth from Zion and the word of HaShem from Jerusalem" (Isaiah 2:3).

* * *

AND IT SHALL BE FOR A SIGN.

The lessons of the Torah are not to remain in the mind. "And you shall know (***veyada'ata***) today and bring it ***down to your heart*** that HaShem is the G-d in the heavens above and on the earth below, there is none other" (Deut. 4:39). The Exodus was the greatest ever revelation in history so far of ***Da'at***-- the "knowledge" that G-d governs this world. The institution of the religion founded upon this event is marked in our parshah with the giving of the first practical commandments through which we keep this knowledge alive from generation to generation and make it palpable and literally tangible in our lives.

The highly tangible act of eating the Pesach sacrifice (or celebrating the Seder night) from year to year keeps the memory of the Exodus alive, stimulating questions from little children, giving the adults the opportunity to hand down the tradition and grow themselves in the process. A farmer's cow or sheep gives birth to a first-born, which he presents to the priest in memory of the saving of the Israelite first-born. A first-born boy is born and must be "redeemed" from the priest. First thing in the day, the Israelite takes leather straps, symbols of bondage, and uses them to bind himself to G-d and literally bind G-d's words and wisdom to his very body, with the Tefilin. "And it shall be for a sign on your hand and for frontlets between your eyes that with strength of hand HaShem brought us out of Egypt" (Ex. 13:16, closing words of the parshah.) Through practical acts of devotion, we bring the knowledge of G-d into our hearts. This is our part in displacing Pharaoh.

BESHALACH

Torah Reading: Exodus 13:17-17:16

Haftarah: Judges 4:4-5:31 (Sephardi ritual) Judges 5:1-31

INTO THE WILDERNESS

*F*airy tales may end happily ever after, but the Torah is an encounter with reality, in which progress and breakthroughs are frequently accompanied by reverses and obstacles.

The climactic drama of the Exodus, related in the previous parshah of ***Bo***, was followed by the entry of the Children of Israel into the Wilderness, the ***midbar***, a place that "speaks" -- ***medaber*** -- teaching day by day. The ***midbar*** is a super-reality, a stark no-man's land where the ultimate existential reality of our lives, wanderers in this often inhospitable world, is writ large. It was fitting that the Torah was given in the Wilderness, a place to which no one can lay claim, a place where no one can take credit. In the wilderness, no one provides hospitality except G-d.

The main event of the "Giving of the Torah" at Sinai is recounted in next week's parshah of ***Yitro*** (and also in the ensuing parshah of ***Mishpatim***, as well as partially in ***Va-etchanan***, the second parshah of Deuteronomy). However, the lessons learned by the Children of Israel in ***all*** their wanderings in the Wilderness are integral parts of this same Torah, as in this week's parshah of ***Beshalach***, which begins to relate their encounter with the harsh reality of the Wilderness after the exuberance of the Exodus.

Directly after the triumphant march of the Children of Israel out of Egypt "with a high hand", they appear to go into retreat, and their former masters come racing after them to recapture them. Directly after they depart from the Red Sea after witnessing the greatest ever freak event in the natural order, they find themselves three days into the

Wilderness with no water to drink. They go further, and they have nothing to eat. They find food today, but will they have food tomorrow? They go further -- and again there is nothing to drink. Suddenly, their deadliest enemies, the Amalekites attack.

The promise is that at the end of the journey lies the "happy ending" -- the Land flowing with milk and honey. But unlike in fairy tales, the path through the speaking, teaching Wilderness of reality is long and arduous, twisting and turning in frightening ways. Each twist and turn in the journey comes to teach a new aspect of faith in G-d: faith in the miracles that take place in and through the workings of nature ("and they ***believed*** in HaShem and in Moses his servant", Ex. 14:31); faith in the miracles through which we receive our livelihood (the root of ***manna*** is the same as ***emunah***, faith); faith in G-d's miraculous power to heal through our keeping the Torah ("I, HaShem am your healer" Ex. 15:26); faith in G-d's power to conquer the forces of evil ("and his hands were faith" Ex. 17:12).

Faith is the sustenance needed to survive in the wilderness of this world and to reach the promised "inhabited land" (Ex. 16:35) that surely lies at the end of the road. The very twists and turns in the road are trials sent to bring us nearer to this sustaining faith. For that reason, it is not written (Ex. 14:10) that "Pharaoh drew near" (***karav***, Pa'al verbal form) to the Children of Israel, but rather, Pharaoh ***hikriv***, Hif'il verbal form -- "Pharaoh ***brought*** closer" (see Rashi ad loc.). I.e. Pharaoh brought the Children of Israel closer: his very onslaught and the fear it caused brought them closer to G-d, forcing them to turn to Him in prayer and faith.

* * *

THE MIRACLE OF THE SPLITTING OF THE SEA

A man once came to Rabbi Yisrael, the Baal Shem Tov, wanting to ask him a question. The man had studied science and philosophy, and according to what he had learned, at the time when the sea split before the Children of Israel, there were natural reasons why it split. Since the sea split naturally, why does everyone make such a fuss about the miracle of the splitting of the sea? This question made the man enormously perplexed, which is why he traveled to the Baal Shem Tov.

Before the man had an opportunity to put his question, the Baal Shem Tov went to the Synagogue and gave instructions to assemble everyone in the town for a sermon. The Baal Shem Tov stood up and said that there are crazy people and unbelievers who find this difficult, but they have eyes yet they do not see. For it is written, "In the beginning G-d -- Elokim -- created." (Gen. 1:1). The Hebrew letters of the name ***Elokim*** have the numerical value of 86, which is the same as that of the letters of the word ***HaTeva*** = Nature. The Holy One blessed be He also created nature. And thus, our sages taught that when "the sea returned to its strength (***eitano***)" (Ex. 14:27), this can be read as if the sea "returned to its ***condition*** (***tana-o***)" (Midrash Rabbah, Beshalach 21:6). From this we learn that when G-d brought about the Creation, He made a condition and incorporated into the very nature of the sea that it would split before the Children of Israel at that precise moment. This makes the miracle even greater, for G-d gave the sea this nature from the very outset of the creation for the sake of the Children of Israel. ***Bereishit***-- "for ***reishit*** -- for the Children of Israel, who are called ***reishit*** = the first". If Israel had not needed this miracle, G-d would not have created nature so."

(From Beit Yaakov -- Teachings of the Baal Shem Tov -- Parshiyot Bereishit and Beshalach).

* * *

THE SONG OF PROVIDENCE

The Shabbat of Parshat ***Beshalach*** is known as ***Shabbat Shirah***, the Shabbat of Song, because the parshah contains the ***Shirat HaYam***, the "Song of the Sea" sung by the Children of Israel after the miracle.

The difference between song (or music) and mere noise is that noise is random and meaningless, while song and music are ordered and communicate a message.

The Children of Israel burst into song after the miracle of the splitting of the sea, because at that moment, they saw clearly that nature is not random and meaningless. It was tailor made for them! The natural realm, random and chaotic as it may seem, is part of and subject to one greater order or system. It is all one song -- the awesome Song of G-d's ***hashgachah***, His "watching over" the world, supervising every tiny detail. Each detail is a note in the amazing beauty of this song. (See Likutey Moharan Part II, Discourse 8:9 and Rabbi Nachman's story of the Exchanged Children).

At the very center of this Song, to which all the world dances, is the vision of the Holy Temple, the House on G-d's Mountain in Jerusalem. This too is an integral part of ***Bereishit***, the letters of which, when rearranged, spell out Bayit Rosh -- the "House that is the Head". "In Your kindness, You have taken this people that You redeemed, You have led them in Your strength to the dwelling-place of Your holiness. You will bring them and plant them on the Mountain of Your inheritance, the foundation of Your dwelling place that You have made, HaShem, the Sanctuary, O G-d, that Your hands have formed" (Ex. ch. 15 vv. 13 & 17).

When we train ourselves to hear the Song of G-d's providence, we can at treasured moments see, with the eyes of faith, the "inhabited land" that lies at the end of the road. It is this vision that gives us the strength to continue with the journey.

* * *

THE TORAH HEALING PATHWAY

Parshat ***Beshalach*** is always read just prior to, or ***on*** the festival of ***Tu Bishvat*** (the 15th of Shevat). Many people think of this as the "Festival of Trees". However, the Mishnah (Rosh HaShanah 1:1) refers to it as the "New Year of ***the Tree***". On one level, this is an allusion to the Etrog tree -- and it is proper on Tu Bishvat to offer a prayer for the Etrog one will take in eight months' time on the festival of Succot, for it is now, after Tu Bishvat, that the fruit begins to develop and grow on the tree. On another level, "***the Tree***" is an allusion to the Tree of Life, which begins sending fresh vitality and life into the world just when spring starts to appear in the Land of Israel and the water from the winter rains enters the trees from the soil, sending energizing sap all through them.

"And they came to Marah and they could not drink the waters for they were bitter. And he cried to HaShem, and HaShem ***showed him*** (or "taught him") ***a tree*** and he cast it into the waters and they were sweetened" (Exodus 15:23, 25).

The "Tree" that sweetens the bitterness of life is the Torah, which provides us with the waters of ***Da'at*** understanding of how evil is joined to good as part of G-d's unity.

The first laws of the Torah were given at Marah: "There He placed for him [i.e. Israel] a law and judgment, and there He tested [the people]. And He said, If you will surely listen to the voice of HaShem your G-d and do what is right in His eyes and listen to His commandments and guard all His statutes, all the diseases that I have put upon Egypt I will not put upon you, for I, HaShem am your healer" (Ex. 15:25-6).

The laws given at Marah were those of Shabbat, the Red Heifer (purifying from defilement from contact with a dead body) and ***dinim***, the laws governing our relations with others (see Rashi on Ex. 15:25). All three are bound up with healing. Only through keeping Shabbat is it possible to heal from the curse of Adam, "with the sweat of your brow you will eat bread". Man is forced to work in the world. The only release from this slavery (Egypt) is to abstain from work for one day of the week, in order to elevate the work of all the days of the week to the service of G-d. The Ashes of the Red Heifer are the source of all healing (***epher*** = ashes, has the same letters as the root ***rapa*** = heal), for if we cannot heal from death and integrate it into our vision of life, we cannot heal from anything. The laws governing our relations with others in our family, marital, business and other dealings are the foundation of social healing, which must go hand in hand with individual healing.

* * *

May we be blessed with health and strength and taste the fruit from the Tree of Life this Tu Bishvat!!!

YITRO

Torah Reading: Exodus 18:1-20:23

Haftarah: Isaiah 6:1-7; 9:5-6

WE ARE ALL CONVERTS

*I*t is fitting that the parshah which tells of the Giving of the Torah at Mount Sinai is named after Yitro (Jethro), Moses' father-in-law -- a convert. Indeed, all those who witnessed the Giving of the Torah were "converts". Thus (as noted in the commentary on Parshat ***Shemot***) the Covenant at Sinai was accompanied by the three components of conversion: circumcision (Rashi on Ex.12:6), ritual immersion in the waters of the Mikveh (Ex. 19:10) and burned offerings (Ex. 24:5). For before G-d, we are all converts -- ***gerim***, "dwellers" in a land and on an earth that is not ours but G-d's. We are all here only by the grace of G-d, utterly dependent upon His kindness and compassion.

Thus no one can claim that the Torah belongs to him by right through ancestral or other merit. There is no room for pride, arrogance or the exploitation of the Torah for worldly advantage. The Torah is not the property of an exclusive caste. It "belongs" only to one who keeps it. The Torah was given in the Wilderness, no man's land, on the lowest of all mountains -- Sinai, the eternal symbol of humility. For only through humility can we "receive" and accept the Torah, which belongs to G-d alone. Receiving the Torah means having the humility to accept it as it is, the way it has come down to us, without trying to "modify" it according to our own ideas and wishes. And when we are willing to accept and follow the Torah as it actually is -- fulfilling ***na'aseh ve-nishma***, "we will (first) ***do*** it and (then) ***hear*** (and understand) it" (Ex. 24:7) -- then we can come to understand how the Torah lifts us out of our slavery to this-worldliness, with its many false gods. Then we can hear the voice of redemption that calls to us every day: "I am ***HaShem*** your G-d who brought you out of the land of Egypt, from the house of slaves" (Ex. 20:2).

Slavery to the idols of the mundane world is ignominious. Yet the Torah accords the greatest honor to those who have the courage to leave this servitude behind and "go out into the wilderness" in search of G-d -- like Jethro. According to tradition, Jethro had investigated every conceivable way of interpreting and living in this world, every world-view and "lifestyle". Only when Jethro came to HaShem and His Torah did he know he had found the truth. "Now I ***know*** that HaShem is great above all the gods" (Ex. 18:11). The Zohar comments: "When Jethro came and said, 'Now I know that HaShem is great.' then the Supreme Name was glorified and exalted" (Zohar, Yitro 69). In other words, the revelation of G-d's light and power is greatest precisely when it comes out of darkness and concealment. Only when we have seen evil and know its power can we understand the greatness of G-d's saving hand. Only one who was a slave truly understands what it means to have been freed. This is "the superiority of the light that comes out of darkness" (Ecclesiastes 2:13).

Thus Jethro the Convert was accorded the honor of having the parshah narrating the Giving of the Torah named after him, and of contributing the hierarchical system of "captains of thousands, captains of hundreds, captains of fifties and captains of tens" through which the Children of Israel are governed. Jethro's name also contains and alludes to the name of another humble convert who was accorded the greatest honor: Ruth the Moabitess, who was the great grandmother of King David, ***Melech HaMashiach***.

* * *

TWO MILLION PROPHETS

Rambam (Maimonides) in "Foundations of the Torah", the opening section of his comprehensive Code of Law, explains the significance of the revelation at Sinai, which was witnessed by at least two million people:

"The people of Israel did not believe in Moses our Teacher because of the signs he wrought. For one who believes on account of signs always has some residual doubt in his heart that maybe the sign was brought about through magic and witchcraft. All the signs that Moses performed in the wilderness were performed to meet specific needs, not to bring proof of his prophecy.

"Then how did they come to believe in him? The answer is: At Mount Sinai, where we ourselves (not a stranger) saw with our own eyes and where we ourselves (not someone else) heard with our own ears the thunderous sounds and flashing lights and how Moses approached and entered the thick cloud. We heard The Voice speak with him as we listened: 'Moses, Moses, go and say to them.' From where do we learn that the Assembly at Mount Sinai and that alone is the final proof of the truth of Moses' prophecy -- proof that leaves no room for further doubt? As it says, 'Behold I am coming to you in the thickness of the cloud in order that the people may hear when I speak with you and also they will believe in you forever' (Ex. 19:9).

"It follows that the very ones to whom he was sent were the witnesses to the truth of his prophecy, and he had no need to perform any further sign, since he and they were both witnesses to the matter. It is like two witnesses who both saw the same thing. Each one is witness that his friend is telling the truth. Neither witness needs further proof of what his friend is saying. Similarly, all Israel were witnesses to the truth of Moses' prophecy and he had no need to perform any sign. For one who believes on account of signs still entertains doubts in his heart.

"Accordingly if a prophet arises and works great miracles and wonders and seeks to deny the prophecy of Moses our Teacher, we do not listen to him and we know clearly that those signs were brought about through magic and witchcraft. For the prophecy of Moses does not depend upon signs, such that we should compare the signs of one prophet to the signs of another. We ourselves saw it with our own eyes and heard it with our own ears. The prophets who deny the truth of Moses' prophesy are like witnesses who tell a person who saw something with his own eyes that it was not as he saw it. The person simply does not listen to them, for he knows for certain that they are false witnesses." (Rambam, Yesodey HaTorah 8:1-3).

* * *

"AND ISRAEL ENCAMPED"

"And Israel encamped there, facing the mount" (Ex. 19:2) -- the Hebrew verb ***vayichan*** ("encamped") is in the singular. They encamped "as one man with one heart" (Rashi ad loc.) -- united. Observing today's rainbow variety of jostling Israelites -- ever-critical, argumentative, obstinate and apparently incapable of agreeing about anything -- it is hard to imagine how all the Children of Israel actually did unite at Sinai to receive the Torah.

This is particularly difficult to imagine for those who have delved into the intricacies of Talmudic law and reasoning, and who know how the Torah repeatedly seems to fly completely in the face of reason and good common sense. How could those two million Israelites collectively agree to accept this elaborate, complex, reason-defying code in all its minute details? What brought them to do so? And the fact is that today's observant descendants of those Israelites, despite the fact of having come from communities spread out all over the world, still all fundamentally agree to accept this code without changing a letter!

The very faith of Jews in the Torah for thousands of years in the face of almost constant adversity and persecution is itself proof of the uniqueness of the Assembly at Sinai, when we all collectively witnessed the same one truth of G-d and agreed to accept the Torah. Only a completely unique divine revelation could have been powerful enough to instill in two million people a faith that has lasted for thousands of years, a faith for which, over the generations, many millions laid down their very lives.

It is ironic that many people today question the historicity of the revelation at Sinai. We live in an age that prides itself on instantly recording its own daily history in the form of incessant news in the press, on TV, radio and Internet. And we are witnesses to the way in which the media have become manufacturers of endless streams of idolatrous images that totally distort the meaning of the world they supposedly reflect.

If we are to begin to internalize the magnitude of the Giving of the Torah, which took place without media coverage, we must try to think ourselves out of our own noisy, sophisticated world. We must try to project ourselves back into the stark, awesome, silent grandeur of the "wilderness", the ***midbar***, where man's existential reality as a ***ger***, a wanderer and a stranger in this world, is writ large. Out of the silence of the ***midbar*** spoke a voice: ***medaber***. And the voice was forever inscribed in the hearts of those who heard it and taught it to their children from generation to generation.

* * *

THE DIFFERENCE BETWEEN A PERSON AND A STATUE

In the above-quoted passage from Rambam about the uniqueness of Moses' prophecy, he states that "the prophets who deny the truth of Moses' prophecy are like witnesses who tell a person who saw something with his own eyes that it was not as he saw it."

The prophets to whom he is referring include those who founded the two major world religions which are rooted in and yet deviate from the Torah: Christianity and Islam. Both drew the bulk of their teachings from the Torah. Yet both implicitly and explicitly deny the finality of Moses' prophecy, seeking to "undo" the laws of the Torah (such as circumcision, the dietary laws, complete Sabbath observance and many others).

The relaxation of the stringencies of Torah law by these man-made religions made them more acceptable to the non-Israelite nations. As Rambam states at the very end of his Code of Law (Hilchot Melachim 11:4 uncensored version): "Man does not have the power to grasp the thoughts of the Creator of the Universe. For our ways are not His ways, nor are our thoughts His. All that happened in the wake of Yeshu of Nazereth and that Ishmaelite who arose after him came only to straighten the way for Melech HaMashiach and to rectify the entire world to serve HaShem together. Thus it is written: 'And then I will turn to all the nations a pure language so that all of them will call upon the name of HaShem and serve Him with one accord' (Zephaniah 3:9). The whole world has thus become filled with the knowledge of the Torah and the commandments. This knowledge has spread to the farthest islands. And when the true ***Melech HaMashiach*** arises and succeeds, they will all immediately know that 'their fathers inherited falsehood' and that their prophets and their fathers deceived them."

Despite the attraction of the two new religions for non-Israelites, neither one of them ever made serious inroads among the Jews. Indeed it was precisely because the founders could not attract the Jews that they turned to the non-Jews for recruits.

In Rambam's ***Igeret Teiman*** (letter to the Jews of Yemen written in 1172 C.E. encouraging them to reject the forced conversion to Islam to which they were being subjected), he explains why the two new religions held no attractions for those who understood the intricate depths of the Torah:

"Their only wish was to compare their lies to the Law of HaShem. But the work of G-d bears no comparison to the work of man except in the eyes of a little child who has no understanding of either. The difference between our religion and the other religions that seek to compare themselves to it is like the difference between a living, conscious man and a statue. The statue is carved out of a piece of wood overlaid with gold or silver or chiseled out of a piece of marble and made to look like a man. An ignorant fool does not know the difference between G-dly wisdom and this artifact made in the form of a man. The statue looks like a man in its structure and outward appearance. But it only seems like a man because the ignorant onlooker doesn't know what is inside either a man or a statue. However, the wise man knows the difference between what is inside the two. The wise man knows that inside the statue is nothing, while the inside of the living man, ***adam***, is filled with truly amazing wonders and works that testify to the wisdom of the Creator -- the nerves, the flesh, the bones, the bodily limbs and all their interconnections."

MISHPATIM

Torah Reading: Exodus 21:1-24:18

Haftarah: Jeremiah 34:8-22 and 33:25-26

*A*s indicated by its name of ***Mishpatim***, "the Laws", much of our parshah is made up of laws -- the basics of the Mosaic code as they apply equally to all Israelite men and women at all times and in all areas of life. These laws flesh out the details of the code for life implied in the Ten Commandments of which we read in last week's parshah of ***Yitro***.

THERE IS NO "BEFORE" OR "AFTER" IN THE TORAH

One of the principles of rabbinic Torah commentary is that "there is no 'before' or 'after' in the Torah". This means that the order in which things are told in the Torah does not always correspond to the order in which they happened -- events may appear out of sequence.

Understanding this principle may help unravel some confusion that can easily arise from a casual reading of the previous parshah and this week's. On the surface, it appears as if the laws contained in our present parshah of ***Mishpatim*** were given to Moses "after" the "main" event of the Divine revelation and giving of the Ten Commandments in the presence of all the people, as recounted in last week's parshah of ***Yitro***. Thus, at the end of last week's parshah we read that "the people stood from afar and Moses approached into the darkness." (Ex. 20:18). Directly afterwards we read that G-d gave Moses a number of commandments, including those relating to the sacrificial altar in the Temple, with which ***Yitro*** concluded. Our parshah of ***Mishpatim*** then follows on immediately with the words: "***and*** these are the commandments that you shall place before them." This makes it appear as if the detailed laws in ***Mishpatim*** were given to Moses "after" the divine revelation to all the people at Sinai.

However, at the end of ***Mishpatim***, after all the laws, we read in Ex. 24:1-18 a narrative portion that recounts for a second time, and in a different way, the event of the Divine revelation at Sinai about which we already read in ***Yitro*** Ex.19-20:1-18. This concluding section of our present parshah goes back in time to Moses' "negotiations" with the people in the days ***prior*** to the Giving of the Torah. "And Moses came and told the people all the words of G-d and ***all the laws***, and all the people answered with one voice and said, All the words that G-d speaks we will do." (Ex. 24:3). The Torah then goes on to tell how, on the actual day of the Giving of the Torah, the first-born, acting as priests, offered "converts'" sacrifices on behalf of all the people, who affirmed their acceptance of the Torah in the words, "We shall do and we shall hear" (Ex. 24:7). Moses then sprinkled the blood of the sacrifices on the altar and on the people to signify the striking of the Covenant.

Which ***were*** "all the laws" that Moses told the people ***prior*** to the "Giving of the Torah" -- the laws of which they declared their acceptance??? Rashi (on Ex. 24:3) tells us that these are the Seven Commandments of the Sons of Noah, Shabbat, honoring father and mother, the Red Heifer and ***dinim*** (laws between man and man) which were given at Marah (***Beshalach***, Ex. 15:25).

In fact, these ***dinim*** are none other than the very laws of murder, manslaughter, theft, robbery, damages, court procedure, etc. that take up the major part of our parshah of ***Mishpatim***. It turns out that these laws too are written in the Torah "out of sequence" -- for they were already given at Marah prior to the "Giving of the Torah" at Sinai.

If many of the laws contained in ***Mishpatim*** were actually given at Marah, why are they written here in our parshah out of sequence, "sandwiched", as it were, between the main account of the giving of the Torah in ***Yitro*** and the second account, at the end of ***Mishpatim***?

Rashi's opening comment on our parshah comes to draw out the lessons implicit in the placement of these detailed laws directly after the account of the Divine revelation at Sinai, immediately following the commandments relating to the Temple altar. "***And*** these are the laws" (Ex. 21:1) -- Rashi states: "The word ***and*** comes to add these (ensuing) commandments to the first (i.e. the Ten Commandments). Just as the first ones came from Sinai, so do these come from Sinai. And why is the section of ***dinim*** positioned immediately after the section dealing with the altar? To teach you to position the Sanhedrin next to the altar" (Rashi ad loc.).

The Sanhedrin is the assembly of Torah sages whose mission is to teach how the laws of the Torah apply in practice in their generation. The appointed place of the Sanhedrin is on the Temple Mount, in the "Chamber of Hewn Stone" (***Lishkat HaGazit***) adjacent to the main Temple courtyard, with the sacrificial altar in its center.

The altar is where man offers his ***korban*** -- his penitence and prayers, through which he comes close (***karov***) to G-d. But good intentions are not enough. Adjacent to the altar of prayer and devotion must be the brain-center of law and organization, through which the teachings of religion and the revelation of the divine are carried into our day-to-day life. This is accomplished through the practice of ***halachot***, "goings" -- ways of "going" in accordance with G-d's law as we go about our daily business in the world.

* * *

THE TORAH CODE

After the heights of G-dly revelation as recounted in last week's parshah, ***Mishpatim*** plunges us into the intricate depths of the Torah code of law. The laws revealed at Marah prior to the "Giving of the Torah, together with those set forth in ***Mishpatim*** and all the other laws written elsewhere in the Torah are all integral parts of the single unified code that was revealed at Sinai (see Rashi on Leviticus 25:1). Since G-d is perfect unity, the entire code was implied in a single flash with the first ***dibur*** ("word") "I am HaShem your G-d" (Ex. 20:2). Corresponding to the Ten Sefirot that underlie all creation, the Ten Words (***Aseret HaDibrot***, the "Ten Commandments") constitute the underlying fundamentals of the entire Mosaic code. In a sense, "All the rest is commentary" -- the six hundred and thirteen separate commandments that make up the code are all details implicit in the essential unity of G-d. All are necessary in order to reveal that unity to the world.

Many in the world pay lip-service to the Ten Commandments, but we do not have to look very far to see that practically all of them are violated in one way or another every day by people all over the world. Societies everywhere are rife with crime and violence, sexual immorality, slander, envy and jealousy. Hardly anyone in the world knows about Shabbat, one day a week of complete rest from technology and business, a day to be with G-d.

The many laws in ***Mishpatim*** constitute the core of the Mosaic code, teaching us how to ***be with G-d*** in ***all*** our involvements and activities in this world.

It is appropriate for the nation that came to Sinai from slavery in Egypt that the code of ***Mishpatim*** opens with the laws of slavery. The law of ***Mitzraim***, Egypt, the place of meitzar, constriction, was that no slave could ever go free. But the first of the detailed laws of the Torah code tells us that the opposite is the case. The Hebrew slave must work for his master for six years, but in the seventh year he goes free. If he chooses to stay on with his master after six years, he may do so, but only until the fiftieth year, the ***Yovel*** ("jubilee"). Time goes in cycles. A person may fall low, but eventually the cycle swings around, and he comes up. The cyclical nature of time implicit in the fourth commandment (six days of work followed by Shabbat) is revealed in the laws of slavery in ***Mishpatim*** to be a redemptive quality. The Sabbath day, the Sabbatical year and the Jubilee (after 7 x 7 = 49 years) all have the power to free man from the various kinds of slavery into which he falls.

Slavery in the literal sense is still widespread in many parts of the world. In addition, many who are supposedly "free" are also "slaves" in one sense or another, whether to their circumstances, to those around them, to deep-seated inner blocks, to urges and desires, to the dictates of the media, fashion, advertisers, etc. etc.

The Holy Zohar, whose commentary on ***Mishpatim*** is exceptionally lengthy, reveals in detail how the laws of slavery in our parshah contain the laws and principles by which souls are re-incarnated in this world. Souls are obliged to "serve" in different incarnations, in order to pay off debts incurred through sins and failures in previous incarnations. All of the other detailed commandments in the Torah also contain mystical allusions. For the revealed code of Torah law, which applies to our lives and everyday business and other affairs, is one and the same as the code through which G-d governs the entire universe on all its different levels. All is unity.

Besides slavery, the code of laws contained in ***Mishpatim*** includes the basic laws of marriage, murder, manslaughter, kidnap, willful injury, willful and unwitting damages of person and property, theft, negligence, loans, law court procedure, ritual and other laws. The code concludes with the laws of the Sabbatical year, the Sabbath and annual festivals, all of which bring redemption into the cycle of time.

At the end of the parshah we read: "And HaShem said to Moses, go up to Me to the mountain and be there, and I will give you the Tablets of Stone, the Torah, the Mitzvah that I have written to teach them" (Ex. 24:12).

The Talmud explains: "***The Tablets*** are the Ten Commandments. ***The Torah*** means the written Torah ("***mikra***"); ***the Mitzvah*** means the Mishnah (=Oral Law); ***that I have written*** -- these are the prophets and the holy writings (***Nevi'im*** and ***Ketuvim***). To teach them -- this is the Gemara, (the deductive principles of the Torah). Teaching that they were all given to Moses from Sinai." (Berachot 5a).

The written Torah, as we read it in the weekly parshah, is an integral unity with the oral Torah. Thus our parshah of ***Mishpatim*** contains the foundations of the laws expounded at length in four out of the six orders of the Mishnah -- the Oral Law. Thus in ***Mishpatim*** we encounter some of the main laws of the order of ***Zera'im*** ("Seeds" - agriculture), including Terumah, the tithe for the priest, and the Sabbatical year. We also encounter the fundamental laws of the order of ***Mo'ed*** (the seasons and festivals), of ***Nashim*** (marriage) and of ***Nezikin*** (damages, property, loans, legal procedure).

At the end of ***Mishpatim*** we read "And Moses came into the cloud and he went up to the mountain, and Moses was on the mountain forty days and forty nights" (Ex. 24:18). Immediately afterward, in next week's parshah of ***Terumah***, the Torah begins to explain the form of the Sanctuary, the prototype Temple, and how it was constructed and inaugurated in the wilderness. This will take up the remainder of Exodus, after which we enter Leviticus and the world of sacrifices and ritual purity. Sacrifices and ritual purity are the subjects of ***Kadoshim*** (holy items) and ***Taharot*** (purity), the last two orders of the Mishnah.

This Shabbat after the synagogue Torah reading, we bless the coming month of Adar – a month in which Israel's Mazal is in the ascendant. ***Meshenichnas Adar marbin simchah!!!*** When Adar arrives, we maximise simchah!!!

TERUMAH

Torah Reading: Exodus 25:1-27:19

Haftarah: I Kings 5:26-6:13

ABOVE SHALL BE BELOW, BELOW ABOVE

From this parshah of ***Terumah*** onwards until the end of the book of Exodus -- five parshahs -- the central theme is the Sanctuary built by the Children of Israel in the Wilderness. The Sanctuary is the prototype of the Holy Temple destined to stand eternally in Yerushalayim.

This parshah explains the design of the Sanctuary and its vessels, while the next parshah of ***Tetzaveh*** explains the garments that were to be worn by those who were to minister in that Sanctuary -- Aaron and his sons. ***Tetzaveh*** also explains the sacrificial rituals that were to inaugurate the Sanctuary and its priests.

After ***Tetzaveh*** comes ***Ki Tisa***, which continues the explanation of the form of the Sanctuary vessels and the sacrifices. When this explanation is complete, ***Ki Tisa*** goes on to narrate the sin of the Golden Calf and how Moses secured atonement for the people through the 13 Attributes of Mercy.

Then come the last two parshahs of Exodus, ***Vayakhel*** and ***Pekudey***, which explain how Betzalel and the other craftsmen actually constructed the Sanctuary and made the priestly clothes. ***Vayakhel*** and ***Pekudey*** repeat practically word for word some of the corresponding passages in ***Terumah*** and ***Tetzaveh***. ***Pekudey*** then concludes the book of Exodus with the account of the inauguration of the Sanctuary and the priests on the New Moon of the first Nissan after the Exodus. This was exactly one year to the day since Moses received the first commandments while still in Egypt: the law of the New Moon and the Pesach sacrifice, prototype of Temple sacrifice.

At the close of ***Tetzaveh*** and Exodus, we read how G-d's Cloud of Glory dwelled constantly over the Sanctuary. Leviticus opens immediately with the Voice of G-d emanating to Moses from between the mouths of the Cherubs in the Holy of Holies, giving him the detailed laws of the Temple sacrifices.

From this overview of the remaining five parshahs of Exodus, we see that the subject of the Sanctuary -- central to the Torah and to the whole world -- is introduced in "sandwich" form. ***Terumah*** and ***Tetzaveh*** explain the intended form of the Sanctuary and priestly garments ***before*** they were executed, when they were in the "mind" and will of G-d. In the middle of the "sandwich" is the account of the sin of the Golden Calf and its atonement through the 13 Attributes of Mercy. Then on the other side of the "sandwich" come ***Vayakhel*** and ***Pekudey***, which tell how the Sanctuary ***idea*** was brought from ***potential to actual*** through the thirty-nine labors of the craftsmen who made it.

At the very center of this "sandwich" structure is the account of the sin of the Golden Calf -- which changed everything for the Children of Israel. In the heady days of the Exodus and the Giving of the Torah, the Children of Israel were elevated to the greatest heights. Then suddenly, forty days after hearing the Voice of G-d at Sinai, in one single orgy they sank to the lowest depths of degradation. From then on they had to learn the terrible pain of retribution, suffering and contrition. This was a loss of innocence parallel to the eating of the fruit of the Tree of Knowledge of Good and Evil.

But God had already prepared the remedy before the illness. Indeed, we might even say that the illness was sent with the very purpose of revealing the great power of the remedy. The remedy for sin is repentance, which saves man from himself and brings him back to the One G-d, bringing him atonement – ***at – one - ment***. The penitential "system" of the Torah is contained within the Sanctuary and its sacrificial rituals, which are a teaching to mankind about how man draws close (KaRoV) to G-d through his ***korban*** ("sacrifice") -- literally, his "coming close". As the way of repentance for having elevated wealth to the status of a god, man is commanded to take gold, silver, copper and the richest fabrics in order to glorify and magnify the One True G-d. Man is taught how to configure the materials of this world so that instead of separating him from G-d through idolatrous uses and configurations, they will serve to draw him ever closer, until G-d Himself "dwells" with man.

Terumah and ***Tetzaveh*** present us the Sanctuary and sacrificial ***idea*** before we have even learned about sin. The lesson of the Golden Calf in ***Ki Tisa*** is harsh. But it is sweetened, because immediately after Moses secured atonement for Israel through the 13 Attributes of Mercy, the very next day he assembled the people and told them to bring gifts of materials and to get busy making the ***actual*** sanctuary, as told in ***Vayakhel*** and ***Pekudey***. Thus the bitterness of sin in ***Ki Tisa*** is "sandwiched" between the sweetness of ***Terumah*** and ***Tetzaveh*** (the Teshuvah ***idea*** in all its innocent purity) and ***Vayakhel*** and ***Pekudey*** (the ***actualisation*** of Teshuvah in the Sanctuary in this world.) [This "sandwich" is reminiscent of how in Temple times, Hillel would eat his Pesach sacrifice with the bitter herbs in a "sandwich" with his Matzah.]

The Torah never wastes a word or a single letter. It is therefore a great wonder that many of the passages about the Sanctuary, its vessels and the priestly garments that we read this week and next in ***Terumah*** and ***Tetzaveh*** are, as mentioned, repeated almost word for word in ***Vayakhel*** and ***Pekudey***. The "mirroring" of the explanation of the ***idea*** in the account of its ***actualisation*** comes to communicate something that is at the very core of the Temple-Sanctuary idea. The Temple or Sanctuary are a "replica" and "mirror" of the Heavenly Sanctuary, which is in the "mind" or will of G-d. They are a "replica" in which the materials of this world -- metals, wood, fabrics, etc. -- are used to bring a "reflection" of heaven into the minds and consciousness of ordinary people.

In this way, what is "above" -- "in heaven" -- actually dwells and exists in material form in this world "below". And through this, "below" becomes "above". "And they will take for Me an offering. And they will make Me a Sanctuary, and I will dwell ***within them***" (Ex. 25 vv. 2, 8).

* * *

JACOB'S CEDARS

"And you shall make ***the*** boards for the Sanctuary from the wood of cedar trees ***standing*** upright" (Ex. 26:15). On this, Rashi comments: "It should have simply said, 'you shall make boards' in the same way as was said of everything else. What are '***the*** boards'? These were boards from those that were ***standing*** ready for this. Jacob our father planted cedars in Egypt and before he died, he instructed his sons to take them up with them when they left Egypt, and he said that the Holy One was going to command them to build a Sanctuary in the wilderness" (Rashi ad loc.)

In the Midrash which Rashi here brings about the wood of the standing boards or beams of the Sanctuary -- the "bones" that enable the entire structure to stand up -- he underlines the conceptual connection between the Sanctuary idea and Jacob.

As discussed in ***Universal Torah*** commentaries on the parshahs in Genesis dealing with Jacob, it was he who made synthesis, order and structure out of the opposing polar tendencies of the two fathers and teachers in whose tents he sat -- Abraham (***Chessed***, kindness and expansiveness) and Isaac (***Gevurah***, power and restraint).

Jacob was the house-builder who built the House of Israel. And Jacob was a genius house-builder precisely because he understood domestic life perfectly. In his first appearance in the Torah (at the beginning of ***Toldot***, Gen. 25:29) he is cooking lentil soup -- using the round lentils as a hint to his father Isaac (who was in mourning for the loss of Abraham, see Rashi) that life and death go in cycles. Jacob's grip on the heel of Esau indicates that Jacob possessed the power to take the simple things of this world (***Asiyah***, Esau) and transform them into communicators of G-dliness.

Thus the components of the Sanctuary-Temple are the same as those of a home. It exists within a defined space, a courtyard, where curtains of modesty separate between what is outside (profane) and what is inside (holy).

The Sanctuary contains different areas. Its very heart is the hearth, the "kitchen". This is where the food is prepared (slaughter of animals) and cooked (on the "oven", the Altar). Within the "domestic quarters" of the House itself, there is a secluded, intimate living area with a lamp (the Menorah) and a table (the Show-bread Table), and a pleasant aroma (from the Incense Altar). Most secluded and intimate of all is the "bedroom", to which no-one except the most trusted has access. This is the Holy of Holies, where the "faithful of His house" may come "face to face" with the King in the height of prophecy.

The Sanctuary and Temple are replete with messages to us about how we must try to build our private homes and structure the lives we lead in them in ways that "reflect" G-dliness and enable G-d to dwell with us here in this world. This is how we lift up and elevate this world.

* * *

TERUMAH - LIFTING UP

The sin of the Golden Calf pulled the Children of Israel down to the depths of degradation. But the remedy existed already from before: ***Terumah*** -- the elevation of mundane objects and materials, gold, silver, wood, fabrics -- through the service of G-d in "homely" ways.

The great beauty of the way of repentance that G-d has provided is that it enables man to repent with honor. Despite having sinned, man is invited to become a contributor. He is asked to give a ***Terumah*** -- to take the gold and silver that he has, the very thing with which he sinned, and "contribute" and "elevate" it so that now it too has its proper place in what becomes a Sanctuary. Then the proper order is restored, and everything sings out the glory of G-d.

One of the ways we "contribute" is through the words of our daily prayers and blessings. For in essence, the Sanctuary is a House of

Prayer. So too our homes should be filled with our blessings and thanks for all the good things of life that we enjoy and with our prayers for all of our needs.

King David (who prepared the way for the Temple) instituted that One Hundred Blessings should be recited daily (Rambam, Laws of Prayer 7:14). These hundred blessings (made up of the morning blessings, the thrice repeated Shmonah Esrey, the blessings before and after two daily meals, etc.) correspond to the hundred ***adney kesef***, "sockets of silver" (Ex. 26:19; Shaarey Orah). These ***adney kesef*** were the solid bases in which the "standing" boards that made up the Sanctuary walls were planted. These "sockets" of solid silver are what kept the boards upright. This silver came from the 100 ***kikar*** of silver contributed by the Children of Israel in response to the command with which our parshah of ***Terumah*** begins: "Let them take an offering.and silver" (Ex. 25:3 and Rashi ad loc.; Ex. 38:26-7).

Kesef, "silver", is related to the word for "longing" -- as in ***kisuf***in. Thus 100 ***adney kesef*** alludes to the hundred times we bless the name of G-d (A-D-N-Y), our Lord, with longing and yearning for His holiness to dwell with us! This small "contribution" on our part is what keeps the entire Sanctuary standing!

Meshenichnas Adar marbin simchah!!!

TETZAVEH

Torah Reading: Exodus 27:20-30:10

Haftarah: Ezekiel 10:-27

LIFE IN THE HOUSE

*I*n the previous parshah of ***Terumah***, the Torah taught us the form and shape of the House of G-d with all its vessels. In this week's parshah of ***Tetzaveh***, we receive instructions about the daily activities that are to take place in that House. The central core of the parshah is taken up with detailed instructions about the making of the garments of those who are to be the ministering attendants in the House -- Aaron and his sons, the priests -- and about the sacrifices that were to be offered during their seven-day initiation.

It may help us to grasp the overall structure of ***Tetzaveh*** by again using the "sandwich" idea. In this case, the top and bottom of the "sandwich" would be the opening and closing sections of the parshah, which give instructions about the "daily life" in the House. ***Tetzaveh*** starts by introducing in its two opening verses (Ex. 27:20-21) the daily lighting of the Menorah candelabrum in the House using the choicest oil -- this opening section would be one side of the "sandwich". Then at the end of ***Tetzaveh*** (Ex. 29:38-45; 30:1-10) we come to the other side of the "sandwich". This consists of the sections dealing with the daily animal sacrifices, meal, oil and wine offerings on the outside Altar, the pleasing fragrance (the incense burned in the House on the golden Incense Altar) and finally (returning to the parshah's opening theme), the daily lighting of the Menorah.

In the middle of this "sandwich" are two considerably lengthier sections. The first gives instructions in fine detail for the making of the garments of those who are to minister in the House -- Aaron and his sons, the priests. The second gives the detailed instructions for what was to be a one-time event in the Wilderness: the 7-day initiation of

Aaron and his sons into the priesthood that was to lead up to the permanent induction of the Sanctuary on the 1st of Nissan. (Because of the central importance of this day in the Torah, we will be returning several times in later parshahs to the description of its events - in ***Pekudey*** at the end of Exodus as well as in several parshahs in Leviticus and Numbers.)

* * *

THE ATTENDANTS -- AARON AND HIS SONS

A basic assumption underlies all sections of our present parshah of ***Tetzaveh***, from beginning to end. The assumption is that the attendants conducting the daily life of the House, about whose daily activities, garments and induction-day we read in such detail, are to be none other than Aaron and his sons.

Throughout our parshah, the entire focus is upon Aaron and his sons, their activities, garments and induction. Indeed it is a fact that the actual name of Moses does not appear anywhere in our parshah from beginning to end, though he is addressed directly in its opening words, ***"Ve-ata tetzaveh"***, "And ***you*** shall command..." and moreover, he was to be the central actor in the priests' induction. [It is said that one reason why Moses' actual name was left out of this week's parshah is because Moses was later to pray -- in next week's parshah Ex. 32:33 -- "blot me out from Your book." However, that prayer had already been answered before it was said, since G-d "blotted out" Moses' name by not writing it anywhere in this week's parshah!]

Addressing now the central assumption -- that it is to be Aaron and his sons who will play the role of ministers in the House of the dwelling of the Holy Presence:

It must be understood that ***ein mukdam o me-uchar baTorah***: "There is no 'before' or 'after' in the Torah". The reason for the appointment of Aaron and his sons and none other to be the priests ministering in the House does not become apparent in the Torah narrative until next week's parshah of ***Ki Tisa***, with the account of the sin of the Golden Calf. Yet even before the reason became manifest, their appointment was already conceived in the mind and will of G-d prior to that event, as we see from this week's parshah of Tetzaveh.

The first-born of the Children of Israel were originally offered an opportunity to become the ones who would serve as the priests. Indeed at the Giving of the Torah, it was the first-born -- the "lads" (Ex. 24:5) -- of the Children of Israel who officiated at the sacrifices, as we read in ***Mishpatim***. However, with the sin of the Golden Calf (told next week in ***Ki Tisa***), the first-born of the Children of Israel failed the crucial test. From that time on, the Priesthood was given to Aaron and his descendants as an hereditary gift for all time.

* * *

HEREDITARY PRIESTHOOD

In an era when public office in virtually all "advanced" countries is theoretically open to all citizens, the role of an hereditary priesthood, which is at the very center of the Torah's system of penitence -- the Sanctuary and Temple rituals -- calls for some explanation.

Much of Genesis is taken up with disputes about who is to serve in the role of the "priest". Cain struggled with Abel. Ishmael fought against Isaac. Esau fought against Jacob. Reuven was the first-born, but Levi took the initiative, Judah, fourth in line, became the leader, while it was the righteous Joseph (against whom all the brothers struggled) who received a firstborn's double portion of two-tribes. And then Ephraim took priority over firstborn Menasheh.

In Exodus: Levi's second son, Kehat, took priority over Levi's firstborn, Gershon. Amram was indeed Kehat's firstborn, yet while the priesthood went to Amram's older son, Aaron, the latter was secondary in prophecy to his younger brother, Moses. The firstborn of the Children of Israel had a brief taste of the priesthood at the time of the Giving of the Torah, 50 days after having been saved from the plague that killed all the Egyptian firstborn. However the Israelite firstborn were displaced from their "birthright" -- hereditary priesthood forever -- owing to the sin of the Golden Calf.

This raises the question of the nature of the priesthood in Judaism, which is relevant to our parshah of ***Tetzaveh***, all of which is devoted to the daily duties of the priests, their garments and their induction service.

It is true that the tribe of Levi (who did not participate in the sin of the Golden Calf), and the Kohanim are in many respects separate hereditary castes. Nevertheless, it remains the case that the ideal social structure of the Israelites as envisaged in the Torah is remarkably free of the social hierarchies and inequalities that characterize even the most "democratic" societies.

In particular, Israelite society is envisaged as one that should be free of any kind of extensive hierarchical network of full-time religious functionaries who act as intermediaries between the people and G-d, and whose service before their passive congregants takes the place of the individual's personal relationship with G-d.

This is true, notwithstanding the fact that only the Kohanim (male descendants of Aaron), and members of the tribe of Levi could actually serve in the Temple, and only the Kohanim could perform certain vital ritual functions (such as purification from leprosy). Nevertheless, the Temple itself had a relatively small number of permanent priestly officials who were responsible for the maintenance of the House. The actual sacrificial services in the House were conducted by different priests every day. Each of the 24 contingents of priests into which the Kohanim were divided served for two weeks out of the year and on festivals, spending the rest of their time teaching Torah among the people in the localities where they lived. The only outstanding exception to this rule, besides the small core of permanent Temple staff, was the High Priest, who spent all his time in Jerusalem, most of it in the Temple itself.

It is certainly correct that the Kohanim were an hereditary priestly caste, who received ***Terumah***, the first gift from everyone's crops, as well as portions of meat, wool and various other gifts. This is what they lived off. The purpose of providing the members of this caste with their material needs was to enable them to devote themselves to a higher-than-average level of devotion (as expressed in eating of Terumah and sacrificial portions in ritual purity) and to the study of the Torah. It was the Kohanim who were expected to be able to play the role of the Torah judges (see Deuteronomy 19:17) in cases of disputes. They were also to play the central role in the "diagnosis" and "purification" of leprosy and other maladies (Leviticus Ch. 13ff.)

Nevertheless, it remains true that despite their exclusive role in the Temple sacrificial services and in the purification from leprosy, the Kohanim were not religious intermediaries who in some sense ***replaced*** the personal connection of the individual with G-d.

The Children of Israel were envisaged as a nation of free, independent small land-owners, each farming his own land and sitting under his vine and fig-tree. Only in dire circumstances would one be sold as a slave to another (as instituted in ***Mishpatim***). Even one who fell into slavery would eventually go free at the end of seven years or in the Jubilee year. In the seventh year, all debts were to be cancelled. Those who had sold their land would get it back in the Jubilee year. The vision was not of a country where most of the wealth is permanently concentrated in the hands of a small elite.

Just as all of the Children of Israel heard the First Commandment, so they were all commanded to serve the One G-d, each through his own prayers and acts of service. The Torah commands that all of the Children of Israel must be holy (Leviticus 19:2). Everyone must strive to go in G-d's ways. Becoming a Nazirite is considered an excess -- the Nazirite must bring a sin-offering! There are no monks in Judaism.

Outside of the Temple itself, Israelite life was intended to be free of an elite of religious functionaries. Although the Kohen and Levi are honored by being called first and second to the public Torah reading, the actual synagogue and its services are run by its members, the majority of them Israelites. The service can only take place if a quorum of 10 Israelites is present. There is no need for an official rabbi as long as somebody present -- any Israelite -- knows how to lead the service and read from the Torah. The "functionaries" in Israelite society are the "captains of tens", "captains of fifties", "captains of hundreds" and "captains of thousands". These must be "men of valor, G-d-fearing, men of truth, hating gain" (Ex. 18:21) -- but they do not have to be Kohanim. In the Torah vision of the Israelite state, membership of the Sanhedrin, the Supreme Court of the state, is not to depend on heredity or wealth but only on Torah wisdom and personal sanctity.

What then is the role of the hereditary Kohanim, whose Temple service, garments and induction are the subject of our parshah of ***Tetzaveh***?

The key concept necessary to understand the role of the Kohen, particularly that of the Kohen Gadol (High Priest), is the concept of ***kaparah*** -- atonement. This and related concepts recur several times in our parshah. The purpose of the precious stones that were attached to the High Priest's shoulders and bore the names of the tribes of Israel was that they should be "remembered" by G-d with favor. The wearing of the ***Tzitz***, the head-plate inscribed "Holy to HaShem", was to secure atonement for impurity. The closing verse of our parshah speaks of how the High Priest must annually sprinkle the golden Incense Altar with the blood of the Day of Atonement sin-offering in order to bring about ***kaparah*** -- atonement.

The institution of the priesthood was not intended to replace individual attachment to G-d on the part of each person through his own devotions. While the Kohanim are charged with maintaining the Holy Temple as the central focus of Israelite and indeed world religious life (for "My House is the House of Prayer for all the Nations), their role in the devotional life of the individual is of significance primarily when the individual, independent "citizen" ***turns aside*** from the path and falls into sin. He is then unable to help himself. If he is liable to bring a sacrifice, he needs a Kohen to offer it for him. If he has what he thinks is a leprous patch on his skin (a sign of a personal deficiency), he needs a Kohen to make the determination and a Kohen to purify him.

The Kohen can play his role as functionary in the Temple services and bringer of ***atonement*** only through standing aside from the rest of the people and demanding more of himself. The Kohanim were distinguished by their unique genetic inheritance as direct male descendants of Aaron, and they protected this inheritance by adhering to higher levels of personal sanctity (such as, that a Kohen may not marry a divorcee, etc.).

The rich, colorful ritual garments of the High Priest embody this concept of separateness, sanctity and atonement. So too, the induction of the priests during their Seven Days of Initiation was characterized by separation, sanctity and the atonement accomplished through the offering of the ox sin offering (atoning for the sin of the Golden Calf) and the eating of peace offerings.

Atonement depends upon the priestly garments and the priests' consumption of sacrificial portions. The original sin of Adam -- of which the sin of the Golden Calf was a "repetition" -- came about through eating. After Adam and Eve sinned, G-d gave them ***clothes*** in order to cover over their nakedness and begin the process of atonement. The priests continue this process of atonement through wearing their unique garments while eating their portion of the sinner's sacrifice.

The hereditary inheritance of the priesthood -- Temple ***service*** -- by the sons of Aaron is justified by the fact that Aaron joined himself to the Torah inheritance through his choice of a wife to mother his sons. For "Aaron took Elisheva the daughter of Aminadav, sister of Nachshon as his wife, and she bore him Nadav and Avihu, Elazar and Itamar" (Ex. 6:23). Elisheva's father, Aminadav, was the Prince of Judah, the tribe to whom Jacob entrusted with guardianship of the Torah, while her brother Nachshon was the first to jump into the Red Sea. Torah knowledge is indispensable for the proper functioning of the priesthood. Without Torah, the priest is helpless -- an ignoramus priest needs a Torah scholar to teach him how to make the correct determination in cases of leprosy.

Through the merit of our Torah study, may we see the Holy Temple rebuilt quickly in our times!!!

KI TISA

Torah Reading: Exodus 30:11-34:35

Haftarah: I Kings 18:1-39 (Sephardi ritual) I Kings 18:20-39

PROVIDING THE MEDICINE BEFORE THE ILLNESS

*T*he lengthy first section of our parshah of ***Ki Tisa*** (the entire first Aliyah in the synagogue Torah reading, up to Ex. 31:18) starts with a number of commandments concluding the account of the Sanctuary, its vessels and the daily services of its ministering priests. Then, with a reiteration and amplification of the Fourth Commandment, the Sabbath, its seriousness (violation is punishable by death) and its holiness as an eternal sign between G-d and Israel, Moses' Forty Days on Mount Sinai after the giving of the Ten Commandments come to an end. G-d gives him Two Tablets of Testimony, but as he readies to go down the mountain back to the people, G-d tells him that the worst had just happened: the people had already violated the Covenant by making a molten idol.

Even before the sin occurred, the commandments with which ***Ki Tisa*** opens provide precisely the remedy for the coming illness, which was rooted within the dark depths of selfish material lust and craving. The Sanctuary as a whole is a remedy for material craving and the lust for wealth. This is particularly true in the case of the mitzvah with which the parshah opens, the ***half-shekel*** which each Israelite was required to contribute to the Sanctuary and for the purchase of the daily sacrifices so as to put food on the "table" of G-d's House, the Altar. The ***half-shekel*** is symbolic of charity and the will to ***give***, as opposed to the selfish desire to acquire and consume. The ***half-shekel*** is the remedy for the appetite for material wealth in itself.

When G-d spoke to Moses, He "showed him a kind of coin of fire, the weight of a half-shekel" and He said to him: "***This*** shall all who pass through the count give -- a half-shekel" (Ex. 30:13 and Rashi there).

This fiery ***half-shekel coin***, which made every single citizen an equal partner in the Sanctuary and its upkeep, was the remedy for material lust and the appetite for wealth. Everyone was to join and be a partner in an enterprise that elevates material wealth -- the finest vessels of gold, silver and copper, the finest fabrics, choicest animals, flour, oil, wine and spices -- by incorporating them in the worship of the One G-d. This is where the display of wealth is truly fitting, a place where each may take a just pride in having a share. Having a joint share with everyone else in the national treasure, the Temple, keeping one's eyes focussed on its splendid golden vessels and their implicit messages -- these are the medicine for the selfish lust for wealth for its own sake.

Differences in wealth and assets were of no significance in this annual half-shekel tax that made each citizen an equal partner in the Temple enterprise. The rich could not give more nor the poor less. Souls cannot be quantified and counted -- each soul has its own unique significance that would be violated by trying to quantify it or assign it a number. What counts is that each person adds his or her own ***self*** and ***will***, and is willing to play his or her part by paying the "head tax" and "casting a vote". Numbers and wealth do not count in the eyes of G-d. What counts is each person's ***will*** to make a contribution -- to have an equal share with everyone else, without pride and without shame, in being part of the whole, feeding the Altar and bringing the fire of G-d's presence into the world.

An integral part of this remedy for the sin of worshipping material wealth and splendor is the keeping of the Sabbath, with which the account of the Sanctuary and its vessels concludes. Observance of the Sabbath is more important even than the work of building the Sanctuary, which must also cease for one day every week. The race to work, build, make and create wealth must stop for one day out of every seven in order to remember that it is not work and material wealth that guarantee security but only G-d's enduring Covenant. What is of prime importance is not our wealth but our soul. One day a week must be for the soul. "And on the seventh day, He rested, ***vayinafash*** -- and became ***ensouled***" (Ex. 31:17).

* * *

THE LOSS OF INNOCENCE

To get a faint grasp of how, forty days after hearing G-d speak from heaven at Sinai, the people could worship a golden calf, it is necessary to understand that the ***Erev Rav*** -- the "mixed multitude" who went up with the Children of Israel out of Egypt -- were by no means a mere rabble of fellow-travelers who jumped on the wagon together with a band of runaway slaves. The Exodus was far more than a slave breakout. It was a religious revolution, in which the entire idolatry-based worldview of Egypt together with its hierarchy of king, priests and wizards was publicly overthrown and defeated. According to the Zohar (beginning of ***Ki Tisa***), the shattering of the existing culture and its assumptions caused some of Pharaoh's leading magicians (the great scientists and philosophers of the time) to join Moses (who was "very great in the eyes of Pharaoh's servants", Ex. 11:3), on this new venture out into the wilderness in search of the One G-d. The Midrashim note that some of these magicians even brought their idols with them when they crossed the Red Sea.

Rabbi Nachman of Breslov, commenting on the two golden calves made later on by Jeraboam, first king of the Northern Kingdom, asks how it is conceivable that he could have deceived a great multitude with such nonsense as worshiping cows. "Certainly this matter contained very deep and profound reasoning. And if a single page of the philosophical writings on which it was based had survived, it would distance many people from G-d and it would be impossible to come close to Him at all. And for this reason, it is a great benefit to the world that the works justifying this idolatry have been lost." (Likutey Moharan II:32). [Likewise it is told in Sanhedrin 102b that the soul of King Menasheh appeared to Rav Ashi, who asked him, "Since you were all so wise, why did you worship idols?" The king replied, "If you had been there, you would have picked up your robes and come running after us." See also Ta'anit 25b, where the angel of the rains is compared to ***egla***, a "calf". The root ***egla*** is also related to ***igul***, a circle or cycle, hinting at how the image of the golden calf was bound up with representing fundamental cosmic cycles.]

"They have turned aside quickly from the path that I commanded them, they have made for themselves a molten ***egel*** and they are prostrating to it and sacrificing to it and they said, These are your gods, O Israel, that brought you up from the land of Egypt." (Ex. 32:8).

Whatever this ***egel*** was intended to represent, it was a deviation from the pathway of absolute monotheism taught at Sinai, which proscribed any kind of graven image. Unlike the path of Sinai, which was intended to lead to the holiness befitting a nation of priests, the festivities around the ***egel*** ended up in "play" (Ex. 32:6) -- the three cardinal sins of idolatry, sexual immorality and murder (see Rashi ad loc.). The molten image, with its sophisticated associated "theology", was at root a wizardly rationalization for material lust.

How it came about that Aaron, Moses' older brother, played a part, albeit unwillingly, in the manufacture of this calf is one of the profound mysteries of the Torah. The two previous parshahs dealt with the elevation of wealth through the incorporation of gold, silver and other symbols of wealth into the Temple service. In ***Tetzaveh*** we saw that at the very center of the Temple service is the High Priest, with his beautiful garments (expressing "splendor", ***Hod***, kabbalistically the characteristic quality of Aaron). Yet suddenly we find that Aaron himself took the gold offered by those who wanted to make the calf, symbol of the ultimate degradation of wealth! This implies that there is a "fatal flaw" in ***Hod*** -- that splendor, even in the service of true religion, may lead to corruption.

[And thus it was that in the time of the Second Temple, the priesthood became corrupt. The "fatal flaw" in Hod corresponds to the sciatic nerve that "jumped" when the angel who struggled with Jacob touched his thigh.]

While Moses was "blotted out", as it were, from the previous parshah of ***Tetzaveh*** (as discussed in last week's commentary), he is the central figure in our present parshah of ***Ki Tisa***. In the previous parshah we saw that the role of the Priest, as epitomized in Aaron, is to secure atonement. But how can atonement come when the priest himself is in need of atonement -- when the splendor of religious service itself has become corrupted because of the inherent "flaw" in this-worldly glory?

Ki Tisa teaches that ultimately, atonement can come only through the Sage, as epitomized in Moses (whose characteristic quality is ***Netzach***, "Victory" -- as when he "argues" with G-d when pleading for forgiveness, see Likutey Moharan I:4). Moses alone "found favor" in G-d's eyes, eliciting the revelation of the Thirteen Attributes of Mercy (Ex. 34:6): Both before the sin and after the sin, G-d does not change. He is always the same: "loving and gracious, patient, and abundant in mercy and truth." True atonement comes from practicing these same virtues: "And you shall go in His ways" (Deut. 28:9).

Repentance is not very glorious -- it is hard to admit that one did wrong, to have to accept the consequences, atone and struggle to change while living with shame and contrition. In order to escape the ignominy of sin, practitioners of religion are sometimes tempted to present an outer face of sanctimony and irreproachability to others and even to themselves, thereby blinding themselves to their own flaws.

This is not the path of religion and repentance taught by the Torah, which gives naked exposure to people's real flaws and shortcomings, including even the errors of an Aaron, a Moses or a David, none of whom were spared from criticism.

The Talmud states: "It was not really consistent with what David truly was that he should have sinned with Batsheva, and it was not really consistent with what the Children of Israel were that they sinned with the Golden Calf. Then why were they made to sin? It was a decree of the King in order to give penitents an excuse" (Avodah Zarah 4b and Rashi there). They were made to sin in order to teach others the ways of repentance ("I will teach sinners your ways", Psalms 51:15). If they could sin, and still bear the pain and repent, then so can others.

While the sanctimonious nations of the world never cease berating and criticizing the Jews and Israel for their supposed sins, the actual followers of the Torah continue with the inglorious work of Teshuvah, scrutinizing themselves for flaws and striving to correct them instead of denying and papering over them. "And He, being compassionate, will atone for sin".

Meshenichnas Adar marbin simchah!!!

VAYAKHEL

Torah Reading: Exodus 35:1-38:20

Haftarah: I Kings 7:40-50 (Sephardi ritual) I Kings 7:13-26

GATHERING OF THE PEOPLE

The parshah of ***Vayakhel*** opens with the words: "And Moses gathered together all the Community of Israel." (Exodus 35:1). According to our sages, Moses' gathering of all of the Community took place on the day following Yom Kippur, when he had secured atonement for the sin of the Golden Calf.

This gathering consisted of all of ***Adat Yisrael***, the Community of Israel. The Zohar (beginning of ***Vayakhel***) states specifically that this Community was made up of all who remained faithful to the true Covenant of Israel, accepting no deviation from the Torah and no prophet other than Moses. The Zohar emphasizes that they could only build the Sanctuary after being purged of all the Mixed Multitude who went astray after the Golden Calf, which was half ox (Edom, Christianity) and half donkey (Ishmael, Islam). Both deviated from the finality of the Torah and the supremacy of Moses as G-d's true prophet, seeking to displace them in different ways by erecting new prophets and intermediaries standing between man and G-d. They and all the nations are excluded from membership of ***Adat Yisrael*** and from contributing to the Sanctuary.

The materials and manpower for the construction of the Sanctuary for the One G-d were to be contributed only by this Community of true Israelites, those willing to abide by the Law of Moses. This accepts no intermediary between man and G-d and permits no form or idol in worship. The only forms permitted in G-d's Sanctuary and Temple and nowhere else are those of the two golden Cherubs over the Ark of the Covenant and the other Sanctuary vessels. The only scripture is the Sefer Torah.

The commandment to build the Sanctuary was addressed to the whole Community of Israel. Each member of this community was to have his or her personal share in this joint national project of building the Sanctuary that Moses was to announce. For the true Israelite, there is no intermediary between man and G-d. Man faces G-d directly. Each one contributes -- and each one has responsibility for his own actions. Only one who truly ***intends*** to do what he does can be said to be responsible for what he does and, if he does good, fairly takes the reward. Only then is there merit in his contribution.

How can one ***intend*** what he does? Taking precedence over all the commandments about contributing to and building the Sanctuary addressed to the Community of Israel is the commandment to observe the Shabbat -- to spend one entire day every week ***wilfully abstaining*** from many kinds of actions and activities.

Moses' discourse to the Community of Israel about the building of the Sanctuary opens with the following words:

"Six days labor shall be performed, and on the seventh day you will have a holy Shabbat of rest in honor of G-d: anyone who performs a labor on Shabbat shall be put to death." (Ex. 35:2).

It is a commandment to labor -- "Six days labor shall be performed". Part of that same commandment is the commandment to observe the Shabbat by willfully abstaining from labor when so commanded. So stringent is this commandment that its willful infringement is punishable by execution. The example of forbidden labor given in the Torah text is that of kindling fire on the Sabbath day, which is infringed by acts as simple as flicking on a light-switch, lighting a cooker or starting a car ignition.

The ability to observe Shabbat and the ability to engage in truly meaningful labor on the other days of the week are bound up together. Only when a person can consciously abstain from action and willfully ***not*** perform a particular range of actions as instructed by G-d on Shabbat can he be said to have true ***intention*** when he does perform the action in honor of G-d on the six days of the week. Only then does his action have true merit.

Only the observance of the commandment to abstain from labor on the Seventh Day in honor of G-d gives true meaning to the building of the Sanctuary in the wilderness and the Temple in Jerusalem in G-d's honor.

* * *

PRAXIS

The greater part of our parshah of ***Vayakhel*** is devoted to a detailed description of how Betzalel and his fellow craftsmen made the Sanctuary and its vessels in accordance with the plan whose details we studied three parshahs earlier in ***Terumah***. While ***Terumah*** taught how they were to be made when they were still on the level of thought – ***be-koach***, in ***potentiality*** -- our parshah of ***Vayakhel*** teaches how they came to made ***be'phoal***, in ***actuality***, on the level of ***Asiyah***, action.

It is significant that all of the laws of what constitutes forbidden ***melachah***, labor, on Shabbat are learned from the 39 archetypal forms of labor that were involved in the making of the Sanctuary on the six days of the week. It is only when we abstain from performing forbidden labor on Shabbat ***because it is Shabbat*** that performing those labors "for G-d" on the six weekdays can be said to be truly intentional and meritorious. The labors that are forbidden on Shabbat are called ***melechet machshevet***, a labor that involves ***machshavah*** -- i.e. it is intentional.

When we observe the Shabbat ***for G-d***, abstaining from forbidden labors because that is His command, this gives the intentional labors that we perform on the other six days of the week in pursuit of our livelihood and all our other needs the sanctity of ***bulding the Sanctuary***. Our intention in pursuing all these needs is that we may serve G-d, pray and keep the commandments. Our going about our daily lives in our homes, at work and elsewhere is all part of ***building***

the Temple, a dwelling place for G-d's presence. For each one of us has our own contribution to make to the construction of this Temple. Each person's mitzvah and good intention help to draw G-d's Indwelling Presence into this world and within the sanctity of our homes.

According to a tradition handed down by the Kabbalah, Betzalel accomplished the "labors" required to build and construct the sanctuary vessels through manipulations of the 22 Hebrew Letters of Creation, as taught in Sefer Yetzirah. Successful manipulation of the letters to produce actual physical constructions in the world without performing any physical action requires the greatness of a Betzalel or the Maharal of Prague, who created a Golem. Nevertheless, even a simple Israelite has the power to "manipulate" the letters of creation by using them to compose prayers to G-d to bless his material efforts in the actual world of Asiyah with success. With the help of G-d, our very words themselves have the power to serve as vessels within which G-d's presence can dwell in this world. Through our words we contribute to building the Sanctuary -- the House of Prayer -- to G-d.

May we soon be worthy to contribute to the Building of G-d's House in Jerusalem quickly in our days. Amen.

PEKUDEY

Torah Reading: Exodus 38:21-40:38.

Haftarah: I Kings 7:51-8:25 (Sephardi ritual) I Kings 7:40-50

A LESSON IN GOOD GOVERNMENT

*T*he parshah of ***Pekudey*** brings the second book of the Torah, Exodus, to an end, concluding the subject of the construction of the Sanctuary, which occupies the last five of its eleven parshahs -- almost half the book.

"These are the ***accounts (pekudei)*** of the Sanctuary." (Ex. 35:21). Following the detailed explanation we have had in the previous four parshahs about the form of the Sanctuary and its vessels, we are now given a full "breakdown" of the "budget" of this national project -- how much gold, silver and bronze, etc.-- together with an exact account of what they were used for.

Much of the silver came from a "head-tax" on the entire nation, while the other materials were contributed by many different people, some wealthy, some poor. All were entitled to know what was done with their contributions. The Torah sets everything forth clearly for all to see.

This Torah lesson about "transparency" in good government is particularly timely today, when corruption is rife in business and government all over the world, and literally billions of dollars of tax-payers' money find their way into private pockets.

When Moses was later accused of bad government (Numbers 16:13-14), he could stand up and pray: "Do not turn to their offering: not a single donkey have I taken from them and I have not harmed one of them".

* * *

THE CENTRAL IMPORTANCE OF THE TZADDIK

The "accounts" of the Sanctuary project include blue, purple and scarlet dyes, one of the most important uses of which was in the garments of the High Priest. This leads us into the detailed account contained in our parshah of how these garments were actually made by Betzalel and his fellow craftsmen. This description of the making of the priestly garments in ***actuality***, on the level of ***Asiyah***, parallels the description in Parshat ***Tetzaveh*** of the form of the garments when they were in ***potential***, in the Divine Will. [Similarly, the description of the actual making of the Sanctuary and its vessels in the previous parshah, ***Vayakhel***, parallels the description of their form in ***Terumah***.]

The world of ***Asiyah*** attains its perfection when we take its best materials -- gold, precious stones, rich, colorful fabrics -- and use them to make the Sanctuary and priestly garments, which give expression to eternal truths about G-d's relationship to the Creation, and how man draws close to G-d. The description of the making of the priestly garments puts the spotlight on Aaron. It is the Kohen-priest, the archetypal Tzaddik, who secures atonement through the Sanctuary services and through his very garments.

Yet the central figure in our parshah as a whole is in fact Moses, the Lawgiver, who established the Sanctuary and the entire system of atonement within which the Kohen functions. Only Moses had the power to take all the different component parts of the Sanctuary, put them together and make them into one.

Our parshah lists in great detail all the component parts of the Sanctuary that were brought to Moses on their completion. The work had been done at great speed. The command to bring the materials was given on the 11th of Tishri, the day after Moses' third descent from Sinai, while everything was ready only seventy-five days later, on the 25th of Kislev. Nevertheless, all the component parts lay there for three months until the appointed time came for the seven-day induction of the priests, followed by the consecration of the Sanctuary for regular services on the 1st of Nissan.

When the appointed time came, Moses alone was instructed to erect the Sanctuary, place all the vessels in position, and conduct the very first services. (Moses officiated as the Priest during the seven-day induction of Aaron and his sons.) Our parshah tells how Moses performed the superhuman task of erecting the Sanctuary all by himself. The detailed account of Moses' induction of Aaron and his sons into the priesthood and the Consecration of the Sanctuary is taken up by the Torah in Leviticus (in Parshiyot ***Tzav*** and ***Shemini***).

Moses' unique role in putting everything together and erecting one Sanctuary is a second lesson in good government besides that of the need for transparent cleanliness, as discussed above. The very foundation of good government and organization is that it should be in the hands of a true Sage, whose only purpose is to serve G-d, as exemplified by Moses (who single-handedly erected the Sanctuary) and King David (who designed and collected all the materials for the Temple). Our generation is waiting for this true Sage to be revealed.

It is hopefully a sign of the imminence of Melech HaMashiach that today, the temporal government has been taken over by unbelievers, as predicted in the Talmud (Sotah 49b): "In the 'footprint' period before Mashiach. government will turn into atheism". Nevertheless, even in this time of exile, as we dream of the building of the physical Temple, we are daily engaged in building a spiritual Sanctuary: G-d's House of Prayer. This is our true national project, and it is accomplished even today when we all contribute our prayers.

In the words of Rabbi Nachman of Breslov:

"Every single prayer that each one prays is a 'limb' of the Shechinah (Divine Presence). All of the 'limbs' and component parts of the Sanctuary are 'limbs' of the Shechinah. And not one Israelite has the power to put all the limbs and parts together, each one in its proper place, except for Moses alone. For this reason, it is necessary to bind all our prayers to the Tzaddik of the generation, as it is written, 'And they brought the Sanctuary to ***Moses***' (Ex. 39:33). And the Tzaddik knows how to put the parts together to make a complete structure, as it says there, 'And ***Moses*** erected the Sanctuary' (Ex. 40:18). It seems as if every day we are crying out to G-d yet we are not saved, and some of our people, the Children of Israel, err in their hearts thinking that all the prayers are in vain. But in truth the Tzaddikim in every generation take all the prayers and lift them up, putting each component and each limb into its proper place, building the structure of the Shechinah little by little, until finally the entire structure will be complete, and then Mashiach will come and finish everything." (Likutey Moharan Vol. 1, Lesson 2).

Rabbi Nachman's above teaching draws out the Messianic allusions contained in the conclusion of this week's parshah of ***Pekudey***, when Moses ***finished*** the work. This was on the 1st of Nissan, when "the Cloud covered the Tent of Meeting and the Glory of G-d filled the Sanctuary." (Ex. 40:33-4).

The month of Nissan -- in the spring, time of rebirth -- has always and will always be a time of redemption for us. As we now conclude our study of the second book of the Torah, the "Book of Names" -- ***Shemot***, Exodus, the Torah focuses our minds on the redemptive quality of the month of Nissan. This is signified by the fact that it was on 1st Nissan that the Shechinah came to dwell among the Children of Israel with the inauguration of the Sanctuary.

The book of Exodus started in a state of exile: "These are the names of the Children of Israel who came to Egypt with Jacob, each with his house." (Ex. 1:1). After their grueling servitude followed by the plagues that afflicted the Egyptians, the light of redemption truly began to shine on the 1st of Nissan: "And G-d spoke to Moses and to Aaron in the land of Egypt, saying: This month is for you the first of the months." (Exodus 12:1-2). After narrating the drama of leaving Egypt, the Splitting of the Sea, the Giving of the Torah and the loss of innocence with the sin of the calf, Exodus concludes with the structure of the World of Repair as exemplified in the form of the Sanctuary.

It was when the Shechinah came to dwell in the completed Sanctuary on the 1st of Nissan that "He called to Moses and G-d spoke to him from the Tent of Meeting." These are the opening words of the third book of the Torah, Leviticus, which introduce the commandments relating to the sacrifices that were to be offered in the Sanctuary. These portions were revealed to Moses on the 1st of Nissan.

* * *

In the merit of completing this cycle in the study of ***Shemot*** and entering the book of ***Vayikra***, may we see the true Sage and Leader of the Children of Israel revealed quickly in our times. Amen.

CHAZAK! CHAZAK! VE-NIT'CHAZEK!

"Be strong! Be strong -- and we will be strong!"

ויקרא

LEVITICUS

VAYIKRA

Torah Reading: Leviticus 1:1-5:26

Haftarah: Isaiah 43:21-44:23

AND G-D SPOKE TO HIM FROM THE TENT OF MEETING

The last five parshahs of the Book of Exodus explained the form of the Sanctuary and its vessels, and Exodus concluded with an account of how the completed Sanctuary was finally erected by Moses on the 1st of Nissan, almost one year after the Exodus from Egypt. With the erection of the Sanctuary, the Cloud of G-d's Glory covered the Tent of Meeting.

"And He called to Moses." (Lev. 1:1). G-d's call to Moses, with which ***Vayikra*** opens, is the immediate continuation of the narrative with which Exodus concluded. Now that the Sanctuary was complete, the next step is for us to learn what is to be done in it. The book of ***Vayikra***, which takes its name from its opening word, thus begins with the detailed commandments relating to the sacrifices, since these were to be the main activity in the Sanctuary and in the Temple throughout the generations.

Leviticus, the Latin name of ***Vayikra***, corresponds to the name used by the rabbis of old when referring to this book: Torat Kohanim, "The Torah of the Priests". The book is so called not only because much of it is taken up with the sacrificial services and other ritual practices (such as purification from leprosy) in which the role of the Kohen-Priest is central. In addition, G-d's challenge to ***all*** of the Children of Israel was to be "a kingdom of ***priests*** and a holy nation" (Ex. 19:6). While only the Kohen-priest may officiate at the offering of sacrifices, they could be brought by all. Many of the other commandments in Leviticus relating to "holiness" apply not only to the Kohen-Priests but to all of us. At the very heart of Leviticus is Parshat ***Kedoshim***, "Be holy." (chs 19-20), which contains the fundamental laws governing man's behavior to his fellows. This is explicitly addressed to all of the Children of Israel (Lev. 19:2). The book of ***Vayikra*** also contains commandments that apply to Gentiles. These include the laws of sacrifices with which our present parshah of ***Vayikra***, opens: the first commandment is that of ***Korban Olah***, the "elevation" or wholly-burnt offering, which both Israelites and Gentiles are eligible to bring.

* * *

TESHUVAH

It is an ancient tradition that little boys who have learned their Aleph-Beit and are just starting to read, commence their study of the ***Chumash*** (Five Books of Moses) with ***Vayikra***. "Let pure souls come to study the laws dealing with purity." For a cynical, sophisticated age that feels entitled to call anything and everything into question, the Torah code of sacrifices and purification may appear ancient, primitive, complicated and irrelevant. But if we are willing to explore the Torah with the fresh eyes of children, ready to take the word of G-d on trust, with faith and belief, we can discover that the sacrificial system contains the keys to repentance and the healing of the soul and the entire world.

The theme of sacrifices enters Genesis and Exodus in a number of places. Adam, Cain and Abel, Noah and Abraham all offered sacrifices. Moses' declared purpose in taking the Children of Israel out of Egypt was to bring sacrifices, and the animal sacrifices brought at the time of the Giving of the Torah were described (Ex.24:5), as were the sacrifices that were to be brought at the inauguration of the Sanctuary (Ex. ch. 29). However, it is here in the opening parshahs of ***Leviticus*** that the sacrificial system of the Torah is laid out in detail. The universal significance of this teaching is brought out in the use by the Torah of the word ***adam*** in introducing the sacrificial commandments: "...when a ***man (adam)*** would bring a sacrifice." (Lev. 1:2). The sacrificial system comes to heal man's alienation from G-d through atoning for his sins and bringing him back into a relationship of peace with Him. This is the ultimate rectification of Adam's sin of eating the fruit of the Tree of Knowledge of Good and

Evil. This sin caused the mix-up of good and evil in this world that is the root of all subsequent sin.

Vayikra begins with the laws of the ***Olah***, "elevation" or "ascending" offering, which could either be an ox, a sheep or a goat, a dove or pigeon, or take the form of a ***Minchah*** offering of wheat in the form of flour or unleavened loaves or wafers. In the case of an animal ***Olah*** offering, the blood of the animal was splashed on the sides of the altar, while its fat and other portions were burned on the altar. The ***Olah*** offering comes to atone not so much for "sins of commission" -- something a person did -- as for "sins of omission", what he failed to do (such as if he failed to fulfil a positive commandment). The laws of ***Olah*** are followed by the laws of ***Shelamim***, the peace-offering, an animal sacrifice whose blood and fat were offered on the altar but whose meat was shared between the priests and the one who brought the offering. The ***Shelamim*** sacrifice is a celebration that signifies that man has made his peace with G-d.

Next come the laws of ***Chatat***, the sin-offering brought for unwitting violation of Torah prohibitions whose willful infringement carries the penalty of excision. Different kinds of animals are to be brought and different procedures of atonement apply depending on whether the sinner is a private individual, the "Prince" (Nasi, king or leader), the Supreme Court (Sanhedrin) or the High Priest. [Rashi on Lev. 4:22 comments: Happy is the generation whose leader is able to admit he made a mistake and who tries to make amends.]

The last part of Parshat ***Vayikra*** contains commandments relating to a variety of ***Chatat*** ("Sin") and ***Asham*** ("Guilt") offerings for specific sins. It is noteworthy that while some of the sins in question are bound up purely with man's relation with G-d (such as unwittingly entering the Sanctuary or eating sacrifices while ritually impure), there are certain sins in man's behavior to his fellow men that also make him liable to a sacrifice. These include the sin committed by one who, having received goods or money on trust, subsequently denies it under oath. This is at once a sin against G-d and against the person from whom he received the goods or money. It is normal and natural for a person to choose a private place without witnesses in order to entrust someone with valuable goods or money for safekeeping. Besides the two people involved, the only other "witness" to the transaction is G-d Himself, who knows what really happened. If the trustee invokes the name of G-d to swear falsely in denial of what G-d knows, this is a denial of G-d Himself. Not only must the trustee return the goods or money together with a twenty-five per cent supplement. He must also make amends to G-d by bringing a sacrifice.

* * *

THE ARI ON THE MEANING OF THE SACRIFICES

The outstanding kabbalist, Rabbi Isaac Luria (Ari) explains that the sacrificial service consisted of elements from the inanimate world (salt), the vegetable world (flour, oil and wine), the animal world (the sacrificial animal or bird), the human world (the sinner, who had to confess his sin over the offering) and the world of the souls (represented by the officiating Kohen-priest). These five realms -- inanimate, vegetable, animal, human and spiritual -- correspond in turn to the "worlds" of which the kabbalah speaks: Asiyah (the material world), Yetzirah ("formation", corresponding to the vegetable realm), Beriyah ("creation", corresponding to the animal realm), Atzilut ("emanation", corresponding to Man) and Arich Anpin, the Crown or Root of Atzilut, corresponding to the soul.

"Know that all the different animals and birds have a soul which descends and is sustained by the ***Chayot*** ('living animals') of the Divine "Chariot" (Merkavah). The pure animals and birds are sustained by the Holy Chariot, while the impure animals and birds are sustained by the Unholy Chariot. Sometimes it happens that a soul falls and a person becomes wicked. As a punishment, this soul might be incarnated in an animal. When this animal is brought as a sacrifice (***Korban***), the effect is to bring this soul back close to G-d again. Through the proper performance of the sacrificial ritual, the soul is brought back to its root and rectified. Even when the sacrificial animal is not an incarnation, it nevertheless contains holy sparks that fell at the time of creation and that are now rectified.

"When the impure animal aspect of man's soul gains dominion over him, it causes him to sin. To rectify this, he must bring an animal as a sacrifice. The burning of the animal on the altar draws down an exalted fire that burns away the sins, drawing cleansing to the person's animal soul from its very root. Since the impurity of the vegetable and inanimate levels is even greater than that of the animal level and also causes people to sin, they too must be represented on the altar in the form of the wine and flour libations and the salt.

"The sin of Adam caused good and evil to become mixed up, bringing a flaw into all the worlds and giving strength to the forces of evil. Accordingly, G-d commanded man to bring together representatives of the inanimate, vegetable and animal realms. and through the service of the priests while the Levites sing, the Israelites stand by and the owner of the sacrifice repents, all of the worlds are cleansed and purified.

"When the Temple stands, the sacrifices elevate and purify all the fallen sparks. Today this is accomplished by the prayer services." (Ta'amey HaMitzvot, ***Vayikra***).

TZAV

Torah Reading: Leviticus 6:1-8:36

Haftarah: 7:21-8:3; 9:22-23

THE ALTAR FIRE

*P*arshat ***Tzav*** is taken up with sacrificial laws and rituals. For many people, it is easier to relate to narrative portions of the Torah or commandments that apply in our day than to those dealing with Temple sacrifices. It is now nearly two thousand years since sacrifices were offered to HaShem in the Temple in Jerusalem: the last time was in 68 C.E., before the Second Temple was destroyed. Many people would find it hard to conceive how the sacrificial system could actually be restored in practice in the foreseeable future, given the apparent geopolitical realities of today. Moreover, nothing could seemingly be more remote from the sensibility of contemporary Jews and Gentiles alike than the daily ritual slaughter of animals, sprinkling their blood and burning their fat and other parts with libations of flour, oil and wine on the Temple Altar. [Instead of accepting the Temple idea, a world unable to make peace watches the willful daily slaughter and injury of human "sacrifices", the civilian and military victims of global war and terror. In the name of what?]

The same world that resents two daily lambs on G-d's Altar in Jerusalem happily slaughters and consumes literally millions of oxen, sheep, and other living creatures every single day for its own enjoyment. While meat, fish, fruits, vegetables and other gifts of G-d's bounty are consumed in homes, restaurants, bars and canteens throughout the inhabited world every day, how many pause for a moment before they eat in order to bless the Giver of that bounty? How many stop to thank G-d after eating and enjoying their food, before continuing with other activities?

The Temple Altar may be more understandable if we think of it as a ***mashal*** or metaphor for the actual table at which we ourselves eat every day, containing lessons about the attitude with which we should go about satisfying this vital natural function. The daily "diet" of animal, wheat, oil and wine offerings on the Temple Altar corresponds to man's daily diet, be it of animal and grain products, fruits, and vegetables or any of the other foods and beverages that go onto his table and into his mouth.

Maybe the reason why some feel uncomfortable about the sacrificial ritual is precisely because it presents our existential situation so starkly in the form of the animal blood, fat and other offerings on the Altar. It is a fundamental law of creation that higher life forms consume lower forms of life in order to subsist. When a lower form of life is eaten and ingested by a higher form, the lower life-form is "elevated" in the sense of actually turning into the body and feeding the activities of the higher life-form. As humans, our blood and fat are made up of materials derived from other, lower levels of existence, mineral, vegetable and animal. Our physical life-functions come to "feed" and serve a higher life-form: the soul.

The Temple Altar and sacrificial system come to guide us to elevate our own blood, fat and energy to fuel the fire of the Service of G-d on the Altar of our own bodies. The Altar fire is a metaphor for the human soul, which indeed can only survive in the human body through a daily diet of "offerings", the various foods that "keep body and soul together". Our bodies "burn up" the various nutrients we take in, just as the Altar "consumes" the sacrifices.

The body requires tending in order to serve as an "altar" for the service of God, just as the Temple Altar had to be tended. Our parshah of ***Tzav*** opens with the mitzvah of ***Terumat HaDeshen***, tending the Altar each morning by removing the ashes, followed by stoking the fire with wood to keep it burning bright. This opening mitzvah of the day in the Temple -- removal of the ashes of consumed sacrifices -- may be compared to what is normally the first physical functioning in a person's day: elimination of wastes to cleanse the body for the service of G-d.

Keeping the Altar fire stoked was the daily task of the priests. So, each one of us has the task of keeping the "altar" of the body, the digestive system and the liver, properly stoked with the right nutrients in the right quantities. As priests of our own bodies, our aim must be to keep the fire of the soul burning brightly every day -- as a "fire offering, a sweet savor for HaShem".

The previous parshah of ***Vayikra*** introduced the subject of sacrifices by setting forth all of the different categories of sacrifices and the various animals, birds or produce that are to be brought in each case. The major part of our present parshah, ***Tzav***, is a continuation of the subject of sacrifices. ***Tzav*** explains the specific procedures accompanying the actual offering of each of the different kinds of sacrifices. The parshah begins with the daily procedure of removing the Altar ashes, because this was the start of the Temple service each morning. Removal of the ashes and stoking the fire were preliminaries before slaughter of the daily ***Tamid*** (Perpetual) sacrifice and burning of its parts on the Altar.

Tzav continues with the procedures accompanying the ***Minchah***-Flour Offering, the ***Chatat***-Sin and ***Asham***-Guilt Offerings, the ***Shelamim***-Peace Offering, and another specific kind of peace offering: the ***Todah***-Thanksgiving Offering for those who have been miraculously delivered from serious danger (illness, captivity, shipwreck or being lost in the wilderness).

Some sacrifices, such as the ***Olah***-Wholly-Burnt offerings and certain other offerings, were "consumed" only on the Altar and were not permitted to be consumed by any humans. However, the priests had a share in eating Sin, Guilt and Minchah offerings, as well as the Peace and Thanksgiving offerings. In the case of the last two, the person who brings the offering also has a share in it together with his dear ones.

The fact that a priest can eat from a Sin or Guilt-offering and thereby accomplish atonement for the sinner is a wonder. So too is the eating of an animal to make peace between man and G-d. What distinguishes holy eating from animalistic eating for the sake of pure self-gratification is the motive of the person who is eating -- his ***kavanah***

(= intention). Having the correct intention is a recurrent theme in our parshah. The priest has to have the correct intention at every stage in the sacrificial ritual.

So too, when we eat, everything depends on our intention. The parshah is teaching us to eat with the intention of stoking the Altar of G-d with nutrients that we can elevate to His service by using this energy for our prayers and our mitzvot day by day. The blessings we make before and after eating serve us to focus upon this intention.

Eating may serve as a means of celebrating, as in the case of the ***Todah***-Thanksgiving Offering. The rabbis stated that in the future, this is the one kind of personal offering that will remain. (Since people will be cleansed of sin, there will be no more place for sin and guilt offerings.) May we be worthy of offering the ***Thanksgiving Peace-Offering*** in the rebuilt ***Holy Temple*** in order to celebrate the true end of war and the inauguration of genuine peace with the coming of ***Melech HaMashiach*** very soon in our times. Amen.

SHEMINI

Torah Reading: Leviticus 9:1-11:47

Haftarah: II Samuel 6:1-7:17

THE EIGHTH DAY

The "eighth day" with which our parshah of ***Shemini*** opens was the first day of the month of Nissan, one year since the Exodus from Egypt. This was the day marked out for the final inauguration of the Sanctuary following seven days of consecration of Aaron and his sons for service as priests. Those seven days had started on the 23rd of the preceding month of Adar. On each of those seven days, Moses had erected the Sanctuary in order to conduct the priestly consecration rituals, in which he himself served as the "high priest", only to dismantle the Sanctuary afterwards. However, on the Eighth Day -- the first of Nissan and first day of the New Year -- the Sanctuary was left standing, so to remain for as long as the Israelites stayed in the same desert encampment. On that day Aaron and his sons fully assumed the role of priests forever after.

The rabbis stated that the first day of Nissan "took ten crowns": It was (1) the first day of creation; (2) first day of the first of the months of the year; (3) the first day of the priesthood; (4) the first day of the Sanctuary service; (5) first day of the inauguration sacrifices of the princes of the twelve tribes; (6) first day for the descent of fire from heaven on the altar; (7) the first day that sacrifices were eaten; (8) the first day that all other altars (such as private altars) other than the Sanctuary altar became forbidden; (9) the first day that the Divine Presence dwelled in Israel; (10) the first day on which the priests blessed the people (*Mechilta*, *Shemini* 1).

In calling this the "eighth" day, the Torah alludes to the fact that, with the inauguration of the Sanctuary, it was the day on which the Israelites completely transcended the natural order, which was brought into being through the "seven days of creation". The latter correspond to the lower seven of the ten Sefirot of which the Kabbalah speaks, corresponding to the "body" (as opposed to the top three, which are the "head").

As long as man does not recognize his true mission in this world and spends his life trying to satisfy only his bodily needs and desires, he is locked within nature, like an animal. However, when he embraces his destiny, willfully configuring and using the material world as a means of drawing closer to G-d, building a Sanctuary and bringing the natural, the animal, as a ***korban***, a "sacrifice" (lit. "a drawing close"), man attains a level that transcends nature. This is the eighth level, that of ***Binah*** (the eighth Sefirah counting up from Malchut, which is the bottom Sefirah). ***Binah*** is the "gateway" to the "head", the brain and the soul (consisting of the top three Sefirot).

When we use our soul-powers -- our willpower, wisdom and understanding, to assert our control over the material and the animal, we can "pass through the gate" into the world of the spirit. This is governed by a law different from that which governs the natural order. The world of the spirit is governed by Torah law. When we pass through the gate, we can know and understand (with ***Binah***) that the natural order is nothing but an arena of challenge created by G-d in order for us to use it to connect back to the Source. As long as we are under the power of nature, this world stands as a barrier holding us back from G-d. But when we assert our spiritual power, this world turns into a gateway through which we can draw closer to Him.

* * *

THE PRICE OF CLOSENESS

So great is the significance of the day of the inauguration of the Sanctuary, the day of man's birth as a spiritual being, that the Torah returns to it in several portions in Exodus, Leviticus and Numbers. ("There is no 'before' and 'after' in the Torah"). In ***Pekudey*** at the end of Exodus, we had the account of how Moses erected the Sanctuary on the 1st of Nissan, drawing G-d's "cloud" to descend so that "His glory filled the Sanctuary". Our present parshah, ***Shemini***, narrates how Aaron and his four sons inaugurated the Sanctuary with special sacrifices, and how G-d's fire descended onto the altar. ***Shemini*** continues with the dramatic story of the offering of "strange fire" in the Sanctuary by Nadav and Avihu, Aaron's first and second sons, leading to their death by fire from heaven. Finally, in ***Naso***, the second parshah of the book of Numbers, the Torah tells of the special offering of Nachshon, Prince of the tribe of Judah, on the 1st of Nissan, initiating the offerings of the princes of the twelve tribes, one by one on twelve consecutive days.

It is one of the profound paradoxes of the Torah that this auspicious day should have been so horribly marred by the death of the two older sons of the leading protagonist in the Sanctuary, Aaron. In the world in which we live, the world of nature and separation, there is no explanation of such a tragedy. As far as this world is concerned, death is the end: how can it be good? If any meaning is to be found in such an occurrence, it can only be through "the eighth day", the level of ***Binah***, understanding, which is the gateway to the transcendent realm of unity, where there is no separation and no death.

If closeness to G-d and entry into the realm of unity came cheap, we would not value them. They come at a price. In what currency can we pay G-d? He does not need our money, our oxen, sheep and other "sacrifices". The price is often paid in pain (***lo aleinu*** -- not on us!!!). Pain robs man of his ability to feel comfortable in this world of separation to which he becomes so attached. Pain drives him to seek relief by trying to transcend the world. Pain is a teacher, a very harsh one.

An event as great as the erection of the Sanctuary and the drawing of G-d's presence into the world could not but come at a great price. The Sanctuary "will be sanctified by My glory" (Ex. 29:3) -- "by those who are My glorified ones" (rabbinic drush, see Rashi on Lev. 10:3, "I will be sanctified by those who are close to Me"). The price was paid by Aaron precisely because his was the pivotal role in the Sanctuary project, which is to configure this refractory material world in such a way that it becomes a vessel, holding and revealing G-dliness. Aaron had all the glory and splendor of this world (***Hod***), as represented in his gorgeous garments. He received the choicest share of the priestly gifts and portions. All this glory had to be elevated to G-d, it could not be allowed to stay in this world and turn into self-glorification.

When we use the wealth of this world for self-glorification, it turns into a golden calf. Aaron is on the very edge. He has all the glory, he wears the wealth of the world on his very person. In order to keep him from going out of his mind with pride, he is struck with a terrible blow, the loss of the flower of his children (their loss in this world, though not in the world of unity). The pain forces him to transcend the world of separation, the material world. Aaron must remain in the world of unity: he must not show mourning or rend his garments. He must stay in the Sanctuary, the Sanctuary of the soul, the world of unity: Keter-Chochmah-Binah. There, the language of our world, the world of separation and pain, does not apply. We can enter that exalted realm only through silent acceptance of G-d's decree. "And Aaron remained silent."

* * *

SEPARATION AND DISTINCTION

Aaron and his surviving sons could not show mourning, because their role was to remain in the world of unity in order to connect others to it. But the Children of Israel had to mourn, because they are the ones who live in the world of separation from which Nadav and Avihu had been torn. It is said that the sin of Nadav and Avihu is that they wanted to dissolve the separation completely and bring the entire world back into immediate unity with G-d. They wanted to redeem evil. They wanted to break through all the barriers. They were drunk with the unity of G-d -- and they went beyond bounds until they were totally burned up inside with G-d's fire.

But G-d does not want us to go altogether beyond the bounds. We may not embrace evil, for G-d created it precisely so that we should reject it despite the temptations. G-d established the world of separation and evil as an arena of challenge for man, in which he must steadily refine and elevate his earthly materialism until he turns himself into a vessel fit to receive G-d's unity. This cannot be done all at once: it must be done step by step, stage by stage.

As an arena of challenge to man, the world consists of good and evil, pure and impure, holy and unholy. Man's task is to use his powers of mind and soul to discriminate between them, to embrace the good and holy while rejecting the impure and unholy. The world is a very deceptive place. The pig displays its cloven hoof as if to say, "I am pure". But the truth is that it is impure, for it does not chew its food over. It does not want to confront its food again, since it always has its nose in the filth.

We cannot allow ourselves to go by appearances in this world: we have to penetrate beneath the surface. The only means we have of doing so is with G-d's Torah, the Tree of Life, which teaches the truth about good and evil in every area of life -- be it what we eat, how we do business, whom we marry and all other areas. Only with objective, outside guidance can we sort out the confusion that came from Adam's eating the fruit of the Tree of Knowledge. When man in his arrogance thinks that he knows -- when he relies on his personal judgments about what is good and bad -- he can go terribly wrong, because there is a serpent within him, the ***Yetzer Ra***, that is liable to deceive him. Making the correct distinctions in this world is at the very center of what we must accomplish here.

Thus the middle letter of the entire Torah, which is in our parshah (the letter ***Vav*** -- signifying "connection" -- in the word "belly" Lev. 11:42), is in a word that alludes to the humiliation of the serpent, who was cut down to size and made to go on his belly (Gen. 3:14). Only by humiliating the serpent and rejecting evil is it possible to connect with G-d. There is no middle word in the Torah, since the total number of words in the Torah is even. The center of the Torah in terms of words comes between the words ***darosh darash*** (Lev. 10:16): "and Moses ***searchingly searched***". Only by searching very hard can we penetrate to the real truth!

The priest is not allowed to drink when he serves in the Sanctuary. Intoxicants and instant religiosity do not bring genuine connection with G-d. Similarly, the rabbi may not drink before giving an halachic ruling. It takes sobriety to distinguish between truth and illusion.

The latter half of our parshah teaches us to discriminate between pure and impure foods, while most of the remainder of the book of Leviticus is taken up with the detailed Torah code through which we separate and distinguish between good and evil in all other areas of life.

Through our assiduous study of the Torah and its teachings, may we find the spiritual strength to take our destiny in our hands and rise to our true mission: "And you shall sanctify yourselves and be holy, for I am holy..." (Lev. 11:44).

TAZRIA

Torah Reading: Leviticus 12:1-13:59

Haftarah: II Kings 4:42-5:19

*I*n the previous parshah, ***Shemini***, the Torah set forth ***torat ha-behemah ve-ha'of***, the laws relating to various kinds of purity and impurity in animals and birds. They came first in the order of Creation. This week's parshah, ***Tazria***, begins a series of parshahs that relate to ***torot ha-adam***, the laws relating to purity and impurity in man, the very crown of Creation. Our parshah takes its name from the greatest of all natural, everyday wonders: a woman's ability to conceive a living child.

THE MIRACLE OF BIRTH

The Midrash states: "We have learned: "What is the form of the embryo when first created? It is similar to a locust: its two eyes are like the two eyes of a fly; its nostrils are like two drops on a fly. Its two ears are like two drops on a fly, and its two arms like two scarlet threads. Its mouth is like a barley seed, its body the size of a lentil. And all its other limbs are contracted inside it like unformed substance (***golem***). And of this it says, "Your eyes did see my unformed substance (***golmi***)" Psalms, 139:16; Midrash Rabbah. Tazria, 14:8).

Says the Talmud (Niddah 30b): Rabbi Samlai taught: To what can the embryo in his mother's womb be compared? To a folded-up writing-tablet placed with his hands on his two temples, his two elbows on his two knees, and his two heels on his two buttocks. His head rests between his knees and his mouth is closed and his belly open. He eats what his mother eats and drinks what his mother drinks. He does not excrete waste lest he kill his mother. And when he goes out into the air of the world, what was closed becomes open, and what had been open is closed. For if not so, he could not live for even an hour. And while in the womb, a light is kindled over his head. With it he gazes and sees from one end of the world to the other, as it says: "When his lamp shone above me" (Job 29:3).

The miraculous entry of the mature embryo into this world in the form of a living baby, embarking on a whole destiny of its own, is accompanied with much physical pain and blood for the mother. By G-d's decree, the baby, if a boy, must be circumcised with pain and blood on the eighth day, initiating him into the Covenant of Abraham. Peeling off the unclean material ***orlah*** foreskin (bound up with nature, which was created in seven days), gives him access to the eighth level, ***Binah***, Understanding. This is the level that is beyond nature, as discussed in last week's parshah, ***Shemini***.

A girl has access to that level in virtue of being female and especially through motherhood, with its pains and joys. Together with the boy's circumcision, motherhood is the first focus of our present parshah, ***Tazria***. Immediately after the birth, the mother must adjust to a new level in life with her baby, boy or girl, in hand. She needs time to recuperate from the birth itself. The biblical laws at the beginning of ***Tazria*** relate to the ritual purification in Temple times for mothers after giving birth. Often questioned is the bird sin-offering which the new mother brings among her other purification offerings. One Midrash says this comes to atone for a sinful thought she may have had at the height of pain in childhood. Another Midrash says that it comes to atone for, "In the heat of sin my mother conceived me" (Psalms 51:7, alluding to Eve's lust).

The Midrash also states that those women who carefully observe the laws of ***Niddah***, purifying themselves as prescribed by the law, will be worthy of giving birth to children who will enter the Covenant of Abraham.

* * *

THE COVENANT OF THE LIPS

The Covenant of Abraham must be inscribed not only on the flesh of the male organ, but in the hearts and on the lips of all of us, male and female. Parallel to the creative organs, which bring the physical person into the world, the lips have the most tremendous power to create realities in the spiritual, psychological and social realms.

If a person refuses to make a covenant with his lips, he may be visited with ***tzara'at***, the "illness" in which his arrogance and malicious deceit in wrongful speech cause "leprous" marks on his "skin". The "skin" is the person's exterior, what can actually be seen, with all its flaws, as opposed to what he may want to present with arrogant deceit to the outside world.

The rabbinic sages unquestionably saw the complex typology of "leprous" marks as actual physical manifestations, discussing detailed grades of skin discoloration and minute differences in size, etc. At the same time, they emphasized that these came about not naturally, by random chance, but as a supernatural spiritual message from G-d contained in the physical symptom.

The entire portion of the Torah dealing with the various kinds of "leprous" marks on different parts of the body and the "quarantine" period of impurity is full of allusions to physical illnesses, psychological, social and even national and international illnesses. The rabbis saw allusions in the names of the "leprous" marks to numerous sins, and to the nations that oppressed Israel.

In the entire process of "diagnosis" of leprous marks, no physician is involved. Indeed, it is not allowed to have a doctor cut out or treat the leprous mark. The diagnosis is in the hands of the ***Kohen***, representing ***Chessed***, G-d's kindness, in shining the light of spiritual insight and truth into the sinner. The only remedy is for the sinner to isolate himself, separating himself from ordinary routine in order to enter a state of contrition and mourning over his sins. He must sit alone, recognizing his uncleanness, warning others, examining his deeds and truly cleansing his heart. Only in this way can he be healed. It is necessary for the Kohen-Priest, the Man of ***Kindness***, to look with his loving eyes at the wound and shine his light into the sinner's soul.

The route to healing and redemption is by looking with the eyes of the priest -- with kindness -- overcoming the morbid illness by revealing the vital goodness concealed underneath.

METZORA

Torah Reading: Leviticus 14:1-15:33

Haftarah: II Kings 7:3-20

LEARNING HOW TO SPEAK

It is appropriate that our parshah, ***Metzora***, with its deep lessons about the purity of speech, is always read shortly before or after the festival of Pesach, whose name signifies, "The mouth speaks". Sefer Yetzirah teaches that the human faculty associated with the month of Nissan is speech. The Seder night, climax of so many arduous preparations, is an exercise in speech: ***Haggadah***, "telling". The story we tell -- the story of our people and of our own inner self -- is at the furthest remove from self-aggrandizement. The story starts with shame, tracing our descent into the depths of degradation, pain and anguish before our miraculous delivery from Egypt. For this, we glory not in ourselves but only in the Holy One, turning our night of "telling" into one of song and praise to G-d.

During most of the recital of the Haggadah, the ***Matzah*** -- the "Bread of Humility" -- lies exposed before our eyes. This is to impress upon us that we must take a humble view of ourselves and our place in G-d's great scheme, for this is the key to using our faculty of speech, man's defining faculty -- in holiness and purity. "Not for our sake, O G-d, not for our sake but for Your Name's sake give glory!"

Speech is truly a double-edged weapon, a "tree of good and evil" the "taste" of which is literally in our mouths. Words can do so much good -- to shine the truth, to encourage, build and strengthen those with whom we live and work... But words can also be used for so much evil -- to deceive, to confuse, to hurt, denigrate and destroy. It is when we are puffed up with ***chametz***, the "leaven" of our own self-importance and rectitude that we are liable to use words aggressively, angrily, without sensitivity. But when we remove the ***chametz*** of self-importance from our hearts in the knowledge that we are G-d's creation -- no more and no less than everyone else -- we can learn to use our amazing faculty of speech with wisdom and love. Then we can join G-d as partners in the work of Creation and the revelation of His truth. Words literally rule over our lives. Can we rule over the words that leave our mouths? Will we rule with arrogance or with humility?

The ***metzora***, literally the "leper", is symbolic of one who abuses his power of speech, being ***motzi-ra***: "bringing out evil". The previous parshah, ***Tazria***, presented an elaborate pathology of the diseases of the soul, such as the "leprous" mark of ***se'eit***, inflated pride, or ***baheret***, the shining white light in which some people constantly seek to present themselves. The first step in the cure for such illnesses of the soul is to receive an objective "diagnosis" from the Kohen-Priest, a clear statement that the mark is ***ta'mey***, impure. Until we name our negative traits correctly, we cannot begin to heal them. Only when we acknowledge the impure for what it is, can we take the first step towards purification. As we saw in last week's parshah, healing of the wounds of the soul requires heart-searching and contrition, which is why the ***metzora*** was sent for a period of isolation "outside the camp".

This parshah of ***Metzora*** begins with the highly picturesque ceremony with which the healed leper begins his process of purification so as to be able to return to normal life "in the camp" with other people. The ceremony required two sparrows together with a block of cedar wood, red-dyed wool thread and hyssop. One of the birds was slaughtered into an earthenware flask of living water. Then the other bird was taken with the cedar, the red wool and hyssop, and together they were dipped into the blood and water in the flask, which were sprinkled seven times on the leper, after which the living bird was sent free (Lev. 14:4-7.).

Can you imagine how hard it was to catch the sparrows in the first place in order to carry out the ceremony? As cats and anyone else who has ever tried to catch a sparrow all know, it is terribly easy for sparrows to fly away. This is why the Hebrew name of the sparrow is ***dror***, "freedom". The very difficulty of catching these birds, which are notorious chatterers, comes to impress upon the ***metzora*** the great importance of catching our speech and chatter ***before*** they fly off. We must learn to take control over what we say, in order to use words intentionally, productively, lovingly, to good effect. Rashi in his commentary on our parshah explains that the wood of the lofty cedar tree was brought "because leprous plagues come on account of arrogance. What is the remedy? The person must lower himself down from his pride like a worm [from whose blood the red dye of the wool thread was derived] and a hyssop" (Rashi on Lev. 14:4).

The use of the two birds in the ceremony is bound up with the double-edged nature of speech, which can be used for either good or evil. The ***metzora*** had to watch as one of the chattering birds was slaughtered in front of his very eyes, teaching him that he must simply kill his evil talk for all time. However, this does not mean that he may not speak at all in future. On the contrary, once he has learned the lesson of humility contained in the cedar, the hyssop and the scarlet thread, the second bird goes free! When we release ourselves from the bonds of pride and arrogance that enslave us, we are freer than ever to explore the great power of pure speech -- "over the face of the field".

ACHAREY MOT

Torah Reading: Leviticus 16:1-18:30

Haftarah: Amos 9:7-15

AFTER THE DEATH OF AARON'S TWO SONS

The parshah, ***Acharey Mot***, introduces the account of the awesome service of the High Priest on Yom Kippur, the Day of Atonement, by noting that this parshah was given to Moses ***after*** -- in the light of -- the death of Aaron's two sons when they offered "strange fire" inside the Sanctuary.

Nadav and Avihu wanted to redeem the entire world and bring it to G-d in an instant -- but they themselves were consumed by G-d's jealous fire. Their endeavor was in the realm of excess. There is an evil in the world that cannot be redeemed: its only redemption lies in being smashed and destroyed forever (just as ***Tum'ah***, ritual impurity, leaves a clay vessel only when it is broken).

At the center of the High Priest's service on Yom Kippur lies the profound mystery of the ***goral***. This was the "lottery" by which one of a pair of identical goats was chosen to be the holy sacrificial offering whose blood would atone for Israel in the Holy of Holies. The other was taken to a remote mountain-crag and cast down to ***Azazel***, the Devil, being quickly broken to pieces on the mountainside. This mitzvah is numbered by the Rabbis together with the purification from defilement from the dead through the ashes of the Red Heifer as among those incomprehensible ***chukim***, "statutes" at which the nations and the evil inclination scoff.

Rabbi Nachman of Breslov once put the question in a graphic form: "In the Purim play, why should one person be chosen to play Mordechai the Jew and live, while another plays Haman and gets hung?"

There is no satisfactory answer to the deepest questions of destiny in this world: it is simply not given to the eyes of flesh and blood to understand why this one is given one role in life and that one another. There is a heavenly ***Mazal*** at work that brings about the ***goral***, "fate". What our parshah tells us is that we are free to choose our path in the world, and that following G-d's commandments guarantees us life.

"And you shall guard my statutes and my laws which, when a man – ***ha-adam*** -- does them, he shall ***live*** through them, ***I am HaShem***" (Leviticus 18:5).

The ***Sifra Devey Rav***, the oldest rabbinic midrashic commentary on Leviticus, goes to some lengths in commenting on this verse to emphasize that this applies to all mankind. "It does not say 'which, when a Kohen or Levi or Israelite does them' but 'when a ***man*** – ha-adam -- does them', including a ***Goy***". Incidentally, this is the exact Hebrew word there. While many gentiles find the word Goy offensive, it should not cause offence. It is simply the standard rabbinic term for one who was not born an Israelite -- "gentile" is the Latin equivalent. In the comment quoted here, the Rabbis were ***emphasizing*** that the Torah path is the universal path, open to Goy, Israelite, Levite and Cohen, as long as they are willing to follow it in truth.

Only one person can play the role of the High Priest. Thus when studying the portions dealing with the High Priest's Yom Kippur service, we are onlookers at the ritual. Yet there is also a deep personal message for us. We study this parshah at this time of the year, as we proceed on the fifty-day ***Sefirat Ha-Omer*** count towards our annual peak, the Giving of the Torah on the forthcoming festival of ***Shavuot***. The season of Counting the Omer is a time for reflection on who we are and what we are trying to achieve. The High Priest's entry into the Holy of Holies on Yom Kippur is a lesson to us to appoint special times for seclusion in order to enter into the personal sanctuary that we must reserve within the depths of our own hearts for true encounter with self and with G-d. One of the best facilitators of this encounter with self and with G-d is the Sweet Singer of Israel, King David. It is customary to give particular emphasis to recital of the Psalms during the Sefirah period, for the Psalms are conducive to healing, repentance, atonement and ***life***.

* * *

The account of the High Priest's Yom Kippur service is followed by a number of commandments establishing the centrality of the Sanctuary in the G-dly service of the community. The prohibition of animal sacrifices outside the Sanctuary, and later, outside the Temple in Jerusalem, forbids each person building his own personal Temple and Altar, whether literally or in the form of pride and self-worship. There is only one place for a literal animal offering. That is Mount Moriah, where Abraham bound Isaac and where Jacob saw the ***Sulam***, the ladder of ascent, that is ***Sinai*** (***Sulam*** and ***Sinai*** have the same gematria.) After the wandering in the Wilderness, the final resting place of the Shechinah for all time is in Yerushalayim, Ir HaKodesh (the Holy City), in the Temple on Mount Moriah.

Among the commandments relating to the slaughter of animals is the severe prohibition against eating blood, which is one of the fundamentals of our daily dietary code. The Shechitah method of slaughter ensures that the vital blood of the animal, strictly forbidden for consumption, is shed at the time of slaughter. The removal of the veins of the animal by the butcher and subsequent salting of the meat according to ritual law ensure the removal of the blood from the meat. This is necessary because an animal spirit resides in the blood. If this blood is consumed by man, he falls from his level and is overcome by an animal spirit. The laws of Kashrut are the very foundation of a diet that ensures that we have a human spirit, and that we think and behave like Bney Adam.

* * *

THE LAWS OF FAMILY PURITY

The third and concluding section of the parshah, which contains the above-quoted verse, "he shall ***live*** through them", lays out the basic family law of the Torah, including the fundamental laws of incest and the various forbidden relationships, including mother and son, father and daughter, brother and sister, adultery, forbidden intercourse during monthly period, prohibition of homosexuality, bestiality, etc.

In more innocent times, some people were taught that certain forms of behavior are fundamentally ***wrong***. The various incest laws of the Torah, which are the Holy root of this code, can be seen in clear letters in our parshah. But anyone who ventures outside the holy camp of the Torah to observe the "wider" world (such as dating services, internet chat-rooms, etc.) can rapidly discover that those interested in any or all of the above prohibitions and perversions can quickly get fully involved in a whole world where they are all freely available. What the internet has begun to reveal appears to be only the tip of the iceberg of the actual behavior of a very large part of the human population. Even in Israel vociferous secularists are openly identified with the reformist line that the fundamental statutes governing human relationships may be freely broken. This is precisely what leads to the breakdown of basic human norms that we witness all around the world today in the name of "freedom" and "liberation".

This is no liberation. The only freedom and life are those promised by the Torah: "And you shall guard My statutes and My laws which when a man will do them, he will live through them, I am HaShem."

The law of Shabbat and the fundamental laws of the code laid down in our parshah are the foundation of the family life which is the basis for the rearing of a new generation -- our children and our children's children. We are all bound to know the basic laws, and if our paths in life bring us to places where these laws are infringed, we must be properly forewarned. It is most important to teach children with sensitivity how they must take care of themselves against strangers and even with friends and close relatives.

The best ways for Jews, Bney Brit, members of the Covenant of G-d, to maintain health and life is through strengthening ourselves with our families and good friends. This is accomplished when we bond together, as we did on Pesach. Now, after Pesach, we carry through the holiness attained during the festival into the days of the year as we Count the Omer -- count the days and learn to value each day, day after day. During the long summer days, we must make time to study G-d's laws, the laws that bring ***life***, celebrating the Shabbat, the Day of Life. Fathers and sons should take time to study G-d's Torah together regularly, and so mothers and daughters.

If all Israel would keep two consecutive Shabbatot, they would be redeemed.

KEDOSHIM

Torah Reading: Leviticus 19:1-20:27

Haftarah: Ezekiel 20:2-20

BE HOLY FOR I AM HOLY

This parshah, ***Kedoshim tihyu***, "Be holy...", was specifically addressed by G-d through His prophet Moses "to all of the assembly of the Children of Israel" (Leviticus 19:2). In the words of the Midrash: "This parshah was addressed to all of the assembly because most of the main bodies of Torah law depend upon it. 'Be holy' -- be pure (***perushim***), separate from the world's vanities. 'For Holy am I, HaShem your G-d': This teaches that if you sanctify yourselves, I consider it as if you had sanctified Me. And if you do not sanctify yourselves, I consider it as if you have not sanctified Me. Could it mean that if you sanctify Me then I am sanctified but if not, then I am not sanctified? No - because it says, '...for I am Holy' -- I am in My holiness whether they sanctify me or not." (Sifra, Kedoshim 1:1).

The code of conduct whose foundations are laid forth in the present parshah gives practical expression to the challenge addressed to the Children of Israel when they assembled at Sinai to receive the Torah. "If you will surely listen to My voice and guard My covenant, you shall be a precious treasure out of all the nations, for the whole earth is Mine. And you shall be for Me a kingdom of priests and a ***holy nation***: these are the words you shall speak to the children of Israel." (Exodus 19:5-6).

Following the account of the Giving of the Torah in ***Yitro***, Parshat ***Mishpatim*** laid down many of the basic laws governing man's behavior with his fellows including the prohibitions of murder, robbery and theft, the laws of restitution for damages, etc. Many of the laws in ***Mishpatim*** are somewhat specialist in the sense that they apply particularly to Dayanim, Torah judges.

However the code laid forth in the present parshah, ***Kedoshim*** applies to everyone, as it is the basic Torah code for everyday life, starting with the respect due to parents and the observance of the holy Shabbat -- which overrides even the former, should any conflict arise.

The next mitzvah in the parshah -- to eat sacrificial portions within their appointed time -- cannot unfortunately be observed today in the absence of the Holy Temple in Jerusalem. However, it is worth noting that correct timing is an important part of G-d's code. Things should be done at their appointed time and not dragged on until all the taste goes out of them. The entire Oral Torah begins with an extensive discussion about the exact time for reciting the evening Shema (Berachot, Chapter 1). It is unfortunate that at times SJT, ("Standard Jewish Time") strays somewhat widely from precision timing. Every moment in life should be treasured, and people's time should not be wasted for any reason.

The mitzvot that follow in our parshah are those of giving gifts of produce to the poor, and of basic integrity: "Do not steal, do not deceive and do not lie to one another. Don't impound your friend's money, don't delay payment for services rendered. Don't unjustly favor either the poor or the rich. don't hate your brother in your heart, give due reproof, do not take vengeance or nurse a grievance against the children of your people, and love your friend as yourself, for I am HaShem".

The code of Holiness contained in our parshah is not one that requires its followers to separate from the material world and live apart in ascetic communities such as in monasteries and the like. On the contrary, true ***kedushah*** comes to a person precisely through living his or her life with family, friends and associates, within the wider community and in the workaday world. Making a living within the boundaries of the halachah, taking into account the needs of the needy, dealing correctly in business, abstaining from all theft and corruption, from hatred, vengeance, etc. etc. It is precisely through keeping these commandments in our everyday material lives, while actually dealing with all that we have to deal with each day, that we become purer.

This "purity" is the ***kedushah***, the "holiness" which is the defining attribute of the path of life set forth in our parshah. In mystical writings, ***kedushah*** is particularly associated with the mental and spiritual faculties of ***Chochmah***, ***Binah*** and ***Da'at***, while the very foundation for their healthy functioning is the purity of ***Yesod***, moral purity.

In giving us a code of "holiness" that governs the way we do business with one another, how we talk to and about one another, as well as so many other details in our lives in the world, the Torah is teaching us to constantly activate our ***Chochmah***, ***Binah*** and ***Da'at*** powers in everyday life. In the words of the Baal Shem Tov, "An everyday barter exchange also involves the Talmudic law of 'exchanging an ox for a donkey'." In other words, everything we do, including in our business lives, is a G-d-given opportunity for discovering buried "sparks" of holiness within the very situations that confront us. We need to activate our minds to recognize the holy potential contained within everyday affairs. Nothing is more evanescent than today: the day is quickly gone. But if we are alert to the mitzvahs we can perform every day, particularly in the realm of "love your friend as yourself" -- which includes all forms of kindness -- we gather great treasures day by day, all of them stored in G-d's memory, where nothing is forgotten.

* * *

THE FOUNDATION

As mentioned above, the spiritual traits of ***Chochmah***, ***Binah*** and ***Da'at*** -- the ability to perceive G-dliness and to grasp the divine wisdom -- are bound up with Yesod, the "Foundation" -- sexual purity. This is the subject of the latter part of this week's parshah. Thus the Torah Code of Holiness in daily life -- ***Kedoshim*** -- comes "sandwiched" between the concluding part of the previous parshah, giving the fundamental incest prohibitions, and the concluding part of this week's parshah, setting forth the penalties for their infringement. This underlines the fact that the true ***kedushah*** depends upon observance of the Torah moral code.

A fundamental principle of Torah law is that wherever a punishment is laid down, the prohibition is also explicitly stated in the Torah. This explains why the incest prohibitions in ***Kedoshim*** appear to duplicate those at the end of ***Acharey Mot***. In fact, there is no duplication: the laws of ***Acharey Mot*** state the prohibitions, while the laws of ***Kedoshim*** state the penalties for their infringement.

At the head of the list of forbidden practices is the giving of seed to Molech (Lev. 20:3). This is explained as a form of idolatry assumed by many to be defunct today in which a father would give over some of his children to be walked by priests through fire as a form of initiation and consecration.

Actual Molech-worship within the technical parameters of the term may or may not be defunct, yet there are indications that various kinds of rituals involving children including pedophilia and actual Satan-worship are practiced in this day and age in many different places in the world. For example, in Australia, a woman who had won a national award for championing victims of childhood sexual abuse has reported a major cover-up of pedophiliac-Satanic activities in the country involving leading politicians, media and business interests, the police and the underworld.

What innocent parents may not realize when they submit their children to television, video, magazines and the other communications media of contemporary society is that they may also be exposing those children to a kind of Molech-worship. Thus, most secular TV and other media, show images of the uncovered human form, many unashamedly erotic, without the slightest compunction. Today images of the uncovered form are so universal that few people can remember the world of a mere fifty years ago, when indecency was still considered shocking.

With all this suggestion and blatant eroticism around them, it is hardly surprising that many teenagers growing up in a secular environment are deeply obsessed with their bodies and their sexuality. The place of the body, sexuality and romance in the mind of many teenage girls, for example, can be seen from a quick survey of the literature they read. What the popular literature does not spell out is the personal pain and agony of so many helpless victims of this culture and their problems of depression, anorexia, substance abuse, thoughts of suicide, etc.

For parents who seek to bring up children who will become and remain true Israelites all their lives, there is no option today but to actively seek out ways of separating them culturally from the secular mainstream. Ideally, the purest environment for young Jewish souls to grow up in is one that is television-free from the youngest age. It is of great importance to protect children for as long as possible from the assault on their consciousness by the unhealthy images and sounds of the contemporary secular media. Only with the power of deep inner conviction together with imaginative educational methods is it possible to fire young people with the zeal for the Torah that alone can immunize them from the evil influences of the prevalent culture which sooner or later they will have to face for themselves.

EMOR

Torah Reading: Leviticus 21:1-24:23

Haftarah: Ezekiel 44:15-31

SAY TO THE PRIESTS

*A*s discussed in Universal Torah ***Tetzaveh***, the Torah conception of the priests and their relationship with the people is radically different from the conception of the priesthood in other traditions. The Kohen of the Torah does not absolve the Israelite of his obligation to forge his own personal relationship with G-d. The Kohen is not an intermediary who performs mysterious rituals that magically guarantee that all will be well for the ignorant worshipper who stands by watching.

In many religions, the priests held or hold a monopoly on religious knowledge, often actually discouraging the pursuit of such knowledge by the masses, whose very ignorance is necessary in order for the priest to maintain his position.

By contrast, the Holy Torah was given as a fountain of truth and wisdom to Israel and to all others who want to drink its waters. The entire people of Israel is intended to be a Kingdom of Priests and a Holy Nation: the goal is for each Israelite to develop, build and cultivate his or her own bond with G-d in every detail of life. How can we do this? We need to learn how to do it. For this reason, pride of place in the Torah tradition goes to the sage and teacher, because he is the one who can tell us how to do this. Even a ***mamzer talmid chacham*** (an outstanding sage who is of illegitimate birth) takes precedence over the High Priest!

In our present parshah of ***Emor***, which is largely taken up with laws specifically relating to the priests, we see that Moses was commanded to instruct not only the priests themselves in these laws but also the Children of Israel. The Children of Israel are not to be excluded from all knowledge and understanding of the priesthood. On the contrary, they too are to study the laws relating to the priests. This is because the Israelites, as a kingdom of priests, have to have a model to learn from. The Kohanim are a kingdom within a kingdom. The Kohanim are to be to the Israelite what the Israelites are to be to the world.

The Temple is G-d's palace on earth: a center-point for all the world to see, in order to contemplate the profundity of the message it contains and thereby to draw closer to the King. Everything about the Temple is about coming closer to G-d, particularly the ***korban*** ("sacrifice", from the Hebrew world ***karov***, "close"). The entire Temple services center upon the sacrificial rites: the daily animal, grain, wine and incense offerings, the lighting of the Candelabrum, and so on. Like life in a royal court, life in the Temple was a spectacle. This was particularly so for the Israelite who brought a personal ***korban***, be it a ***Shelamim*** ("Peace") offering, or an ***Olah*** and particularly a ***Chatat*** - Sin-offering.

The animal is substituted for the person to undergo the slaughter, flaying, cutting and burning the sinner really deserves. (Those who worry about the alleged cruelty to the animal should first go and complain about the millions of animals daily slaughtered all over the world, often with great cruelty, as "sacrifices" for the gratification of men's selfish lusts. To understand the meaning of the ***korbanot***, we must be willing to think of the Temple as it actually was and will be, not try to adapt it to man-made moral "standards".)

The ***Sefer HaChinuch*** (explaining the meaning of the 613 commandments) discusses the sacrificial rituals at length in Mitzvah #95: Building the Temple. The ceremony consisted of various stages: ***semichah*** (the penitent's laying on of hands on the animal's head), ***shechitah***, the slaughter of the animal, ***kabbalah***, collecting of its blood and sprinkling it on the altar, the flaying and cutting of the carcass, salting of the meat, the burning of the altar portions and eating by the priests of their share. The ***Sefer HaChinuch*** explains in detail how the different stages of this unsettling and even shocking ceremony all communicated an unforgettable lesson to the penitent about how man must bring his animal side under control. We are to learn how to "slaughter" and elevate our animality by devoting our energies to G-d's service and thereby burning our fat on His altar. (See also Nachmanides' commentary on Leviticus 1:8).

The priests in the Temple, who conducted these ceremonies, were actors in a drama that was calculated to awaken people and induce them to think and repent rather than to hypnotize them with hocus-pocus. The role of the priest was as a facilitator, enabling people to understand the lesson for themselves.

Carrying the obligation to serve as ministers in the House and Court of G-d, the priests are a nation set apart, and are subject to an even more stringent code than the Israelites, as laid out in our parshah of ***Emor***. They are not allowed to defile themselves for the dead except in the case of their closest relatives. They are strictly forbidden to blemish their own bodies. They are not allowed to marry a divorcee or a woman who has been involved in a relationship tainted by immorality, etc. The Kohanim are to be a completely pure breed, fit to serve as G-d's ministers on earth. The true Kohen is to be an exemplar in his very life of the elevated purity to which every Israelite should aspire, each according to his or her level.

The ultimate exemplar is to be the ***Kohen Gadol*** ("high priest"). Although the ***Kohen Gadol*** appears in costumes that are most gorgeous by the standards of this world, he must remain completely separated from this world. This is because his task is to keep our eyes focussed upon G-d's world. Thus the ***Kohen Gadol*** is not allowed to defile himself with the dead even in the case of his closest relatives. For in G-d's world, there is no death but only life.

Everything about the Temple is designed to lift us up above the often tawdry world around us and to teach us how to draw closer to the underlying reality of G-d. For this reason, the Temple must be a place of the imposing splendor and beauty. Everything must be in the best repair. Not a flagstone must be loose nor an altar stone chipped. The vessels must be the finest gold and silver. And so too, the ministers themselves must be people of pleasing looks. Our parshah details the physical blemishes that disqualify a priest from participating in the Temple service itself (though not from eating sacrificial portions). The parshah also details the blemishes that disqualify an animal from being offered as a ***korban***. Everything offered to G-d has to be the very finest and most beautiful. So too, we must seek to beautify our offerings of prayers, our mitzvot and acts of kindness, and take care that they should not be blemished.

* * *

THE CYCLE OF THE YEAR

The calling of the ***Kohanim*** was very exalted. The separation and purity demanded of them is not required of the Israelites, who on the contrary are required to be involved in the world -- farming, manufacturing, selling and buying, raising families, etc. As discussed in the commentary on the previous parshah, ***Kedoshim***, it is precisely through bringing every area of our actual lives under the wing of the Torah that we attain holiness.

Only the Kohen Gadol is to remain within the Temple precincts or in his nearby home in Jerusalem all the time. The people are to be throughout the country, going about their lives. For the Israelite, the relationship of G-d is one of "running and returning": "running" in the sense of regularly rising above the mundane to make a deeper connection with the underlying reality of G-d, but then "returning", in the sense of going back to grappling with everyday reality.

The Torah appointed a rhythm of weekly, monthly and seasonal ***Mo'adim***, "appointed times", whereby the Israelites rise above the mundane and restore and strengthen their connection with the divine. Our parshah is one of several in the Torah (Ex. ch. 23; Numbers ch. 23; Deut. ch. 16) that set forth the cycle of festivals and their associated practices, each with its own particular focuses.

In our parshah (Leviticus ch. 23) one of the main themes that runs through the account of the various festivals and their associated Temple practices is that of drawing ecological balance and agricultural blessing into the world. During the ***Aliyah Le-Regel*** -- the foot-pilgrimage to the Temple on Pesach, Shavuot and Succot -- the Israelites would leave the work of making a living and tilling the ground in order to participate in ceremonies whose purpose was to bless that work with G-dliness. Pesach, and Shavuot are particularly bound up with grain, which is man's staple food. The Matzahs eaten on Pesach may be made from one of the five kinds of grain. On the second day of Pesach, at the beginning of the grain harvesting season, an Omer measure is to be brought from the newly-ripened barley crop. During the coming weeks, while the wheat-harvesting is going on, the Sefirah count directs our minds forward to Shavuot, when a "new grain offering", the first wheat offering from the new crop -- two loaves of leavened bread -- was brought.

The observances of Succot are particularly bound up with the water-cycle. The four species of Etrog (citron), Lulav (palm branch), Hadass (myrtle) and Aravot (willow branches) all require ample water. Succot comes after the hot, dry summer of Eretz Israel, prior to what should be the rainy season. We take these four species in our hands and pour out our hearts like water in thanks and praise, hinting to our heavenly Father how totally dependent we are on His blessings and mercy.

The chapter in our present parshah of ***Emor*** relating to the festival cycle leads us in the direction of the following parshah, ***Behar***, which sets forth the commandments relating to the cycles of Sabbatical and Jubilee years, which are also bound up with agriculture, ecological balance and reverence for the earth.

* * *

HIDDEN CYCLES

Besides the cycles of festivals and Sabbaticals that give time its rhythm, the world is also governed by cycles that are often not apparent, because one generation does not know what happened in previous generations and therefore cannot understand how what happens today is cyclically rooted in what happened earlier.

To understand the incident of the ***megadef*** ("blasphemer") in the closing section of our parshah (Leviticus 24:10ff), it is necessary to understand that "the son of the Israelite woman who was the son of an Egyptian man" was in fact the issue of an illicit relationship. Our rabbis teach that Shulamit bat Divri was the wife of the Israelite whom Moses saw being beaten by an Egyptian the first time he went out to visit his brothers. The Egyptian would daily drive the Israelite out of his home and send him to his labors, thereafter going in to his wife. (See Rashi on Lev. 24:10 and on Exodus 2:11).

There is a deep counterpoint in the positioning of this episode in Parshat ***Emor***, which centers on the special purity demanded of the priests. Shulamit bat Divri is the exemplar of the opposite: immorality. While the holiness of the priesthood requires separation and the making of distinctions between pure and impure, fine and blemished, she sought to erase distinctions, greeting everyone with a naive "Peace be upon you, peace be upon you". As if friendly chatter is enough to turn evil into good. It was Shulamit bat Divri's endeavor to erase distinctions that laid her open to the immoral relationship which led to the birth of the blasphemer. The latter, however, discovered that, whether you like it or not, this ***is*** a world of distinctions. While the blasphemer was an Israelite through his mother, he had no tribal affiliation, since this comes only through the father. Accordingly, the blasphemer had no place in the Israelite camp.

Contemporary political correctness will cry out in the voice of Shulamit bat Divri that he should have been given a place -- isn't it unfair that he should be excluded because of a quirk of birth? Endless similar questions can be asked about other commandments in our parshah. Why should a blemished priest not be allowed to serve in the Temple? Why should a divorcee not be allowed to marry a priest? etc. etc.

Rashi brings a midrash that the blasphemer "went out" (Lev. 24:10) in the sense that he departed from the Torah: he mocked the idea that the Sanctuary Show-Bread (subject of the preceding section), which was eaten by the priests when it was nine days old, was a fitting institution in the Sanctuary of the King (Rashi ad loc.). The blasphemer could not accept G-d's Torah the way it is. He wanted to adapt the Torah fit his own personal views.

There was a way that even the blasphemer could have found his place. As quoted at the outset, even a ***mamzer talmid chacham*** has precedence over the High Priest. If the blasphemer had been willing to submit himself to G-d and accept the position G-d put him in, he could have been saved. But he was not willing to submit and instead he opened his mouth and poured out a torrent of abuse.

Over sixty years previous to this, when Moses saw this man's father striking Shulamit bat Divri's husband, Moses knew that there was no potential. "And he looked here and there and he saw that there was no man [that no man would come forth from him to convert, Rashi] and he struck the Egyptian" (Ex. 2:12). The rabbis taught that Moses "struck" him by invoking the Name of HaShem. It was precisely this name that the son of the Egyptian's illicit relationship blasphemed. Prior to the Giving of the Torah, Moses inflicted instant justice on the father. However, after the Giving of the Torah, Moses was subject to the Torah like everyone else and he had to wait to hear from G-d how to deal with the blaspheming son.

The account of the punishment of the blasphemer includes related laws of punishments for killing and the damages that must be paid for inflicting injury to humans and animals. The cycles of crime and its penalties and payments revolve from generation to generation, but this is not apparent to the onlooker who sees only the here and now and does not understand what was before and what will come afterwards.

BEHAR

Torah Reading: Leviticus 25:1-26:2

Haftarah: Jeremiah 32:6-27

THE LAND BELONGS TO G-D

"To G-d belongs the land and its fullness, the earth and its inhabitants." (Psalms 24:1). "The heavens, the heavens belong to G-d, but the earth He ***gave to the sons of Adam***. The dead will not praise G-d nor all who go down to desolation. But we will praise G-d from now and forever! Halleluyah!" (Psalms 115:16-17).

*O*ur present parshah, ***Behar***, and its "sister", next week's parshah of ***Bechukotai***, which in some years is read on the same Shabbat, explain under what conditions the Earth and its treasures are given in trust to the sons of man, and when the trust is taken back by its rightful Owner -- if men breach the deed of trust, which is the Torah, G-d's Covenant.

The social, economic, ecological and environmental lessons of ***Behar*** are particularly urgent today, when men act as lords of the Earth, owning and controlling vast tracts, depleting and destroying her gifts, despoiling her of her treasures for their own short-sighted gain and pleasure, without ever pausing to consider: Who really owns all this? For what purpose did He make it? On the contrary, the Torah commands us to appoint seasons and special years in which we all reflect on Who owns everything and learn to respect His creation.

Behar continues with the theme of the cycle of time, which was also central in last week's parshah of ***Emor*** in the section dealing with the annual cycle of festivals (Leviticus ch. 23). The section in ***Emor*** began with the first of all of G-d's "appointed seasons", the Holy Shabbat, which is the crown of G-d's Covenant. ***Behar*** takes the concepts of "Six days of work, one day of rest" a level higher, dealing with the cycle of years, which is measured in circuits of 7 x 7 Sabbaticals, followed by the fiftieth Jubilee year.

Our parshah of ***Behar*** thus begins with the Shemittah cycle in which the land is to be worked and tilled for six years, after which it is to be left "fallow" throughout the seventh year. The Torah gives us a picture of an idyllic world in which independent owner-farmers are raising their wheat and grains for bread and tending their vineyards for wine. After all their gifts to the poor and tithes to the priests and Levites etc. during the six years of labor, they are to go a step further in the seventh year, giving their very fields and vineyards back to their true Owner. In the seventh year, they are not allowed to work their own land. Instead, they must open their gates to everyone so that all can have a share in the fruits from the holy Table of G-d -- the produce of Israel in the Shemittah year has a special sanctity. Even the animals have their share in the fruits of the Shemittah year -- for like us, they too are G-d's guests on His amazing Earth. The Shemittah cycle is a fundamental rhythm in time designed to help us constantly keep in mind that G-d is the true Owner -- of all the world around us and of our very selves.

The fifty-year Jubilee cycle takes us to even higher levels of this awareness. The Jubilee cycle is like a gracious cosmic game in which even the losers eventually get to go back and have a fresh start all over again -- because G-d, the true Owner and Master of all the land and its inhabitants, is truly compassionate. Even in the idyllic world of independent land-owners, one tends to be more successful, while another is less successful. In time, one is forced to sell his land and even his house. Then he falls into debt, and eventually he becomes enslaved. In the Jubilee year, signaled by the trumpeting of the Shofar of Freedom on Yom Kippur of that year, all the slaves go free and all the fields and orchards go back to their original owners.

In our parshah, the Torah sets forth the code of laws applying to ownership of land in particular, and also of other forms of property, and under what conditions. The laws in our parshah include those of sale, and of business honesty and integrity. The forms of property include people's own selves: under the law of slavery, one person might become the "property" of someone else, whether in the legal or economic sense, or in the spiritual sense, where a person may even fall so low as to sell himself to some form of idolatry.

Rashi on Leviticus 26:1 explains the "moral logic" underlying the sequence of laws set forth in our parshah: "At first the Torah warns about the observance of the Sabbatical year. But if a person is greedy for money and falls under suspicion of violating the Sabbatical year, he ends up selling his possessions. That is why the Torah juxtaposes here the laws of sale, including the sale of moveable articles. If the person still does not repent, he ends up selling his hereditary land. If he still does not repent, he ends up selling his house. If he still does not repent, he has to borrow on interest. in the end he sells his very self, not just to an Israelite, but even to an idol-worshipper."

Yet even the most degraded goes free in the Jubilee year, in which the blast of the Sinai trumpet of Freedom on the Day of At-One-ment signifies that all the debts have been paid through the redemptive power of Binah, the Fiftieth Gate. This theme of freedom in our parshah is particular relevant to us in the present season, as we count the days of the Omer in the seven-fold count of the days and weeks leading up to the Fiftieth Day, the Day of the New Offering, season of the Giving of the Torah: Freedom.

At the very heart of the entire system of redemption set forth in the Torah through the festival cycle and through the Sabbatical and Jubilee cycles lies the Shabbat, which is the very essence of the Sinaitic code. When Moses first asked Pharoah to free the Israelites, all he requested was that they should go "into the wilderness" (away from the technology of civilization) in order to liberate themselves from slavery to earthly lords of the land like Pharaoh. The commandment of Shabbat was given at Marah (Exodus 15:25), prior to the Giving of the Torah at Sinai. The concept of Shabbat is built into the concept of the Manna, which appeared for six days of the week with a double-portion on the sixth day. Shabbat is the fourth commandment. Immediately after the Ten Commandments in Exodus ch. 20, the Torah begins ***Mishpatim*** with the laws of slavery, which involve the Sabbatical and Jubilee concepts.

Now in ***Behar***, as we approach the conclusion of the elaboration of the Sinaitic code (***Bechukotai*** sets the seal on this, while the name of our parshah -- "On the Mount" -- reminds us of Sinai) the Torah returns to the theme of Shabbat as being at the very center of the Covenant. The concluding verse of our parshah is: "Guard My Sabbaths and have reverence for My Sanctuary, I am Hashem" (Leviticus 26:2). The entire time-scheme set forth in ***Behar*** -- the Shemittahs and Jubilee year -- is founded on the concept of Shabbat. Then in the following parshah, ***Bechutokai***, we see that the vengeance of the Covenant is built around a structure of seven-fold punishments for the spiral of sin caused by the violation of the Shabbat.

It is a strange irony that the observance of the Shabbat as set forth in the Shulchan Aruch, the practical Code of Jewish law, is something that most of the contemporary world finds impossible to accept. While the entire world accepts the concept of the Work and Leisure cycle, the world is unable to accept that a person may voluntarily take upon himself to abstain from all kinds of activities on the Sabbath day, and so too in the Sabbatical year, in order to show that he takes upon himself the Kingdom of Heaven, the world of the true Sabbath.

No serious political or intellectual commentator today would take seriously the idea that the complete observance of Shabbat and Shemittah, including abstinence by Israelites from the 39 prohibited labors on Shabbat and all the prohibited labors of Shemittah, could be the key to the redemption of Israel and saving the world ecology.

This contemporary neglect of the concept of Shabbat as a serious concept, is in stark contrast to the centrality of the Shabbat in the prophetic vision of the world of the future, in which the Sanctuary in Yerushalayim is at the very center.

"For so says HaShem to the castrated who will guard My Sabbaths and choose what I desired and who hold by My Covenant. And I have given them in My House and within My walls a place and a name better than sons and daughters, I will give him an eternal name that will never be cut off. And the sons of the strange people who will be attached to HaShem to minister to Him and to love the name of

HaShem, to be to Him as servants -- all who keep the Shabbat and do not transgress it, and who hold by My Covenant -- I will bring them to My holy Mountain and make them rejoice in the House of My Prayer, their whole-offerings and peace-offerings will be for favor on My Altar, for My House will be called The House of Prayer for all the peoples. Thus says HaShem, Who gathers the scattered of Israel -- more will I gather upon him and those of his who have already been gathered." (Isaiah 56:4-8).

In other words, in the world of truth, where everything belongs to G-d (as opposed to the world of the lords of the land, where everything is falsehood) the pride of place goes to those who weekly take on the discipline of Shabbat, abstaining from every form of the 39 forbidden labors as explained by the sages, in order to receive the holiness of the day.

It is in strange contrast that the observance of Shabbat and the Shemittah in the Land of Israel are today matters of contention, with a majority of the population apparently not against blatant violation and defiance of the Shabbat, which is publicly favored by leading judges, politicians and commentators.

In order to save Israel, there needs to be a full-scale international program to explain to Jews, Christians, Muslims and people of other faiths that the observance of Shabbat and Shemittah by true Israelites, with the support of Gentiles, is in fact the very key to bringing prosperity and blessing into the entire world.

The observance of Shabbat and of Shemittah is an art-form, in which man submits himself to a code which focuses his mind on the ways we interact with and manipulate the environment on the days of the week and during the non-Sabbatical years.

It is through abstinence from manipulating the environment for one day of the week that we learn how to elevate our activities on the other six days, and we turn our daily work into the work of building a sanctuary of holiness around us here in this world. Observance of

Shabbat and Shemittah enhance our respect for the natural world around us and for the various grades and levels of life and being. The Shemittah teaches respect for the environment and ecology.

Shabbat is the key to the entire redemption: "If Israel will keep two (consecutive) Shabbatot, the Son of David will come immediately."

BECHUKOTAI

Torah Reading: Leviticus 26:3-27:34

Haftarah: Jeremiah 16:14-17:14

IF YOU WILL GO IN MY STATUTES

*O*ur parshah, ***Bechutokai***, puts the seal on the book of Leviticus, which is the "heart" of the Torah (Genesis being the "head", Exodus the "arms", Numbers the "legs" and Deuteronomy the "mouth", Malchut). ***Bechutokai*** marks the conclusion of G-d's revelation to Moses in the Sanctuary in the camp at Sinai and the sealing of the Sinaitic Covenant, while the coming book of Numbers recounts the journeying of the Children of Israel on their way to the Promised Land.

As the seal on Leviticus, the book of the "heart", ***Bechutokai*** addresses the two sides of the heart: love and fear. Our love of G-d is aroused by the promises of blessing if we will ***go*** in His statutes, while our fears are aroused by the dire punishments for failure to do so.

What does it mean to ***go*** in His statutes? This is explained by Rabbi Nachman of Breslov:

"The life of Torah and Mitzvot should be one of constantly striving to move forward from level to level in our fulfillment of the actual commandments. In every commandment that we carry out, there is a level of meaning that we can grasp within our minds, yet at the same time, the mitzvah has profoundly deeper meaning that is now beyond our grasp. These two levels are those of ***na'aseh*** ("we will do") and ***ve-nishma*** ("and we shall hear") respectively. ***Na'aseh*** applies to that which is within our grasp now, the physical mitzvah with its plain intention – ***we will do***. We must go ahead and do it now on the simple level even if as yet we do not have deeper understanding, even if the level of ***ve-nishma***, ***and we shall hear*** -- understanding -- is still beyond us. To ***go*** in G-d's statutes means to strive constantly to turn that which is as yet beyond us -- our ***ve-nishma*** -- and make it into our ***na'aseh***, something that we ***can*** meaningfully accomplish. This is brought about when we pray to G-d to help us in our practice and to give us deeper understanding. Deeper understanding also depends upon deeper study.

When we thus turn what was our ***ve-nishma*** into a new level of ***na'aseh*** -- because we now incorporate our newly attained, deeper insight into our practice -- we thereby discover that a new level of ***ve-nishma*** opens up ahead of us. It is this higher level of ***ve-nishma*** that we must now strive to attain and turn into a new, higher level of ***na'aseh*** for ourselves. We must continue this way striving to go from level to level, constantly integrating new levels of understanding into our practice. Thus, we constantly ***go*** from level to level in our practice." (Likutey Moharan Part I, Torah 22)

* * *

AND IF NOT.

Rashi in his commentary on ***Bechutokai*** explains how the terrible penalties for failure to follow the path of the Torah are built upon a seven-fold schema, because the essential cause of the exile was the violation of the Sabbath and the Sabbatical years. At the very core of the sins that invoke the terrible cycle of punishment are seven basic sins, each of which drags the next in train: (1) Neglect of study. (2) Neglect of practice. (3) Despising others who practice. (4) Hatred of the sages. (5) Preventing others from practising. (6) Denial of the Divine origin of the commandments.(7) Denial of the existence of G-d.

Graphic illustrations of the fulfillment of all of the terrible penalties described in our parshah in actual Jewish history are recounted in the Midrash. The infringement of the seven basic sins causing the exile has been a recurrent theme in all of Jewish history from biblical times until today. The rebellion of the Ten Tribes under Jereboam son of Nevat against the House of David under Rechav'am represented a craving for greater license than was permitted by the House of David, whose royalty depends upon constant study of the Torah and in particular the oral tradition. Under the northen king Ahab [whose influence is said to have been worldwide], hatred and persecution of the sages -- the prophets -- became institutionalized. Later on, the Assyrian King Sennacherib's chief spokesman marching against Jerusalem under Hezekiah was a renegade Jew, Ravshakeh.

After the end of the Babylonian exile, the return to the land and the building of the Second Temple, new challenges to the authority of the Torah arose, such as from those who denied the afterlife or the oral law, or denied the giving of the Torah at Sinai. Among the most notorious enemies of the Torah were those who hellenized in the Second Temple period, when it was "politically correct" to be Greek. The festival of Chanukah commemorates the miraculous saving of the authentic Torah pathway from the assault upon it by Greek culture.

Rabbi Moshe ben Maimon, the Rambam (Maimonides) wrote a letter known as ***Igeret Teiman*** encouraging the Jews of Yemen to remain faithful to the Torah and give their lives if necessary rather than submit to forced conversion by their Moslem rulers. In this letter, Maimonides explains the difference between the assault upon the Torah by Greek thought and the assault upon the Torah by Christianity and Islam.

The Greek philosophers denied the existence of G-d and the revelation at Sinai and accordingly provided justification for preventing Jews from practicing the Torah, e.g. Shabbat, circumcision, etc., leading to open violation and vilification of the Torah by the Hellenists. Greek philosophy was a direct assault upon the Torah, leaving the Jews of the time with a choice -- whether to go in the way of the Torah or of the Greeks.

On the other hand, Christianity and Islam did not blatantly repudiate the entire Torah of Moses. What they did was to establish alternative 'Torahs" that were more acceptable to non-Jews, leaving the Jews of their respective periods with a different kind of choice: whether to remain faithful to the traditional Torah of Moses or to follow an alternative "Torah".

Hatred of the sages of Israel is deeply entrenched in Christianity, because the claims of its founder and his followers about his divinity were a direct assault upon the authority of the sages and an attempt to steal the Torah from its true guardians, the House of David under Hillel (as later handed down in the Mishnah and Talmud). The adherents of the new religion wrote their own "Torah" openly mocking the Torah of Moses, as when their leader is displayed licensing the plucking of grain on the Sabbath for charitable reasons against the protests of the "Pharisees", who are depicted as being mean. In the writings of the new religion, the Pharisees (i.e. the rabbis of the Mishnah) are characterized as the evil face of institutionalized religion. The new religion drew all of its teachings from the Torah, but detached them from the accompanying stringencies of the Law, while attaching them instead to its own devotional system focussing on its own saints and heroes. Particularly after the conversion of Saul (Paul), who was a Pharisee, the new religion institutionalized the systematic vilification of the Torah tradition of the rabbis, turning the written Torah (Torah, Nevi'im & Ketuvim, TaNaKh) into a mere introduction to its own new "Torah" or "Testament", which was meant to replace the Sinaitic Covenant.

Denial of the pathway of the Torah of Sinai -- the written Torah and the oral Torah -- is thus deeply built into the very structure of Christianity, which became the dominant religion in the western and many other parts of the world and one of the main foundations of its culture, together with that of Greece and Rome. As Christianity gained strength, persecution of Torah-observant Jews together with burnings of Torah scrolls and Talmuds became a regular occurrence.

Denial of the Torah given to Moses at Sinai is also inherent in Islam, the founder of which claimed to have supplanted Moses as the ultimate Prophet. The founder of Islam was initially enamored of the Torah of Moses, but wanted to adapt it in his own way. Angered at the stubbornness of the Jews in resisting his changes, he established his own new "Torah" as an alternative to the "old" Torah. Islam saw itself as the stick with which to beat the recalcitrant Jews who despised and neglected their own Torah. In the writings of Islam the "People of the Book" are depicted as renegades to their own teachings.

During the long exile since the destruction of the Second Temple, the Jews who have remained faithful to the Torah of Moses have been surrounded until today by a most formidable cultural assault against their own tradition from the two younger sister religions, Christianity and Islam. These two have gained the ascendancy and taken all the glory, parading their own alternative "Torahs" in the face of the Torah of Moses.

It is understandable that over the generations, many Jewish souls, subject to this cultural onslaught, have fallen victim to the allurements of the surrounding religions. In addition, since the time of the European renaissance and the "Age of Reason", secularism has become a new alternative to religion of any kind, creating yet another allurement from the stringent code of Judaism, which looks more irrelevant than ever in the modern world.

In this way, the Torah of Sinai has been apparently completely marginalized by almost the entire world. The Sinai tradition is guarded by seemingly powerless networks of rabbis and their students, sitting in the Yeshivahs, daily studying the oral tradition as brought down in the Talmud, and by the numerically tiny proportion of the world's population who are Torah-observant.

What is it about the real Torah that makes those who love her cling to her even in the face of adversity on every side? Throughout the generations until today, those who keep the Torah of Moses and abstain from the 39 forbidden labors on the Sabbath have been the butt of every jester and jeerer. Meanwhile Christianity, Islam and every other religion are on the ascendant, including the religion of Satanism and the universal religion of self-indulgence and material consumption.

What love is it that makes those who strive to follow the authentic Torah of Moses continue day after day in the face of all this? How do we keep on ***going*** in the Torah, even though her face is shrouded in a dark cover -- for in this upside down world, the deeper meaning of the Torah is not revealed?

But if we keep studying the Torah, she will reveal her face to us. The way to keep ***going*** in the Torah is to ***go on studying*** the Torah!

In the merit of our study of the book of Leviticus and our ongoing study of all the Five Books of Moses, may we be blessed with all the blessings of our parshah: "If you will ***go*** in My statutes."

CHAZAK! CHAZAK! VE-NIT'CHAZEK!

"Be strong! Be strong –and we will be strong!"

במדבר

NUMBERS

BAMIDBAR

Torah Reading: Numbers 1:1-4:20

Haftarah: Hosea 2:1-22

IN THE WILDERNESS

*I*t was fitting that the Giving of the Torah took place in no-man's-land amidst the stark desolation of the Wilderness. Here no temporal king could claim that he played host to the event, thereby meriting a special share in the glory. The Children of Israel were chosen to receive the Torah not because they were the most glorious, but because their hearts had been broken through exile and slavery. For the only way to receive the Torah is through humility, symbolized by the lowly Mount Sinai.

Having been appointed as guardians of the Torah, the task of the Children of Israel was to bring it up from Sinai to the Promised Land, from which they were to shine its light to all the inhabitants of the world. Genesis traces the roots of the Torah and of the souls of Israel who were to be its bearers, and Genesis is thus the "head" of the Torah. Exodus is the "hands", describing how G-d redeemed the Children of Israel from slavery in Egypt "with a mighty arm" and made them into a unique nation through the gift of the Torah and the presence of His Sanctuary in their midst as the focus of their national life. Leviticus is the "heart" of the Torah, setting forth its main laws in all areas of life.

Now we come to the Book of Numbers -- the "legs" -- tracing the journeying of the Children of Israel on foot through the wilderness to the borders of the Promised Land, with all the accompanying trials and tribulations. Our parshah of ***Bamidbar*** begins in the Wilderness of Sinai, almost a year after the Children of Israel's arrival to receive the Torah. By now, they had been taught all the main laws of the Torah, and the Sanctuary was in place and fully functional. The next stage was to take to the road and carry the Ark of the Covenant -- encompassing the entire Torah -- up to the land. The commandment to Moses with which ***Bamidbar*** opens, to take a census of the people and organize them by tribes, was a preparation for their departure from Sinai, which is narrated in ***Beha'alotcha*** (Numbers ch 10).

As described in our parshah, the twelve tribes of Israel were to be encamped around the Sanctuary in four groups of three tribes each. When they traveled through the wilderness, they were to travel in the same formation. The positions of the twelve tribes were the same as those of Jacob's twelve sons when they carried his funeral bier from Egypt to the Cave of Machpelah.

Ramban (Nachmanides) opens his commentary on ***Bamidbar*** by pointing out that the way the people encamped around the Sanctuary was directly parallel to the way they encamped around Sinai at the time of the Giving of the Torah. We find in the following parshah that they were commanded to send those who were ritually impure away from the Sanctuary and out of the camp (Numbers 5:1ff). This parallels the command to Moses to put boundaries around Mount Sinai at the time of the Giving of the Torah -- for "the stranger who draws near will die" (1:53; 18:7). At the end of our present parshah, we learn that even the Levites, whose task was to carry the Sanctuary parts during their travels, were forbidden to see the Sanctuary in its "moment of shame" while being dismantled (Numbers 4:20). Correspondingly, the Israelites at Sinai were forbidden to break through and go up the Mountain in order to feast their eyes.

These and other parallels point to the profound conceptual link between the Sanctuary (and Temple) and the Giving of the Torah. The Giving of the Torah at Sinai was a one-time event: the Torah "came down" from heaven to earth, providing man with a ladder of ascent to G-d. Having come into this world, the Torah had to remain the central focus of our attention forever afterwards. The Ark of the Covenant with the Tablets of Stone and Moses' Torah scroll thus had pride of place in the Holy of Holies at the very center of the Sanctuary, with the Twelve Tribes encamped around it. [Similarly, in the Synagogue, it is customary to read the Torah from a desk in the middle of the Synagogue among all the people.]

From the Wilderness of Sinai, the Children of Israel were to carry the Ark of the Covenant up to the center-point or "navel" of the earth in Jerusalem, "...for the Torah will go out from Zion and the word of HaShem from Jerusalem" (Isaiah 2:3). This was the spot where Jacob dreamed of a ladder joining earth back to heaven. The Hebrew word for ladder is SuLaM, which has the same numerical value as SINaI (=130).

* * *

THE TRIBES OF ISRAEL

The Zohar states that the form of the Sanctuary corresponds to the form of the work of Creation. Thus the various different areas making up the Temple courtyards and buildings correspond to the different "worlds" discussed in the Kabbalah (as explained in "Mishkeney Elyon" by Rabbi Moshe Luzzatto, ***Ramchal***, translated in "Secrets of the Future Temple").

The arrangement of the twelve tribes in four camps around the Sanctuary corresponds to the "four camps of the Divine Presence" and the "four camps of angels" that channel the flow of divine sustenance into the world. These are aspects of the ***Merkavah*** ("Chariot") seen by the prophets, representing the system of providence through which G-d governs the world. The four camps correspond to the four roots of Creation (Kindness, Judgment, Compassion and their manifestation in reality: "Kingship") and to the four elements (Water, Fire, Air and Earth, which is the "vessel" of the first three). The various different names and numbers making up the account in our parshah of the census of the Twelve Tribes consist of codes and ciphers that are bound up with the root forces in the spiritual and physical worlds.

The difficulty which many find in relating to sections dealing with the different tribes and their names and numbers, is compounded by the fact that today the majority have become disconnected and even alienated from their own "tribal" roots after thousands of years of exile and wandering. Originally the consciousness of tribal affiliation among the Children of Israel was very powerful, as is evident from the end of Parshat ***Emor***, where the episode of blasphemy was caused when members of the tribe of Dan refused to allow the son of the Egyptian to camp with them because his lineage was flawed.

Today, however, few Jews even know which tribe they come from, although the majority (besides Kohanim and Levites) assume that they are from the tribes of Judah or Benjamin, which were the only two that did not disappear when the Ten Tribes went into exile prior to the destruction of the First Temple. (Some believe that the Sephardic communities of Spain and Morocco came from the tribe of Judah while the Ashkenazi communities of Germany and Poland came from the tribe of Benjamin. This is mentioned by Rabbi David Kimchi -- ***Radak*** -- in his commentary on the Bible.)

Besides being unaware of their own tribal affiliation, many Jews are also quite unaware that many people throughout the world whom they consider to be Gentiles actually believe themselves to be the Children of Israel. Moreover, in many cases they believe they ***do*** know to which tribe they belong. This includes enormous numbers of people in the Indian sub-continent, Africa and South America etc. as well as the Mormon Church, which considers America today to be the home of the Ten Tribes, and prominent members of British and European royalty and aristocracy, who believe they are the true Israelites (without explaining why they do not observe the Sabbath or other Torah laws).

Just to complete the mix-up, if you were to ask most Jews today to enumerate the different components that make up the nation, the answer would not be the twelve tribes but rather: ultra-orthodox, orthodox, traditional, conservative, reform, secular-right, secular-left, etc. etc.

Our fragmentation and disarray in today's sophisticated "civilized" world is in sorry contrast with the order of the camp in the wilds of the desert that saw our birth! Perhaps we need to develop a new way of looking at the different types that make up the people of Israel in terms of the order set forth in ***Bamidbar***: how near are they to the Sanctuary-Temple idea or how far away?

NASO

Torah Reading: Numbers 4:21-7:89

Haftarah: Judges 13:2-25

THE LONGEST PARSHAH

Parshat ***Naso***, with 176 verses, is the longest parshah in the whole Torah, and the Midrashic commentaries, particularly the aggadic Midrash Rabbah, are also exceptionally lengthy. It is fitting that this parshah is usually read on the Shabbat after the festival of Shavuot celebrating the Giving of the Torah, when our love of the Torah is renewed and we receive new vigor and energy to devote ourselves to our studies. We are now enjoying the longest days of the year, and the long Summer Shabbat should give us plenty of time to explore the beautiful mysteries of this parshah.

* * *

NO "BEFORE" AND "AFTER" IN THE TORAH

As noted in a number of previous commentaries, the sequence of parshahs and sections in the Torah is not always chronological, and Parshat ***Naso*** is one of the prime cases.

The opening of our parshah, dealing with the census of the Levitical families, is a direct continuation of the previous parshah, ***Bamidbar***, the closing section of which started the narrative of the Levitical census. The command to Moses to conduct the census of the people was given "on the first day of the ***second*** month" of the year after the Exodus (Numbers 1:1), and Moses did so forthwith. After completion in Parshat ***Naso*** of the account of the census, the Torah ***jumps back*** chronologically to the first day of the ***first*** month of the year after the Exodus -- the day of the inauguration of the Sanctuary.

The chronological jump is not obvious immediately. However, the section after the Levitical census deals with commandments that relate to the newly inaugurated Sanctuary: sending the ritually impure out of the camp, the sacrifices of the ***Sotah*** (the wife suspected of infidelity), and the ***Nazir*** (who vows not to drink wine, cut his/her hair or become defiled by the dead), the priestly blessing (which was given in the courtyard outside the Sanctuary, and was instituted by Aaron on the day of its inauguration). The lengthy closing section of Naso narrates in detail the dedications and sacrificial offerings of all the Princes of the Twelve Tribes of Israel on the twelve inaugural days of the Sanctuary, starting on the 1st of Nissan. Although the date is not written explicitly in our parshah, it says: "It was on the day of the completion by Moses of the erection of the Sanctuary." (Numbers 7:1). We are already familiar with this most auspicious day from our studies in Exodus and Leviticus.

The Torah continues dwelling on the 1st of Nissan and associated themes into the following parshah, ***Beha'alot'cha***, and there the date is given explicitly: "And G-d spoke to Moses in the wilderness of Sinai in the second year after their going out from the Land of Egypt ***in the first month***" (Numbers 9:1). Rashi (ad loc.) tells us that this verse indeed is the written proof that there is no "before" and "after" in the Torah.

In other words, the various parshahs and sections of the Torah are not necessarily arranged in chronological sequence but thematically. This indicates that adjacent passages in the Torah whose subjects may not on the surface appear to be interconnected do in fact have profound interconnections. This gives rise to the rabbinic method of interpreting passages in the Torah according to their ***semichut***, "proximity" to one another. Our parshah contains a case in point in the rabbinic comment on why the section about the ***Nazir***, who vows to abstain from wine, comes directly after that about the ***Sotah***, the unfaithful wife. "Everybody who sees the damage done by and to the Sotah will want to abstain from wine, which is what brings to fornication" (Rashi on Numbers 6:2).

* * *

THE GIVING OF THE TORAH AND INAUGURATION OF THE SANCTUARY

As noted earlier, ***Naso*** is always read on the Shabbat after Shavuot, anniversary of the Giving of the Torah. Clearly there is a deep link between the Giving of the Torah and the Inauguration of the Sanctuary/Temple and its associated commandments, which is the theme of the greater part of ***Naso***. On this, one of the longest Shabbatot at the height of summer, when the world is in full bloom around us, the Torah keeps our minds focussed on the 1st of Nissan, the "New Year", time of rebirth, the day of the Consecration of the Sanctuary.

On the day the Sanctuary was consecrated, the Torah descended from Sinai with its awe, thunder, lightning and earthquakes and was brought in the golden Ark of the Covenant, under the wings of the Cherubs, into the ultimate serene tranquillity of the Holy of Holies. This was the vision of Jacob, the founding father who built the House of Israel: that the Torah should come down from its lofty heights and dwell inside the Sanctuary -- not only in the actual, external Sanctuary, but in the home of every Israelite and the heart of every Israelite. When we bring the Torah into our homes and our hearts, it becomes the vessel of peace and blessing that radiates light all around us, just as the blessing of the priests radiates from the Sanctuary (and today, during the priestly blessing in the synagogue, from before the Ark, housing the Torah scrolls): "May the Lord bless you and keep you...". For the study of Torah itself confers blessing. For the entire Torah is woven of the names of G-d, and "in every place where I shall cause My name to be mentioned, I will come to you and bless you" (Exodus 20:21).

* * *

IN THE HOME AND IN THE HEART

At the center of Parshat ***Naso*** are two lengthy sections that bring the Torah of the Sanctuary directly into our very homes and hearts: these are the sections dealing with the laws of the ***Sotah***, the wife suspected of infidelity, and the ***Nazir***, who vows to abstain from wine, cutting his/her hair and defilement from the dead.

At the very center of the true Torah home is the love between husband and wife, which is the very foundation of the ***binyan*** -- the "building" or structure of the family. True love between husband and wife is very jealous: true love brooks no outsiders and third parties. The unity of husband and wife must be complete, face to face, without a trace of a shadow in between.

It is hard even to speak of the purity of love between husband and wife in a world in which third parties are accepted as a normal part of life. It is this rampant immorality that breeds broken homes, broken hearts, children who grow up between one home and another, knowing little or nothing of family, roots and kinship.

Completely opposite is the morality emanating from the Ark of the Covenant in the Holy Sanctuary: "This is the Torah of the Sotah." Strange as it may seem in the context of contemporary (im)morality, the ceremony of the Sotah, the wife suspected of marital infidelity, one of the most awesome rituals of the Temple, is intended as a bulwark of family purity.

In normal everyday life husbands and wives are constantly coming into contact with all kinds of other people in various different contexts, and it is only natural that relationships can form even in societies that are sexually segregated (as in Temple times) let alone in contemporary mixed society.

The Sotah ritual -- administering the bitter waters to the wife even as she protests her innocence in the face of suspicions of infidelity -- was intentionally very frightening to the woman involved and to all who saw it. Here we see the Temple, where the ritual would take place, as a kind of theatre where a spectacle is held up to the entire nation in order to teach a deep lesson.

The bitter waters are the truth-tester of the Torah (quite different from lie-detectors). Mixed with the water was earth from the floor of the Sanctuary (archetype of the Israelite home as it should be) and the dissolved ink of the letters of Torah verses and curses written on the scroll of the Sotah, including the holy name of G-d. What is the truth? Did she or didn't she? Is she lying or is she telling the truth?

The actual Sotah test in Temple times only works when the husband himself is absolutely beyond reproach on any level in all of the commandments relating to sexuality -- the foundation of the Covenant. On such an ideal level of purity, love is fierce and love is jealous. Suspicions may arise. The holy waters of the Sotah can dispel them. For this it is worth dissolving and washing off even the holy name of G-d: to make peace between man and his wife, or to make them separate.

Today, in the absence of the Temple, the Sotah waters take on a different significance, more allegorical. In actual life, without ideal levels of purity, suspicions and strange thoughts do often creep into the best of relationships. It is not infrequently through the bitter waters of suffering that the truth really comes out, one way or the other. And when the bitter waters prove that there was never any disloyalty at all, the resulting rebirth of love and vigor brings new, stronger children into the world, strengthening the home with the joyous mother of children at its center.

[In the Midrash, the Sotah is the Jewish nation, suspected of infidelity to G-d because of their dalliance with the nations, tested by the bitter waters of suffering.]

* * *

THE NAZIRITE

The Hebrew word ***Nazir*** is today used for a monk, but the Torah has no place for such celibacy, and only the prophet Moses and certain true Tzaddikim were permitted to separate themselves from "the way of the world". The Torah ***Nazir*** was not one who separated himself from the world as a recluse from normal life. (On the contrary, the laws of ***Nazir*** are bound up with family life: a man may make his son a ***Nazir***, he may invite his wife to take the vow of ***Nazir***, nullify her vow, etc.) The Nazirite vow is one that would in Temple times be taken on by a regular, normal person who did not want to separate himself from the entire world, but did want to set extra limits on his own behaviour, over and above what the Torah requires of everyone.

Following on from the above-quoted Midrash -- "Everybody who sees the damage done by and to the Sotah will want to abstain from wine, which is what brings to fornication" -- the ***Nazir*** living in the real world full of immorality wants to set for himself or herself extra personal boundaries against anything that may even lead to such immorality -- wine and anything connected with wine, and even fancy hairstyles! The Nazirite may not defile himself with the dead, for while death exposes the folly of worship of the body, fears of aging and death often drive people to seek out the pleasures of the body compulsively.

The section dealing with the Nazir sets forth the detailed laws of the Nazirite vow, yet implies that taking on specific vows is not encouraged by the Torah. Among his sacrifices, the Nazirite has to bring a sin-offering for abstaining from permitted pleasures, as if what the Torah itself prohibits is not enough. When we take on vows, sometimes the tests become overwhelming, and may cause us to break them unwittingly (like the Nazirite who becomes unwittingly defiled by contact with the dead.).

What the Torah wants from us is the true labor of the heart: commitment. A vow is an explicit verbal commitment that we make, creating a Torah of our own, something that goes beyond the letter of the law. It may be in the form of a personal boundary. It may be in the form of a specific commitment. Jacob, the founding father of Israel, builder of the home, was the first one to make a vow. At Mount Moriah, the Temple Mount where Jacob dreamed of the ladder (***Sulam*** = ***Sinai*** = Giving of the Torah), he woke up and set up the Temple foundation and vowed to give a tithe of all he received to G-d. The

Torah that came forth from the Sanctuary (Leviticus 1:1) begins with a vow -- that of a person who wants to offer a sacrifice in the Temple: "When a person would offer an offering" (Leviticus 1:2).

The Nazirite vow is much more demanding than a one-time sacrifice: it is a commitment to a very strict discipline -- complete abstinence from grapes and wine, no haircutting to emphasize the opposite of body-oriented immorality, etc. In the present day world in which we lead our lives, the actual Nazirite vow is not a practical possibility, but we certainly all know ways in which it is desirable to hedge ourselves in with personal boundaries that help separate ourselves from that which is negative and evil in this world of Good and Evil.

What is asked of us is to make our personal boundaries and adhere to them without expressing them in the form of specific vows. The danger of the vow is that during the initial enthusiasm in which it is made, we may not see prospective difficulties that could make it impossible to adhere to it. What is asked of us is not to tie ourselves up in verbal commitments that we cannot keep, but rather, to make an inner commitment -- the commitment of the heart -- to what we know to be good, and then do everything in our power to adhere to our commitment.

* * *

TWELVE STYLES

The concluding section of ***Naso*** deals with the sacrifices of the Twelve Princes on the twelve inaugural days of the Sanctuary. It is striking that these were one-time sacrifices, yet we read these portions of the Torah several times during the year: they are publicly read in the Synagogue during Chanukah, and in some Synagogues they are read from a Torah scroll on the first twelve days of Nissan.

In last week's commentary discussing the names of the Princes and numbers of the tribes of Israel in the Wilderness, I made reference to the fact that in the Hebrew Torah, all of these are ciphers, codes and letter-permutations that bring entire worlds upon worlds into being. The same is true of the portions dealing with the sacrifices of the Twelve Princes, each of whom brought identical offerings on twelve successive days.

One of the reasons why the Midrash Rabbah on ***Naso*** is so lengthy is because not only does it contain extensive drashot on the ***Sotah*** and ***Nazir***, etc. It also contains very lengthy drashot showing that although each of the Twelve Princes brought identical offerings, in each case they had an entirely different meaning and intention, each wondrous, each amazing.

And so too, each Israelite dons the same Tallit and Tefilin, abstains from the same forbidden labors on Shabbat, gives Tzedakah, does Chessed. But in each case the meaning and intention of each act is entirely different. The hidden intentions in the heart of each one. The hidden efforts.

And G-d has joy from them all. All are His children. All are members of the Twelve Tribes of Israel, the House of Jacob.

BEHA'ALOT'CHA

Torah Reading: Numbers 8:1-12:16

Haftarah: Zechariah 2:14-4:7

* * *

*A*fter the dedication of the Sanctuary -- the portable Temple and repository of the Torah -- the Children of Israel were almost ready to start the journey to the Land of Israel. The purpose was to fulfill the mission of Abraham, the founding father: to take the Ark of the Covenant up to Jerusalem so that the light of the Torah would shine from Mount Moriah to the entire world.

The opening sections of ***Beha'alot'cha*** set forth some final details relating to the Sanctuary and its services (the lighting of the Menorah, the inauguration of the Levites and their service, the law of the Second Pesach). The Torah then relates the miraculous Divine providence visible in the encampment and journeyings of the Children of Israel in the wilderness. The sections dealing with the Sanctuary conclude with the command to Moses to make trumpets, after which the Torah relates the Children of Israel's momentous first journey from Sinai towards the Promised Land.

* * *

UNTIL THE FLAME GOES UP BY ITSELF

Rashi explains the thematic connection between the opening verses of ***Beha'alot'cha***, about the Menorah, and the concluding section of last week's parshah of ***Naso***:

"When Aaron saw the dedication offering of the Princes of the Tribes, he became demoralized because neither he nor his tribe was with them. The Holy One blessed be He said to him: By your life, yours is greater than theirs, because you kindle and tend the lights" (Rashi on the opening verse of our parshah).

The Consecration of the Sanctuary and the offerings of the Princes were events of cosmic significance containing the keys of Creation -- but they were one-time events. The service of Aaron and his tribe were daily.

The service of the Priest (Aaron, Chessed) is to light the Menorah. Each one of us is the Priest in charge of the lighting of our own Candelabrum: allowing the light of ***Da'at***, the understanding of G-d, to shine out from its source, in the Sanctuary, before the Holy of Holies, into our souls, minds and hearts. But how can we attain Da'at? "An amazing wonder is ***Da'at***, it is exalted far above me, I cannot reach it" (Psalms 139:6). How can a human being possibly attain the light of ***Da'at***, knowledge of the Infinite G-d? This is the work of the priest, whose task is to tend the lights and kindle them.

Rabbi Nachman explains that the lights of the Candelabrum that each one of us, as priest, must tend, are the seven lamps of the face: the two eyes, two ears, two nostrils and the mouth. We tend the eyes by not looking on evil (i.e. by not gazing at and lingering over evil temptations, and by seeing not the bad everywhere but the good). We tend the ears by heeding the words of the wise and their reproof. We tend the nostrils by breathing into ourselves the fear and awe of G-d, knowing that our very lives depend upon Him. We tend the mouth by not speaking falsehood – ***evil speech***.

The priest must light the lamps "until the flame goes up by itself". Rabbi Nachman explains that when we do our work of tending the lamps, as detailed above, ***Da'at*** will come upon us of itself, and we will be able to understand things that we could not understand before. ***Da'at*** is obviously a spiritual understanding which we may not even be able to put into words. Spiritual understanding is metaphorically called "light", and "shines" in the form of "Seven Clouds of Glory" (i.e. from all directions). These are a surrounding canopy of holiness. From this canopy -- dark in relation to its Infinite Source, but a protective cloud radiating light to the camp below) shines the light of ***Da'at***. The way to attain this light is by tending the lamps of the Menorah, as above. (Likutey Moharan I:21).

* * *

THE LABOR OF THE LEVITES

After the account of the daily service of the Priest (***Chessed***) in each one of us, we come to the inauguration of the Levites (***Gevurah***) and their service: the guarding of the Sanctuary/Temple and singing during the sacrificial services.

In the Generation of the Wilderness, the Levites carried the parts of the portable Sanctuary on the journeys. The highest service was that of carrying the golden Ark of the Covenant through the wilderness until it would reach its place in the Holy of Holies in Jerusalem. From there the light of the Torah would shine to all the world.

It is said of the carrying of the Ark of the Covenant that, while its bearers were apparently carrying it, in truth it was carrying its bearers. However, this was a one-time service of the Levites in the Generation of Wilderness. After the entry into the Land of Israel, the essential service of the Levites that remained for all times was that of singing during the Temple services.

Why does this require ***Gevurah***? It may seem that singing is a simple, pleasant task that should be associated with ***Chessed***. Yet we see with our own eyes how hard it is to sing. It's not the singing itself that is so hard: in fact, once you start, like the Ark of the Covenant, which carried its bearers, the song carries you. What is hard is to ***start*** singing.

This is sadly apparent in today's ***Mikdash Me'at***, the "portable Temple" that should be the Sanctuary of the Children of Israel in all their habitations, the ***Beit Kenesset***, the House of Gathering of the Children of Israel -- the ***Synagogue***. There are some in which a good (or bad) Chazan is paid to sing, and occasionally a choir, and this may be inspiring. In many, however, there is an embarrassed prayer leader and a heavy congregation reluctant to get any form of ***singing***.

It is this heavy, depressed reluctance to start singing (people start looking at their watches) that must be overcome with ***Gevurah***, forcing ourselves to sing. The act of "force" need not be brutish. Often all that is needed is just starting to lightly hum the ***nigun*** (melody), then keep going until the grace and beauty of the melody itself takes over, and the Ark of the Covenant carries its bearers.

The commandment of the Service of the Levites completes the account of the Sanctuary indicating the supreme importance of song in the Temple/Synagogue Service. Singing in prayer is a unique human ability that even the angels wait to hear. It is the crowning moment of the Service. We may want to hurry the prayers so we can get away from the Synagogue, but instead we "slaughter the animal", "sacrifice ourselves" and stand there singing instead. The song is made up of air, ***ru'ach***, spirit. The song is ***Gevurah***, sifting the animal ***ru'ach***, the side that wants to run away and occupy ourselves with the secular world, from the uniquely human ***ru'ach*** -- the air of our songs. This air or ***ru'ach*** is the vessel through which the even higher faculty of ***Da'at*** is able to enter and dwell, and then everything is complete: the Meat is on the Table (the sacrifice), the Lights are kindled (the Menorah) and the Choir are singing.

* * *

THE SECOND PESACH

"The Second Pesach" has two senses in connection with our parshah. In the first sense, so far there had only been one Pesach: the night of the Exodus from Egypt. The celebration of the one-time Second Pesach, a year later, free in the Wilderness, recipients of the Torah, with the Sanctuary newly erected, was itself an event. It showed that the Exodus, as the foundational event of the People, was henceforth to be institutionalized as an annual experience with the slaughter of the lamb on Passover.

The sacrifice could only be offered by those in a state of ritual purity. So central to the attachment of the Individual to the Nation is this annual sacrifice (failure to bring the sacrifice makes one liable to excision) that some provision had to be made for those who were unable to bring it in its proper time on the 14th of Nissan. This might be because they were far away and unable to reach the Temple, or because of defilement for any one of a number of naturally recurrent reasons (contact with the dead, menstrual impurity, etc.) Accordingly they were given a "second chance" on the annual ***Pesach Sheini***, Second Pesach (in the second sense of the term!) institutionalized now in Torah law.

The Torah narrates in our parshah how this vital national law, integral to the annual functioning of the Temple as the central focus of the Children of Israel, came to be revealed because when G-d commanded them in the wilderness to observe the one-time "Second Pesach" on 14th of Nissan, one year after the Exodus, a number of people in the camp were ritually impure.

Knowing there was no way they could participate in the celebration of this awesome one-time event -- institutionalizing for all time the annual celebration of the anniversary of the Exodus with the eating of the Paschal Lamb, they felt they had ***lost out***. They felt denied this central act of communion with fellows because of extraneous natural reasons: they had to attend to the dead.

"Why should we be worse off, not to be able to offer the sacrifice of HaShem in its appointed time among the Children of Israel" (Numbers 9:7). (The offering of the Paschal Lamb in the Sanctuary/Temple was accompanied by the full Levitical choir and orchestra singing the Hallel, an awesome experience.)

"Why should we be worse off?" There was no way that they could offer the Sacrifice but they longed to be able to. It was their longing that elicited the commandment of Pesach Sheini, the annual "Second Pesach" that gave a ***second chance*** to those who lost out the first time -- a tremendous act of love and compassion.

Longing and yearning elicits love and compassion. It is our longing for the Second Pesach, the Pesach of ***Geulah***, when we too, now impure through contact with the dead etc., will have a ***second chance*** and won't have to feel we lost out because we didn't experience the Pesach in Jerusalem.

* * *

THE CLOUDS OF GLORY AND MOSES' TRUMPETS

As indicated above, the Clouds of Glory constitute an exalted state of consciousness in which a high ***Da'at***, knowledge of G-d, dwells, because we seek to sanctify ourselves and order our lives in the proper order (the Israelite camp). With ***Da'at*** one can understand that everything that happens is under G-d's control: there are times when you stay still for different periods, times when you have to venture and journey for different periods.

We may wonder when we will come to the end of the journey through the wilderness? When will we reach the Promised Land? We know when the Generation of the Wilderness reached the Promised Land, but when will ***our*** generation get there? When will we see the Ingathering of the Faithful to the Holy Temple on Mount Moriah, from which the Torah will shine to the world? When will ***we*** sing the Hallel in Jerusalem?

The answer is given in our parshah, in the commandment given to Moses: "Make for yourself two trumpets of silver." (Numbers 10:2).

Moses is the central ***neshamah***, the root soul of all the Children of Israel. Moses, who brings the ***Torah*** to Israel, must be in command. In his hand are the trumpets to summon the Children of Israel and their leaders together. In addition, in the Temple, the Priests had trumpets which were sounded.

One of the occasions for sounding these Trumpets of Moses -- Trumpeting the ***Torah*** of Moses -- is in times of war. "When you come to war in your land against the enemy oppressing you [such as now], and you shall ***blast on the trumpets*** [the trumpets of the Torah of Moses] and you will be remembered before the Lord your G-d and you will be saved from your enemies" (Numbers 10:9). The verse speaks of war in the land against ***the*** enemy. Asks the Midrash: "Who is ***the*** enemy? This is in the war of Gog and Magog, after which there will no longer be any enslavement to the nations" (Sifrey).

It is in this war against Gog and Magog that we will be remembered before G-d when we hear the blast of the Trumpet of Moses, making us remember the Torah of Sinai.

* * *

THE JOURNEY THROUGH THE WILDERNESS

The Torah account of the one-time journey of the Generation of the Wilderness is a paradigm of the entire history of the Children of Israel. Before we arrive at the trials and tribulations, the Torah sets forth the ideal form in which the Children of Israel advance through history, organized into tribes and families travelling in formation.

As the Children of Israel set off on their journey from their historical place of encampment at Sinai, where the Torah came into the world, Moses (root soul of the Children of Israel, ***Hevel*** or ***Abel***) makes his eloquent appeal to Jethro, the archetypal ***Ger Tzedek***, Righteous Proselyte (***Kayin*** or ***Cain***) to link and journey together (reconciled brothers: ***tikun***).

Only when the Jew and the Righteous Gentile link together on this journey through time can the Torah dwell in the Promised Land and shine forth from Mount Moriah. [Yael, righteous proselyte wife of Hever HaKeini, Jethro's descendant, delivered Israel from Sisera; Ruth (same letters as Jethro) was the great grandmother of David, who made the Torah rule in Israel. Shemayah and Avtalion, Rabbi Akiva and Rabbi Meir and many other important Israelites were from families of proselytes. Sometimes the proselyte shames the Israelite, because the proselyte exposes his weaknesses, having become tired after years on the road, while the proselyte is fresh with the clear vision of the beginning, the Exodus, which we have to re-experience each year at Pesach.

* * *

THE INVERTED NUN'S

"And it was with the travelling of the Ark, and Moses said: Arise HaShem and let your enemies be scattered and those who hate you will flee from before you. And with its resting, he will say: Return HaShem to the tens of thousands of thousands of Israel" (Numbers 10:35-6).

In the Torah scroll, these two verses, the opening verses of the sixth Aliyah, are preceded and followed by an inverted letter ***Nun***. The two verses are thus set off apart, as a separate entity. (A scroll with 85 letters, corresponding to the number of letters in this parshah, halachically has the same status as a Torah scroll and must be treated with the proper respect.) The two verses are of central importance in the entire Torah. It is when Moses stands up, blasting forth the ***Torah of HaShem***, that G-d's providence is shown in scattering the enemies of Israel and returning His indwelling Presence to the longing and yearning thousands and thousands.

The rabbis taught that although we normally speak of the Five Books of Moses, there are really seven, because these two verses constitute a separate book by themselves. The two verses divide the Book of Numbers into all that came before and all that comes afterwards. What came before is one book. What will come afterwards is another. And these two verses are a book in themselves, making Seven Books of the Torah. These are the Seven Clouds of Glory that accompany us on all our journeys, shining the light of ***Da'at*** to us at all times.

Why was it necessary to make a separation between all of the Book of Numbers that came before these two verses and all that comes afterwards? With the census of the people, erection of the Sanctuary and the ordering of the Camp of the Israelites in its proper order, the entire Order of Creation in its ideal form was complete.

From now on, the task was to actually take the Torah up to Zion. To go on the journey. Actually implementing and adhering to the Torah day to day on the arduous journey of life, amidst all the trials of the wilderness is an entirely different story.

The two verses separate between the Ideal and the Actual. One of the two verses speaks about a state of war. The other speaks about a state of peace. In each case it is Moses who must speak, to bring the Divine Presence upon Israel. "And Moses said... And he will say."

* * *

THE SCHOOLBOY RUNS AWAY

The rabbis said that they left Sinai like a schoolboy running from school (or like worshippers after the service). There is a side that simply rebels against the discipline of Torah and Mitzvot, the same dry diet of words and letters on a scroll, songs, prayers and more prayers, day after day. "***Manna***". Spiritual sustenance. Great! But what about some French Fries?

As soon as the real, actual hardship of the wilderness become apparent during the first three days of the journey, the first complaints began to be heard about ***flesh***. Man is made of two sides, the Spiritual and the Physical: that is his entire challenge in life. Dinning out the Trumpets of Moses, Trumpets of the Torah, are the cries of our appetites and desires for physical comforts and pleasures like in Egypt, where they come ***chinnom***, "free" (free of the burdens of Torah and Mitzvot, see Rashi on Numbers 11:5).

The admixture of yeast in the dough, the ***Erev Rav*** ("Mixed Multitude", the opposite of the Righteous Proselyte, the fallen ***Hevel***, Bilaam) raise their voices in ***lashon hara***, evil speech, about the dull, boring diet: the Manna. The source of all evil lies in evil speech. [Thus today, in the time of exile in the war of Gog and Magog, aspersions are cast upon the Diet of Moses, Manna, Torah, and upon Moses himself, in the form of the true Talmidey Chachamim, who are considered to smell putrid in the time of Mashiach. The aspersions are cast by the ***Erev Rav***, those who lust for the material world and those led astray by them.]

Moses could not take it. If his voice was not going to be heard, what was the point of living?

The only solution was to spread the spirit of Moses around among the people, kindling from Moses' ***Menorah*** of Prophecy and lighting up 70 other Prophets, making a Sanhedrin of 70 Elders with Moses, the root of the Tree, at the Center: the King. These would bring the prophetic spirit back to the people.

When Moses is King, order is restored, ***Da'at*** reigns, and we learn that material lust is from the side of death and must be buried. That first stop on the journey through the wilderness was named "The Graves of Lust" -- "for that is where they buried the people who had the lust" (Numbers 11:35). It is necessary to overthrow the ***Erev Rav*** and to make Moses the king.

* * *

THE UNIQUENESS OF MOSES

Our parshah contains G-d's own testimony about the uniqueness of "My servant Moses, who is faithful in all My House." (Numbers 12:7). This too was occasioned by a one-time event, a nearly fatal sin of ***lashon hara*** that is to be inscribed daily in our memories: "Remember what the L-rd your G-d did to Miriam on the road when you went out of Egypt" (Deuteronomy 24:9). Miriam criticized Moses.

Even the saintliest are human. Sometimes even they may be tempted to cover over and disguise their own faint residue of pride under a veneer of piety. "Why is he any different?"

Only Moses is beyond all pride. "And the man Moses was very humble more than all man on the face of the earth" (Numbers 12:3).

Evil speech kills. The punishment is "death" -- leprosy, the withdrawal of life and vitality from the flesh.

Only Moses can bring healing. "G-d, please, heal -- please -- her". The voice of Moses must be heard.

SHELACH LECHA

Torah Reading: Numbers 13:1-15:41

Haftarah: Joshua 2:1-24

*W*ith the arrival of the summer solstice and the longest day of the year, we are now standing on the threshold of ***Tekufat Tammuz***, "the season of the month of Tammuz", the hottest time of the year. For long hours every day, Eretz Yisrael is bathed in dazzlingly bright light. It is appropriate that kabbalistically, this season is associated with the human faculty of vision. (The tribe associated with the month of Tammuz, which begins in little more than a week's time, is Reuven – ***Reu-ben***: "***See***! A son!")

The theme of purifying and refining our principle faculties was introduced at the beginning of the previous parshah, ***Beha'alot'cha***. As discussed in our commentary, the seven lamps of the Menorah allude to the seven "lamps" of the head: the two eyes, two ears, two nostrils and the mouth. The highest of all are the eyes, and the visual image of the Menorah with which ***Beha'alot'cha*** begins ("according to the ***vision*** that HaShem ***showed*** Moses") initiates a series of parshiyot all of which prominently feature the faculty of vision.

As we will discuss presently, this certainly applies to ***Shelach Lecha***, with its theme of "spying out the Land". It also applies to the ensuing parshiyot: In ***Korach*** we find that Korach rebelled because he was deceived by his own ***vision***, while all the Children of Israel ***saw*** that the Staff of Aaron sprouted. In ***Chukat*** we learn that when sprinkling the blood of the Red Heifer, the priest had to ***look*** towards the entrance of the Sanctuary, while the bitten Israelites had to ***gaze*** at the bronze serpent. "And Balak ***saw***..." (Numbers 22:2). "And Bilaam ***saw***…" (24:1). "And Pinchas ***saw***..." (25:7) "And HaShem said to Moses, Go up… and ***see*** the land that I have given to the Children of Israel" (27:12).

* * *

SPYING OUT THE LAND

The theme of vision is paramount in ***Shelach Lecha***. The parshah begins with G-d telling Moses to send men who "will ***spy out*** the Land of Canaan which I am giving to the Children of Israel". The parshah ends with the passage recited by every Israelite in the ***Shema,*** morning and evening: "They will make for themselves ***Tzitzit*** on the fringes of their garments… and you shall ***look*** at it and remember all the commandments of HaShem and you shall do them, ***and you shall*** not ***go spying after your hearts and after your eyes*** that you went astray after them." (Numbers 15:38-39). The same word for spying occurs in the opening and closing verses of the parshah, highlighting the importance of the theme of vision throughout the parshah. The Tzitzit are the remedy for faulty and sinful vision.

In the words of Rashi's comment on the latter verse (Numbers 15:39): The heart and the eyes are spies for the body, and they act as the body's agents in sinning. The eye sees, the heart desires and the body carries out the sins." The fringes of the Tzitzit surrounding us on all four sides, are a visual reminder of G-d's presence everywhere. The blue ***techeilet*** thread in the Tzitzit is the color of the sea, which is a reflection of the color of the heavens, the seat of G-d's glory.

Tzitztit is the first mitzvah to which a young boy is introduced (customarily at the age of 3), because this mitzvah comes to remedy the vision of the eyes, which caused Adam's downfall. "And the woman ***saw*** that the tree was good for food and it was desirable to the ***eyes***… and she ate and she gave also to her husband with her" (Genesis 3:6).

Likewise, it was deceptive vision that led to the fall of the Children of Israel forty days after the revelation at Sinai. "And the people ***saw*** that Moses' was delayed in coming down from the mountain." (Exodus 32:1). According to the sages, Satan deceived the people with a "desert mirage" of Moses being carried up dead to heaven. They didn't want an invisible leader. They wanted one they could see with their own eyes. "And the people gathered against Aaron and said to him, Rise, make us gods who will go before us." (Exodus 32:1). They couldn't stand not being able to see G-d. They felt impelled to violate the Second Commandment against making graven images. They wanted a visual representation of the divine -- the demanded to see the unseeable -- but their representation turned into an idol, giving a license to lust.

In the sin of the Golden Calf, the heart went astray after the image before the eyes. The sin took place at the very height of ***Tekufat Tammuz*** (season of Vision), on the 17th of the month. The sin of the Golden Calf led to all the subsequent trials and tribulations of the Children of Israel, represented in the Forty Years of Wandering in the Wilderness (for it is only after 40 years that a person attains ***Binah***, "understanding" -- Avot 5:21). Although the decree of forty years wandering was specifically incurred through the sin of the spies, Rashi (on Numbers 14:33) tells us that "From the moment they made the calf, this decree arose in His Thought. Except that He waited for them until their measure was filled, as it says (Exodus 32:34): 'On the day of my visitation I will visit upon them their sin' ".

The forty-year penalty corresponded to the forty-day journey of the Twelve Spies from the Wilderness around the Land of Israel. This also took place during ***Tekufat Tammuz***, one year after the sin of the Golden Calf. The spies left at the end of Sivan, they were travelling around Israel during the entire month of Tammuz, and they arrived back at the Israelite camp in the Wilderness only on the 9th day of the month of Av.

On their tour of the land, the spies saw exactly what they wanted to see. With the exception of Joshua and Kalev, they rejected the vision of the forefathers, Abraham, Isaac and Jacob. They did not want to accept the traditional report that their ears alone had heard: that G-d promised to take them to a land "flowing with milk and honey". They could not take it on trust. They wanted to check it out with their own eyes and decide for themselves. And they saw what they wanted to see: a real place, a land governed by natural laws, where people live and die. A beautiful land, but one which it was against all the laws of nature that the puny ex-slave Israelites could conquer in the face of a sea of entrenched Amalekites and Canaanites. "And we were in our own eyes as grasshoppers, and so we were in their eyes" (Numbers 13:33).

The sin of the spies was a failure of faith. They allowed themselves to be misled by the external appearance of the natural world into a colossal failure of nerve, despite all the promises given by G-d that He would bring them to the land. The faith of Israel does not depend upon what the eyes see. On the contrary, we declare our faith wrapped in the Tallit, clutching the Tzitzit by our hearts, closing our eyes to the visual world around us and covering them with our hand: "Shema Yisrael, HaShem is our G-d.!" Only Joshua and Kalev closed their eyes to external appearances, knowing that with G-d's help, it is possible to "bend" nature. "We will go up and take possession of it, for He can -- we can -- (conquer) it."

Eretz Yisrael looks like a regular country with houses, roads, fields, forests and mountains, etc. (as Rabbi Nachman put it, "these actual stones and houses"). Yet in reality, the law of the land is totally beyond nature. It is: "A land that HaShem your G-d cares for constantly, the ***eyes*** of HaShem your G-d are on it from the beginning of the year and until the end of the year" (Deut. 11:12).

Every Israelite recites the law of the Land of Israel twice daily, morning and evening in the Shema: "And if you will surely listen to My commandments. And I will give the rain of your land in its season...and you will eat and be satisfied. Guard yourself lest your heart seduces you and you go astray... and you will be lost quickly from the good land which HaShem is giving you" (Deut. 11:13-17).

Perhaps the spies feared the people could not live up to the level of the law of the land, and they preferred an easier, more natural way of life outside of Israel. As leaders of their tribes, the spies conducted an ingenious operation of public opinion manipulation, using skillfully chosen words to implant in the people's minds a vision of the impossibility of achieving their natural destiny that led them all to tears. (This the spies achieved with words alone, even without the use of television, which is the Satan's ultimate deceiver of eyes.) "And all the community cried out, and the people ***wept*** on that night." Tears come from the eyes, the organs of vision. With our tears we try to wash away the bad that our eyes have seen.

The people should have focussed their vision on that which is beyond nature -- the miracles that had been performed for them. This should have given them the faith that G-d has the power to fulfill His promises. (See Rashi on Numbers 14:11). Those who had seen the miracles and still did not believe in G-d would not see the land. "All the men who see My glory and My signs that I did in Egypt and in the Wilderness, yet have tested Me in this ten times, and have not listened to My voice -- They shall not see the land that I have sworn to their fathers, and all who despise Me shall not see it" (Numbers 14:22-3).

Yet immediately after the imposition of the decree, the Torah continues with a series of commandments that can only be fulfilled in the Land of Israel, including the laws of the wheat, oil and wine libations that accompany animal offerings in the Temple, and ***Challah***, the gift of the first portion of one's bread to the priest (Numbers Ch.15). The positioning of these commandments directly after the narrative of the spies is a reminder that even though the exile ("forty years") may be lengthy, eventually Israel will inherit the entire land and have the merit of offering its choicest produce in the Temple and on the table of the priests. [The Challah, separated by the woman and given to the priest, rectifies Eve's sin of giving the forbidden fruit to Adam.]

KORACH

Torah Reading: Numbers 16:1-18:32;

Haftarah: I Samuel 11:14-12:22

* * *

KORACH'S ENVY

*I*n the account of the sin of the Ten Spies in the previous parshah of ***Shelach Lecha***, we learned about the painful consequences of distorted vision in man's relation with G-d. The Spies and those who listened to them lacked faith in G-d's promise to take them to the Land of Israel, allowing outward appearances to deceive them into thinking they would be unable to conquer it. The sin could be rectified only through a protracted exile that comes to teach us that, in spite of outward appearances, G-d is in fact leading us to ultimate, complete possession of the Land.

The distortion of vision that is the theme of our present parshah of ***Korach***, a distortion which led to such dire consequences for Korach and those who listened to him, was of a different nature. In Korach's case, the distortion lay in the way man views his fellow man: Korach could not bear to see another more prominent than himself. "Why is Moses the king, Aaron the high priest. and Korach just another Levite?"

The sin of vision of the spies is deeply rooted in the sin of eating the fruit of the Tree of Knowledge. Just as the outer appearance of the fruit made Eve lose faith in what G-d said about not eating it, so too the spies wanted to see things for themselves and make their own decisions -- and they lost their faith. Korach's sin of vision, on the other hand, is rooted in Cain's jealousy of Abel, whose offering (the prototype Temple sacrifice of Aaron) found favor in G-d's eyes. "Why is Abel the priest?" Cain wanted the whole world for himself -- so he killed Abel. So too Korach was envious of Aaron's eternal role as the high priest of G-d's Temple, and he tried to destroy him.

According to the Midrash, Korach's "starting point" is to be found at the end of the previous parshah, giving the commandment of Tzitzit, where a single blue thread is tied with seven white threads as fringes on the four corners of our garments. [Issues relating to the use of white linen threads with the blue ***techeilet*** woolen thread are also bound up with Cain and Abel: the offering of the former was of linen, while the latter offered sheep.] The question that Korach asked was: "If a person is wearing a garment that is entirely ***techeilet***, does it also require Tzitzit?" When Moses answered that it does, Korach ridiculed him: "If a single blue thread is enough to fulfill the duty of Tzitzit for a white garment, surely a garment that is entirely ***techeilet*** doesn't need Tzitzit!"

Korach wanted a garment that was all ***techeilet***, all kingship and grandeur. He did not want to be reminded that the only King is G-d, all around us, in all directions. Korach wanted the kingship and grandeur for himself: he was all ***techeilet***, all ***Gevurah***. According to rabbinic tradition, Korach possessed amazing wealth. Everything was for himself, yet in rebelling against Moses and Aaron, Korach played the democrat, the people's champion: "All the community, all of them are holy, and ***HaShem*** is within them, and why do you lord it over the Assembly of ***HaShem***?"

Korach's rebellion was against the authority of Moses (the rule of law), but he justified it with an appeal to people's highest ideals: "Everyone is holy -- so why do we need priests and rabbis?" Korach used his wealth and prestige to whip everyone up into a frenzy against Moses.

The first word of G-d's command to Moses and Aaron -- "***Separate*** yourselves from this assembly and I will consume them." (Numbers 16:21) gave its name to a doctrine that was espoused by Rabbi Moses, the Chatam Sofer (1762-1839) leader of European Jewry in his time, in response to the proponents of religious and cultural assimilation. The doctrine is that of ***Hitbadlut***, Separation. At a time when assimilationist thinking was spreading rapidly among the Jews of

Europe, the Chatam Sofer urged his faithful co-religionists to separate themselves in every possible way from anyone who deviated from the Judaism of the Shulchan Aruch, the Code of Torah law.

Today, assimilation has become so universal that the Torah faithful have little option but to run after the assimilated and try to help them find their way back to G-d. Nevertheless, having an understanding of the origins of ***Hitbadlut*** may help us in trying to unravel the knots of ***machloket*** (conflict) in which our communities are so tied up. For ***Hitbadlut*** remains the key to the separatist attitudes shown by some in the observant community until today. The essence of ***Hitbadlut*** is to try to distance oneself from those who represent a culture and way of life that are in rebellion against G-d's Torah as we have it from Moses.

The assimilation movement made rapid inroads among Jews everywhere from the 1800's onwards because of the strength of its appeal to those who felt caged in by the centuries-old restrictions on Jewish social and economic life. While assimilation had its theorists and exponents (from Moses Mendelson onwards), what gave it such power and influence was the fact that it was sponsored by a clique of extremely wealthy Jewish sponsors (= Korach) who were themselves in flight from the Torah of Moses. They used their influence in the countries in which they lived to establish synagogues, educational and cultural institutions that deviated from the traditional pathway. Indeed, they have been so effective that they have succeeded in making what is essentially a deviation appear mainstream, whereas the authentic Torah of Moses appears purely marginal. What could be more of a distortion of vision?

* * *

HELL

The punishment of Korach and his band was that "they went down alive to She'ol" (Numbers 16:30). The bible commentator ***Or HaChaim*** (Rabbi Chayim ben Attar) explains (ad loc.) the use of the word ***She'ol*** (which has the connotation of "borrow") as a term for

Hell. "The explanation is that the earth did not have power over them to kill them, but they were left alive, and the earth gave them as a deposit to Gehennom".

Many seekers of the truth of the Torah are confused about what place She'ol, Gehennom or Hell really play in the Torah worldview. In the Bible, the word used for hell is, as in our parshah, ***She'ol*** (see also Genesis 42:38 and Deuteronomy 32:22).

Throughout the Talmud, the standard term referring to hell is Gehennom, but this does not appear in the Bible at all except as the name of a location just outside ancient Jerusalem -- Gey Hennom, the "Valley of Sighs". This was where there was an idolatrous temple to Molech, to whom children were dedicated by being passed over fire (making the children scream or "sigh").

The confusion over what hell really is derives precisely from the fact that all false religions and cults use precisely this idea to strike such fear into the hearts of their led flocks that they will be psychologically locked into the cult all their lives. Going down to hell alive is precisely what is so frightening about the idea, as it means that death is not a refuge of unconsciousness from the threatened pains of hell. On the contrary, "hellfire and brimstone" preachers delight in reminding their audiences how, despite the excruciating pain of the threatened fire and freezing cold, etc., there is no death and no relief in hell, only more and more pain. All this as the punishment of those who dare stray from the cult!

In the Five Books of Moses, the prime sanction that is threatened for disobedience against the Torah is not hell, but rather the tribulations of This World (as in the curses in Leviticus chapter 26 and in Deuteronomy chapter 28). However, Hell is also threatened: "For a fire is kindled through my wrath and it will burn to the depths of ***She'ol***." (Deuteronomy 32:22). The Talmud teaches that unconsciousness and insensitivity provide no relieve in hell. "The worms of the grave are as hard to the dead person as a needle in living flesh" (Shabbat 13b). But the Torah also explicitly states that "When the wicked person turns from all his sins that he did and guards all My laws and practices justice and charity, he will surely live. All his sins that he did will not be remembered against him; through the righteousness that he practiced he will live" (Ezekiel 18:21-22).

The psychological power wielded by priests and cult-leaders over their hypnotized flocks lies in their implicit claim that it is they themselves who determine who will suffer in hell and for what crimes (i.e. betrayal of the cult). However, the Torah teaches that G-d alone determines what each one must suffer, and that a person suffers only for those actions for which he bears responsibility, and not for the crimes of others. ("It is the soul that sins that will die. A son will not bear the sin of a father and a father will not bear the sin of the son. The righteousness of the righteousness will be upon him and the wickedness of the wicked will be upon him" -- Ezekiel 18:20).

The Torah view is that while hell is certainly painful, it is compassionate in the sense that the sinner pays for his sins in order to be cleansed of them and thus prepared for reconciliation and true communion with G-d. Thus the Torah teaches that there is a time-limit to hell, while the final reward is eternal.

Rabbi Nachman of Breslov commented that while we believe in the eternal reward (Gan Eden), and while it ***may be*** that Olam Ha-Zeh, "This World", exists somewhere or other, the place we are in now would for many people appear to be Gehennom, in view of the terrible suffering many people go through here. May all that we may have suffered here be our atonement, and may G-d speedily grant relief from all our troubles and sorrows.

The Talmudic rabbi Rabbah bar bar Hannah relates (Bava Batra 74a) that he was taken by "an itinerant merchant" to a place in the wilderness where Korach and his band were swallowed up. There was a fissure in the crust of the earth from which smoke was rising, and the heat was so intense that some drenched cotton-wool lowered into it on the end of a spear was scorched immediately. The merchant asked him what he could hear. He heard voices crying out: "Moses and his Torah are true, while Korach and his band are deceivers." The merchant told Rabbah that Korach and his band were rotating in the fire of hell like meat on a spit, and that every thirty days they would complete a circuit and could be heard saying the same thing: "Moses and his Torah are true.". This fits in well with another teaching of Rabbi Nachman: that the essential pain of hell is not so much physical as the pain and shame at having been wrong all along. If we have been wrong, let's admit it!

* * *

THE TORAH ECONOMY

The account of Korach's challenge to Moses and Aaron is followed by the laws relating to the sacrificial parts and Terumah (gifts of grain, oil, wine and other produce) given to the priests in return for their service in the Sanctuary, and the tithes which the Levites received in return for theirs.

In Temple times, these gifts made up a substantial part of the livelihood of the priests and Levites, who were thus left free to pursue their work of going out among the people and teaching them the Torah. Since the study and teaching of the Torah are not per se economically productive activities (though they are the source of all blessing, spiritual and material), the only way they can be seriously pursued is when each member of the wider society takes a share in supporting them.

In the words of Rambam (Laws of Shemittah and Jubilee 13:12-13):

"The tribe of Levi did not have a share in the land of Israel or in war booty together with their brothers, because they were separated to serve HaShem and minister to Him and to teach His righteous ways and laws to the multitude. Accordingly they were separated from the ways of the world, they do not fight in war like other Israelites and they do not have a share in the land or attain material power. They are the army of G-d and G-d is their share and inheritance.

"And not only the tribe of Levi, but every single person from all the inhabitants of the world whose spirit encourages him and whose understanding leads him to separate himself to stand before G-d and serve Him, to know G-d and go on the straight path. G-d will remove from his neck the yoke of the "many calculations" that people seek for themselves. For this person has sanctified himself as a holy of holies, and HaShem will be his portion for ever and ever and G-d will provide him in this world with what suffices him, just as G-d provided the priests and the Levites with their livelihood. And thus King David said: HaShem is the portion of my share and my cup: You sustain my lot!"

CHUKAT

Torah Reading: Numbers 19:1-22:1.

Haftarah: Judges 11:1-33.

THE BEGINNING OF THE END

Now that we have passed the summer solstice, the days are still long but imperceptibly they are starting to get shorter, as we move inexorably closer to the end of the year and the coming New Year and Days of Awe. The Hebrew letters of the present month, Tammuz, are the initial letters of the phrase ***Z-man T-eshuvah M-mashmesh U-va***, "the Time of Teshuvah is getting closer". The letters of next month, ***Av***, are the initial letters of ***Elul Ba*** - "Elul (month of repentance) is on the way". After the month of Av comes Elul itself, and soon afterwards, Rosh HaShanah, Simchat Torah and the conclusion of the annual reading of the Torah.

In the previous parshah, ***Korach***, we passed the mid-point of the book of Numbers (Numbers 17:20). Korach's conspiracy is not explicitly dated in the Torah narrative, but is considered to have taken place early on during the wanderings of the Children of Israel in the wilderness. The Torah passes over the 38 years of wandering after the sin of the Spies in almost complete silence -- except for a list given later on of the stopping points on the journey, Numbers ch. 33, Parshat ***Mas'ey***. In our present parshah of ***Chukat***, we move almost imperceptibly from the initial period in the wilderness following the Exodus and the Giving of the Torah, right to the end of the 40 years of wandering and the first stages of the conquest of the Land of Israel.

Parshat ***Chukat*** begins with the commandment of burning the Red Heifer and using its ashes for purification from defilement from the dead. This commandment was among the first given to the Children of Israel directly after the Exodus and the Crossing of the Red Sea (Exodus 15:25, see Rashi there). The section about the Red Heifer as we have it in ***Chukat*** (Numbers ch. 19) is also listed in the Midrash (Sifra) as one of those given to Moses on the 1st of Nissan one year after the Exodus, the day the on which the Sanctuary was erected.

The positioning of the section of the Red Heifer here -- as we move into the latter part of the book of Numbers and on towards the end of the Torah -- is bound up with its thematic relationship with other sections of our parshah. The commandment of the Red Heifer, which comes to purify from defilement from contact with the dead, is followed immediately by the narrative of the death of Miriam. ("The death of Tzaddikim atones like the sacrifices" -- Rashi on Numbers 20:1). The death of Miriam took place in the last year of wandering in the wilderness, on the 10th of Nissan, exactly a year before the crossing of the Jordan and the entry into the Land. This is the first clue to dating the events in this parshah. The ensuing lack of water in the wilderness caused Moses and Aaron to strike the rock, leading to the decree that they would not enter the Land but die in the wilderness. Moses takes Aaron up Mount Hor to die, while Elazar, his son succeeds him as High Priest. We suddenly have to confront the loss of the elders and leaders of the generation. How do we deal with death?

Without our even noticing the transition, the older generation are leaving one by one, having been replaced by a whole new generation. The new generation -- who are actually the old generation in new bodies -- are now moving inexorably forward to the end and the goal - the Land of Israel. The Generation of the Wilderness have passed on, and the Generation of the Conquest now begin their advance.

As the Torah directs our eyes to the end goal of the wandering in the wilderness -- entry into the Land to fulfill the Torah there -- it first focusses our eyes upon the end goal of man, which is death: "This is the Torah: when a man dies." (Numbers 19:14). For unless we come to terms with death, we cannot truly live. Death is a fact, perhaps the main fact, of life. We are forced to confront it at some time or another. In order to come to terms with it, we have to learn how to look at it.

Thus Parshat ***Chukat*** takes its place in the series of parshiyot read during the bright summer months of Tammuz, time of Teshuvah, that teach us how to look at various different aspects of life in the correct perspective. ***Beha'alot'cha*** taught about the purity of vision in general. ***Shelach Lecha*** taught about viewing the world -- and our own selves -- with the eyes of faith despite outward appearances. ***Korach*** taught about how we look at others who may be better than ourselves. ***Chukat*** now comes to teach us how to look at our mortality, death, the end goal of life, in the right perspective -- for with the right perspective, we can transcend death.

Today, even though recently we were promised a new order of peace, the world has been plunged before our eyes into an era of global war. Every day we are bombarded with gruesome and horrific images of bloodied, burned, mutilated bodies. It has long ceased to be surprising to hear of new daily outrages in locations far and near. We are hardly aware of how dulled our sensitivities have become to injury, death and suffering. If we were to start weeping as we should, would we have enough tears for all the suffering in the world?

Rabbi Nachman of Breslov teaches that the only way we can transcend suffering is by trying to focus our vision on the faraway, ultimate goal of the entire Creation, which is surely completely good. Rabbi Nachman says we must even close our eyes to this world -- close them tight -- so as to keep focussed on this ultimate, transcendent goal, which is to bring the entire universe to perfect unity and completeness through G-d's hidden guidance and providence. (Likutey Moharan 1:65 "Garden of the Souls".)

While no-one can fathom the depths of meaning of the Red Heifer -- any more than we can fathom the real meaning of death and of life -- we are free to search for hints of meaning in this fascinating commandment, which is the key to complete redemption. This depends upon the restoration of the ashes of the Red Heifer, because only when we are able to be purified from impurity from contact with the dead can we go up to the Temple, source of ***life***, and carry out all its rituals in the proper way.

What causes defilement from contact with the dead is not the soul of the dead person. It is the physical remains of his or her body. The death and decomposition of the body are very repugnant: they threaten us, both as health hazards and because they undermine our pride and dignity as living human beings. They remind us of our mortality -- "You are earth, and to the earth you will return" -- but we cannot live with such intense awareness of the vanity of the physical world. We are commanded to cover the body, bury it in the earth, put it out of sight. We should not pre-occupy ourselves with the dead (as did the Egyptians). Our job is to keep living, to keep marching to the end goal -- "the Land of Israel".

Thus the priest (son of Aharon, signifying light and vision) takes the pure Red Heifer -- its redness signifying the harshness of ***Din***, Strict Judgment, and ***Gevurah***, Might. The priest sheds the heifer's blood -- breaking its power. The priest gazes towards the the Holy of Holies and sprinkles the blood of the heifer towards it. This sprinkling of the blood of the Red Heifer towards the Holy of Holies was integral to the whole ceremony, which was performed on the Mount of Olives at a spot directly aligned towards the gates of the Temple. The body of the heifer was then burned on a woodpile and minute quantities of its ashes were mixed with water from a living source to be sprinkled with hyssop on people and utensils that had become defiled.

In breaking the power of Strict ***Din***, the priest had to look towards the Holy of Holies, because this is the ultimate goal of all Creation, the place of complete unity, peace and perfection. Defilement from the dead is very depressing. (The chapters on this subject in Rambam's Mishneh Torah can also be somewhat depressing, as they deal in detail with different parts of the body in varying stages of decomposition, etc.) In order to live we cannot occupy ourselves with death. We must be aware of our mortality, but we must separate ourselves from physical death. The souls of the dead go on living on their plane, and so must we on ours. The seven days of purification from defilement with the dead are seven days of separation from what ought to be the abnormal -- the decaying dead body, which has to be buried and put away -- in order to return to the Land of the Living. It is necessary to be sprinkled with the ashes of the Red Heifer on the third and seventh days of the week in order to draw renewed strength by repeatedly looking toward the Holy of Holies.

Like the priest breaking the force of severe ***Din*** by gazing towards the Holy of Holies, we too, in order to keep living, must keep our gaze focussed on the Holy of Holies. The Holy of Holies in our lives should be our times of prayer and Torah study, and, in the family context, quality time with our dear ones and especially spouses. These are the best support through all the vicissitudes of life.

* * *

"ARISE, O WELL." (Numbers 21:17)

The living waters with which the ashes of the Red Heifer are mixed are one of several references to water in our parshah. Notable among the other references are the "Waters of Strife" -- the waters that Moses and Aaron extracted from the Rock, which cost them the privilege of leading the Children of Israel into the Promised Land. This section of the Torah is of course no less profound than the preceding section about the Red Heifer. Rabbi Nachman saw his explanation of Moses' striking the rock (Likutey Moharan I:20) as being the key to all of his Torah discourses. The bare essence of Rabbi Nachman's teaching is that even the saintly Moses should not have sought "water" -- Torah insight and inspiration -- "by force", i.e. in the merit of his good deeds, his "rod", as a "right". Rather, he should have wept and begged for the waters of Torah as a gift, through prayer. Thus Moses had to atone for his error with the 515 prayers that he offered in the hope of entering the Land of Israel.

It was the death of Miriam that led to the lack of water which made Moses strike the rock. For throughout the forty years of wandering, a miraculous well accompanied the Israelites in the merit of Miriam. Miriam (having the connotation of bitterness) symbolizes the soul of the suffering true Torah scholar ("eat bread with salt, drink water by measure") through whose merit Torah insight comes into the world to inspire the generation. When this soul departs the world, there is a terrible thirst for water, with no one having the power to enlighten and inspire. Each generation needs to dig for the waters of the Torah anew.

The history of Miriam's well is not written explicitly in the Torah text but only allusively. The allusions are brought out in the Aramaic Targum and in Midrashim brought by Rashi on certain verses in our parshah -- such as Numbers 20:10-11 and 21:15ff. This well of the waters of inspiration accompanied the Israelites on all their journeys in the wilderness and provided water for the camp at each of their stopping places. When Miriam died, it disappeared, but it returned in the merit of Moses and traveled with the Israelites on the last stages of their journey through the wilderness. When they entered the Land under Joshua (on 10 of Nissan, anniversary of the death of Miriam), the well also entered the land. It traveled to the Kinneret (Sea of Gallilee), where it is said to be visible from mountains to the east as a kind of "sieve" on the surface of the sea. From the depths of the Kinneret, the well is said to feed the waters of Israel's most important water reserve. (The Ari is said to have taken R. Chayim Vital on a boat and given him a cup of this water to drink, after which R. Chayim Vital understood the teachings of his master.)

The final stages of the journey of the Israelites through the wilderness and the first stages in the conquest of the Land of Israel are recounted in our parshah. Their geography is somewhat obscure to many, as they took place in what is today the kingdom of Jordan, which for political reasons remains temporarily out of bounds for Torah lovers. The Israelites were headed to ***Arvot Mo'av***, the "Plains of Moab" east of the River Jordan facing Jericho. There they assembled prior to the entry into the Land in order to hear the final discourses of Moses, which make up the book of Deuteronomy.

Our present parshah describes their journey there. From the wilderness, they advanced around Edom (S.E. of Yam HaMelach, the "Dead" Sea) and Moab (to the east of the southern part of Yam Hamelach), crossing the River Arnon, which flows into the Yam HaMelach from the east, midway from north to south. The Arnon, which meets the sea via a spectacular mountain gorge, is the boundary between Moav, which the Israelites were forbidden to conquer, and the territories to the north, which had been conquered by the Emorites. The narrative of the Israelite conquest of the latter territories begins in our parshah.

The parshah relates that the miracles of the crossing of the Arnon were comparable with the miracles of the crossing of the Red Sea (Numbers 21:14ff.). The Emorites were waiting for the Israelites in caves in the gorge below, but the two sides of the gorge miraculously came together, allowing the Israelites to walk safely above. The Well of Miriam, which traveled with the Israelites, flushed the blood of the dead Emorites out of the gorge so that the Israelites could see the miracles performed for them.

Thus, forty years after the Generation of the Exodus had sung to G-d when they came up from the Red Sea, the Generation of the Conquest sang again as they witnessed the first miracles of the conquest. "That was the well of which HaShem said to Moses, gather the people and I will give them water. Then Israel sang (lit. ***will sing***) this song: Arise, O well!" (Numbers 21:16-17).

The conquest of the Land depends upon Miriam's well -- the well of Torah insight and inspiration. May we soon hear the song of the conquest of the Land for the Torah, for the Holy of Holies and for the glory of HaShem -- quickly in our days!

BALAK

Torah Reading: Numbers 22:2-25:9.

Haftarah: Micah 5:6-6:8.

* * *

The story of Bilaam and his talking donkey is one of the most strangely picturesque sections of the whole Torah. It is said that one Shabbat, while the holy Rabbi Yitzchak Luria, the Ari, was taking a short nap, his attendant noticed the master's lips moving in his sleep. When he awoke, the attendant asked him: "Master, what were you studying?" "It was a lesson about Bilaam's donkey," replied the Ari. "But if I were to try to explain to you what I learned in those few minutes, the introductions alone would take hundreds of years."

Since the Torah states that "there did not arise another prophet in Israel like Moses" (Deut. 34:10), the rabbis inferred that while there never arose another prophet in Israel of the stature of Moses, there did arise a prophet of comparable stature among the other nations. This was Bilaam, who was sent to the nations so that they could not argue that if they had had a prophet like Moses, they would not have rebelled against the Torah. The Torah describes Bilaam as "knowing the knowledge of the Supreme" (Numbers 24:16). Yet instead of reproving the nations and bringing them to the service of G-d, Bilaam's advice to them was to untie the reins of chastity that had hitherto bound the Children of Noah and to let wild immorality loose on the world.

According to the Ari, Bilaam is one of three who had the same soul: Laban, the antagonist of Jacob; Bilaam, the antagonist of Moses, and Naval the antagonist of King David (I Samuel, Chapter 25). The initial letters of the three make up the name of NaVaL, who cast his evil eye on G-d's anointed, David Melech HaMashiach, just as Laban cast his evil eye on Jacob and his children and Bilaam cast his evil eye on

Moses and the Children of Israel. [The three are fallen parts of the soul of Abel, whereas Moses embodies the rectified Abel.]

As the adversary of Moses, who brought the Torah to Israel, Bilaam is the chief adversary of Israel. To look at him from the outside, one might easily have been deceived, for this arch prophet of the Seventy Nations may well have appeared on the surface as a supremely pious and spiritual individual. The Torah itself testifies that he received prophecy from HaShem. Presumably Bilaam was constantly engaged in meditations and rituals, and surrounded by priests, monks and other acolytes. A turn of expression in Ethics of the Fathers explains how we find out who is the true Bilaam: not from his external piety and spirituality, but by observing the actual traits of those who are his students and followers. "Whoever has these three traits is of the students of the wicked Bilaam: an evil eye, a haughty spirit and an expansive appetite" (Avot 5:19). Rashi, in his commentary on our parshah, shows where in the narrative Bilaam exhibits these traits (Numbers ch. 22 v. 13 & 18; ch. 24 v. 2).

Bilaam is the very epitome of those who choose This World, the world of extraneous splendor, glory, wealth and appetite, over the World chosen by Abraham, Jacob, Moses and the Children of Israel: the World of Truth. Having chosen This World, Bilaam cannot but look askance at the Children of Israel, whose eccentric religion appears to make no sense in terms of the visible logic of the material world. Israel's existence is such an affront to the world chosen by Bilaam that he feels compelled to "cast the evil eye on them" -- to demonize and curse them. His haughty spirit is offended that this nation of escaped slaves seeks to rein in man's material appetites and desires and elevate them in the service of G-d.

While Moses brought the knowledge of G-d to the world -- the Tree of Life -- what Bilaam embraced was the other side of knowledge: the Tree of the Knowledge of Good and Evil. Bilaam demanded the right to know and experience every side of the world to the full, without boundaries or limitations. "Knowing the knowledge of the Supreme". This desire to know everything, including the innermost face and slimy underside of the material world, is expressed in the rabbinic statement that Bilaam had intercourse with his donkey (Sanhedrin 105b). The donkey is symbolic of materialism in general (***Chomriut***), as indicated by the generic Hebrew term for donkey, ***Chamor***. Wanting to "have it all", Bilaam was diametrically opposed to the Israelite path of self-restraint and discipline.

It is part of G-d's deep plan for man in this world that there should exist a world-view and mindset that is diametrically opposed to that of the Torah in order for man to be subjected to the test of free will. We are indeed constantly confronted with and challenged by this mindset in the predominant materialist culture that surrounds us on every side in the contemporary world. It is the mindset that tells us that we are in this world to enjoy everything it has to offer according to the way we feel, without having to be bound by the dictates of a restrictive religious code of conduct that constantly seems to be telling us what we must do next and what we must not do.

The deepest mystery of creation is that G-d gave man free will to do as he chooses, yet G-d directs man in such a way that in the end, he has no option but to acknowledge that G-d is right. This mystery is contained in the story of Bilaam, who was determined to curse Israel and tried every way possible to get G-d to agree, but in the end was forced to bless Israel, even against his will.

Bilaam wanted to be completely free: to be in the driver's seat, "riding the donkey" -- going where he chose in the material world. The irony is that the donkey itself rebelled, and refused to go where Bilaam wanted. Bilaam wanted to know and enjoy the side of the world where there is no G-d, no restraint, no pangs of conscience, only the donkey, the animal. But the donkey itself opened its mouth! The term for the donkey in our parshah is ***Aton*** -- alluding to the 22 letters of the Aleph Beit, from Aleph to Tav, and to the Fifty Gates of Understanding (the final letter of ***Aton***, Nun, has the numerical value of 50). Bilaam was forced to see that the material world itself is made up of "letters of the alphabet" -- spiritual significance and purpose. Bilaam could not escape from G-d's truth.

G-d "bridled Bilaam with a halter and put a hook in his mouth, the way a man bridles an animal to take it where he wants" (Rashi on Num. 23:16). Bilaam was forced against his will to bless the Children of Israel. The bridling of Bilaam comes to teach us the profound lesson that although it may appear on the surface that the forces of evil are riding high without control in the world, in fact G-d has evil on a leash like a dog. G-d allows evil only just as much rein as suits His deep plan for the world.

The Talmud states that "from the blessings of that wicked man you learn what was in his heart. He wanted to say that they should not have synagogues and study halls -- "How goodly are your tents, O Jacob". The Indwelling Presence should not rest upon them -- "...and your sanctuaries, O Israel". Their kingdom should not continue -- "...like streams they extend". They should not have olive trees and vineyards -- "like gardens by the side of a river". Their odor should not waft forth -- "Like aloe trees planted by G-d". They should not have kings of stature -- "...like cedars by the side of waters". They should not have a king who is the son of a king -- "water will flow forth from his source". Their kingdom should not hold sway over the nations -- "...and his seed over the many waters". His kingdom should not be daring -- "...his king will be high above Agag". His kingdom should not be fearsome -- "...and his kingdom will be exalted" (Sanhedrin 105a).

From this Talmudic passage we learn what gives Israel its strength: its synagogues and study halls, and its kings -- the true kings who follow in the path of King David, the archetype of the true Tzaddik.

"How goodly are your tents of Jacob." Everything is founded on the sanctity and purity of Israel's "tents and habitations" -- the Torah home, where man and wife unite in holy love to bring new souls into the world and nurture them in the ways of G-d. It was precisely this sanctity that Bilaam sought to attack in advising Balak that the best way to get the better of Israel would be by promoting immorality. Thus Bilaam's advice was to ensnare the Israelite men with the Midianite girls, who would quickly persuade them to go after the god of immorality. This was diametrically opposed to the way of Moses, causing a plague that threatened the entire nation. They were saved only through the heroism of Pinchas, who zealously stood up for HaShem when everyone else was confused.

PINCHAS

Torah Reading: Numbers 25:10-30:1

Haftarah: I Kings 18:46-19:21

PINCHAS, PRINCE OF PEACE

*"P*inchas son of Elazar son of Aaron the Priest turned away My wrath from upon the Children of Israel in his zealousness. Therefore say: I hereby give him My Covenant of Peace" (Numbers 25:11-12).

The opening verses of our parshah of ***Pinchas*** follow immediately after the account of Pinchas' heroic act given at the end of last week's parshah, ***Balak***. The Prince of the tribe of Shimon was publicly flouting Moses' authority by taking a Midianite princess for himself in front of his brothers, in front of Moses and in front of the whole Assembly of Israel. His claim was that if Moses could marry the daughter of the Priest of Midian, why should he not also be allowed to take a Midianite woman?

The humble Moses was speechless. The meaning of his marriage with Tzipporah was too exalted to be explained in a public forum. Nobody could remember the halachah. In the consternation over this public scandal, the law was concealed from everyone's eyes. Everyone was weeping. The Prince of the tribe of Shimon was publicly flouting the prohibition against intermarriage by taking a Midianite princess into his tent, and political rectitude was saying "Let them". The aim was to open the floodgates to casual relations with people of all nations without discrimination, leading to intermarriage, assimilation and the erasing of all boundaries between holy and profane.

There is profound irony in this challenge to the authority of Moses, the Levite. It was Jacob's second-born, Shimon, who had joined his next younger brother, Levi, in the act of zealousness that earned them the anger of their father (Genesis Chapter 34, see ***Universal Torah*** -

Vayishlach). This was the vengeance on the inhabitants of Shechem for the kidnapping of their sister Dinah. The inhabitants of Shechem had agreed to become circumcised, but for the wrong reason: it was not the Covenant of Abraham that they wanted, but the Israelite girls.

The present challenge to the Covenant of Abraham came from the wicked Bilaam, who advised Balak, king of the Moabites, that the way to undermine the holiness of Israel was by enticing the Israeli boys with their girls, who would then pull out their idols and make the Israelites worship them. Ironically, in this test, the Prince of the tribe of Shimon uses his characteristic trait of ***Gevurah*** in zealous championship of complete personal freedom, challenging Moses' Levitical zeal for the Covenant -- which imposes restraints on the satisfaction of our physical appetites -- and Moses was speechless.

Only Pinchas remembered -- young Pinchas, the son of Elazar, who was now High Priest after his father, Aaron. Fear was keeping everyone else's mouths gagged as the true Israelite code of morality was publicly mocked. Pinchas himself was in a minority of one. He was in mortal danger of being publicly lynched for daring to challenge contemporary political rectitude. Even so, he courageously took up his spear, went straight into the tent after them and pierced the two of them in the act through their private parts, bringing them out thereafter on the spear to show everyone.

The law that Pinchas championed is stated clearly by ***Rambam*** (Maimonides) in his Code. "An Israelite who has marital relations with an idol-worshipper from one of the other peoples or an Israelite woman who has marital relations with an idol-worshipper are liable to 40 lashes by Torah law. The Torah forbids only marriage, but one who has casual relations with a non-Israelite is liable to the penalty of lashes by rabbinical decree because it leads to marriage. Anyone who has relations with an idol-worshipper, whether in the context of marriage or casually, if he performed the act publicly, i.e. in front of ten or more Israelites, ***if the zealous attack and kill him they are praiseworthy and valiant*** and this is a Law given to Moses on Sinai, and the proof is what Pinchas did to Zimri."

This particular law about zeal is hedged with numerous qualifications: the zealot may only strike them at the moment of the act. If the zealot came to the Rabbinic Court and asked permission to kill, they do not give such a ruling. (Mishneh Torah, Issurey Biyah, Forbidden Relationships ch. 12, 1-8).

It is forbidden to take the law into one's own hands. Only a person of the supreme purity and saintliness of Pinchas could do what he did. The point is not to legitimize killing, which has already gotten completely out of hand in the sad, bullet-torn, explosion-shattered world in which we live today. Far more important is to understand the actual severity of the crime for which the Torah allows a saint like Pinchas to single-handedly kill the perpetrators when this is absolutely necessary at that moment for the honor of G-d and the sanctity of the People of Israel. In the words of Rambam: "This practice (of casual relations and intermarriage) causes one to become attached to the idolaters, from whom the Holy One blessed be He has separated us, and to turn away from HaShem and betray Him" (ibid.)

Pinchas' valor lay in standing up for what is right and true even though it flew in the face of the prevailing orthodoxy, and he was in mortal danger of getting lynched. Pinchas did not flinch from stating the Torah law, even when it was unpopular, and for this he was given G-d's Covenant of Peace.

Our age is obsessed with the search for peace. How ironic that the more everyone runs after peace, the more it eludes us. Every plan that is supposed to bring peace seems to lead only to further strife and violence. Could it be that those who are so zealous for peace would be more effective if they were to apply their zeal to the search for G-d and His Torah? The authentic Israelite pathway to peace is recited daily at the end of the morning prayers: "Rabbi Elazar said in the name of Rabbi Chaninah: The students of the wise increase peace in the world, as it says: 'And all of your children are students of G-d, and great is the peace of your children'. Read the Hebrew word for children in that verse not as ***banecha***, 'your children', but as '***bonecha***', your ***builders***!' "The way to build true peace is through studying and keeping the Torah.

* * *

INHERITING THE LAND

Approaching the end of the forty-years in the Wilderness, the new generation of the Children of Israel stood assembled in the plains of Moab near the Jordan River, facing Jericho, poised to enter the Promised Land. The land was to be divided among those counted in the census that G-d now commanded Moses to take. As we approach the conclusion of the Book of Numbers and come towards the Book of Deuteronomy, the theme of the Land of Israel and how we are to live in it becomes increasingly prominent. One of the first lessons we learn is from the fact that the land is to be divided fairly among all the people. The vision is one of a nation of equal, independent homestead owners possessing family pride as opposed to one in which a minority of wealthy property-owners exploit and manipulate a migrant population lacking strong family roots, alienated and cut off from the land.

In Torah law, land is considered the best and surest property -- movables (let alone paper wealth) cannot compare. While sale and purchase of land takes up a sizeable part of Torah law, the sages counselled not to part with land whenever possible, and certainly not ancestral land. Land should be held and transferred from generation to generation. Our parshah introduces the Torah law of inheritance (see also Deuteronomy 21:16ff). The law was given by G-d to Moses in response to a question raised before him concerning inheritance by daughters. The question was raised by the daughters of Tzelaphchad, who had died of his own sin in the wilderness leaving no sons. They asked for their father's share of the land to be given to them so that his family name should not be diminished among his brothers.

The daughters of Tzelaphchad longed and yearned for the Land of Israel. They could not bear the thought that their family would not have a part and a share in the land.

In the words of the Midrash: "When the daughters of Tzelaphchad heard that the Land was to be divided among the males but not the females, they all gathered together to take counsel. They said, 'Not like the love of flesh and blood is the love of G-d. A person of flesh and blood has more love for the males than the females, but He who spoke and the world came into being is not that way. Males, females, His love is for all! As it is written: 'His love is over ***all*** His works' (Psalm 146)

The Midrash continues: "... Rabbi Nathan said.: The power of women is more beautiful than the power of men. The men said, 'Let us appoint a head and return to Egypt' (Numbers 14), but the women said, 'Give us a share of the land' (Numbers 27:4)."

* * *

THE MANTLE OF LEADERSHIP

Land may pass from father to son (or daughter) but leadership must pass not by inheritance (unless it is genuinely deserved) but from a true leader only to a true student. As we start to approach the end of the Torah, issues relating to the end of life (such as inheritance) are more to the fore. This is the case in our parshah, where Moses is instructed to ascend the mountain to see the Land for which he so yearned, after which he was to die.

Characteristically, Moses' first thought at that moment was not for himself but for those he would be leaving behind. "And Moses said to HaShem: Let HaShem, the G-d of the spirits of all flesh, appoint a man over the Assembly, who will go out before them and come in before them and who will bring them out and bring them in, and the Assembly of HaShem will not be like a flock that has no shepherd" (Numbers 27:15-17).

The appointment of Joshua as Moses' successor to lead the Children of Israel into the Land of Israel involves the mystery of ***semichah***, the "laying on of hands" whereby the Master gives Torah authority to the

Student. Joshua deserved this because of his assiduous devotion to Moses and his constant study of the Torah: "He had been Moses' attendant from his youth" (Numbers 11:28) "and his attendant Joshua the son of Nun was a lad who would not move outside the tent".

[Rabbi Nachman of Breslov explains the mystery of ***semichah*** and how the "hand" signifies the transfer of wisdom in Likutey Moharan Part I, Discourse 61 #2.]

* * *

"AND THE LAND WILL GIVE ITS PRODUCE"

Directly after the account of the appointment of Joshua to lead the Children of Israel into the Land, the Torah enters into a lengthy section detailing the sacrifices in the Temple every day, on Shabbat, on the New Moon and on each of the festivals throughout the year. The juxtaposition of the two sections is explained in the commentary of ***Ramban***, (Rabbi Moshe ben Nachman, Nachmanides). "Having said, 'Among these you shall divide up land', G-d completed the exposition of the law of the sacrifices that they should perform in the land."

There is an integral connection between the inheritance of the Land and bringing sacrifices to the Temple every day, every week, every month and on every festival. The Temple is at the very center of the land in all three dimensions of existence: time, space and soul. The souls of the people who inhabit the land must to be focussed on the Temple both in terms of time and space. In terms of time, they must be focussed on the Temple through the services that must be performed at specific junctures in time: in the morning and afternoon (times of the daily sacrifices), on the Sabbath, on the New Moon, and particularly on the three pilgrim festivals, when the whole nation must come up to Jerusalem.

Space is intimately bound up with these very services in the Temple at these various junctures in time. This is because the Temple services are centered on the produce of the Land. Our parshah details the various sacrifices of lambs, oxen, wheat, oil and wine on the Temple Altar daily, on Shabbat, the New Moon and all the Festivals. The regular offering of these token gifts culled from the produce of the Land elevates and brings blessing to all of the fruits of the Land.

Unique among the offerings on the Altar are those on the festival of Succot ("Tabernacles"). On the first day, the offerings included thirteen oxen, on the second day twelve, and so on. The total number of oxen offered on the seven days of the festival was seventy, corresponding to the seventy nations of the world, for whose blessing and welfare Israel is also charged with responsibility. It is our prayer that both Israel and the nations will quickly realize that peace and blessing will come only from the Temple services and not from empty peace plans.

On Succot even the humblest of all has its place on the Altar: water. The Midrash tells us that at the time of Creation, the waters cried out to G-d that everyone has a place on the Altar -- oxen, sheep, wheat, barley, oil, wine. All except for water. The waters threatened to engulf the world until G-d promised them that on the festival of Succot, Israel would offer a libation of humble water on the Altar, accompanied by ***Simchat Beit HaSho'eva***, "the Joy of the Water Drawing", which was so great that it brought people to prophecy.

The water libation on Succot is not written explicitly in the Torah but only allusively. Three seemingly minute anomalies in the Hebrew phrasing of the laws of the offerings of the second, sixth and seventh days of the festival of Succot, enable us to trace the letters of the word Hebrew word ***mayim*** -- ***water*** -- running through the Hebrew text (see Rashi on Numbers 29:18).

May we constantly drink the waters of the Torah, "and this book of the Torah will not move from your mouth, and you shall meditate in it day and night in order to guard and perform all that is written in it, for then you will have success in your paths and then you will be wise" (Joshua 1:8).

MATOT-MAS'EY

Torah Reading: MATOT: Numbers 30:2-32:42;
MAS'EY: Numbers 33:1-36:13.

Haftarah: Jeremiah 2:4-28; 3:4; 4:1-2

*W*e now complete our annual study of the book of ***Bamidbar*** (Numbers) by reading its two lengthy closing parshiyot, ***Matot*** and ***Mas'ey*** together. Some years each of these parshiyot is read on its own Shabbat, but in most years these two parshiyot are read on one Shabbat so as to ensure that we begin reading the book of ***Devarim*** (Deuteronomy), with its central theme of ***teshuvah*** -- coming home to G-d -- on the last Shabbat prior to the fast of the 9th of Av commemorating the destruction of the Holy Temple.

As discussed in earlier commentaries, Genesis is the "head" of the Torah, Exodus the "arms" (the "outstretched arm" of redemption), Leviticus the "heart", Numbers the "legs" (journeying through the wilderness to reach the Land) and Deuteronomy the "mouth", trumpeting forth: "Hear O Israel!" Coming at the end of the book of Numbers, these two parshiyot show us the Children of Israel at the end of their journeying in the wilderness, assembled in the plains of Moab, facing Jericho, poised to enter the Land. It was here that Moses delivered his final discourses, which make up the book of Deuteronomy. The various Messianic themes and allusions in this week's double parshah make them appropriate reading for the central Shabbat of the Three Week period of mourning for the lost Temples, which is a preparation for the Restoration quickly in our days. [***kinot***, "lamentations" = ***tikun***, "rectification.]

PARSHAT MATOT

The uniqueness of the prophecy of Moses is seen in the opening words of Parshat ***Matot*** introducing the laws of vows. "And Moses spoke to the heads of the tribes of the Children of Israel saying, '***This*** is the word that G-d has commanded.'" (Numbers 30:2). There are various levels of prophecy, which may come through "a clear glass" or through a "dim glass". The latter is the case in countless verses in the prophetic literature where the prophet says "***Ko*** -- So said HaShem", indicating that the words of the prophecy are ***like*** -- resemble -- the actual Truth, yet they are merely similar, an evocation of something that in itself is actually much higher. Moses himself also prophesied using the comparative expression ***Ko***, as in Exodus 11:4. However, as Rashi points out (in his comment on Numbers 30:2), unique among all the prophets, Moses also used the expression ***Zeh hadavar*** -- "***This*** is the word", the actual word of G-d. For Moses revealed the very ***pnimi'ut***, the "inner essence" of G-d, like no other prophet.

* * *

WORDS AND COMMITMENTS

An important theme in Parshat ***Matot*** is the care with which we must use words and language because of their very great power -- language is the "glass" that may either reflect or obscure the truth. "When a man wants to make a vow to HaShem or to swear an oath placing a prohibition upon himself, he must not profane his word. He must do according to all that comes forth from his mouth." (Numbers 30:3).

We live in an age when streams of verbiage flow forth at us in such quantities from all directions -- billboards, papers, magazines, TV, radio, Internet and on and on -- that we can easily become almost completely desensitized to words, their meaning and importance. We take it for granted that politicians make promises and undertakings which they have no intention of keeping; that "experts" shoot forth with torrents of instant comment which are as enduring as rotten fruit; that commercial advertising has turned the destruction of language into an art-form; that the media are filled with every kind of irreverence and unholiness.

As a medicine against this desensitization, the Torah asks us to think hard about the words we bring forth from our own mouths, and particularly the personal commitments we make. While we often focus on language as the means of communication with each other, with ourselves and with G-d, the concept of the vow is one where we use our G-d-given gift of speech to elevate ourselves spiritually. One might take a vow to dedicate something of worth to the Temple or charity, or to erect a personal boundary and abstain from some undesirable behavior that has proved a pitfall for oneself and others. The father of the vow was Jacob, when he came to Mount Moriah and had his dream of the ladder. In the morning, he set up a stone, the prototype Temple Altar, and vowed that if G-d would protect him and provide his needs, he would make this the House of G-d and tithe all he received (Genesis 28:20). [David the Messiah also swore and vowed he would not rest until he found a place and a dwelling-place for G-d, the Holy Temple -- Psalms 132:1-5.]

Because of the extreme seriousness of an oath or vow to G-d, the Torah Codes advise us not to take actual oaths or vows unless we are thoroughly conversant with the intricacies of their laws. Much of the discussion in the relevant Talmudic tractates of Nedarim, Nazir and Shevuot is bound up with careful analyses of the meanings and implications of different kinds of phraseology. The larger part of the section on vows in our parshah is taken up with special laws that apply to vows made by an unmarried, betrothed or married woman, which may be nullified by her father and/or husband. This is because vows she may make even with the best intentions could cause complications in her domestic life that might affect others (e.g. if she were to vow to abstain from certain foods or not to use cosmetics, etc.). Her freedom is circumscribed by her responsibilities to others, and the Torah gives her father and/or husband the last word on whether to uphold her vows. Indeed we should not make vows or commitments that can affect others detrimentally. The point is not to deter us from making commitments, but rather to impress upon us the care with which we should go about making them and the seriousness with which we must uphold them.

* * *

THE WAR AGAINST MIDIAN

It is significant that the final war fought by the Children of Israel prior to their entry into the land was the war for sexual morality -- to rectify the degradation of the sin of ***Baal Pe'or*** as described at the end of Parshat ***Balak***. The crafty Bilaam knew that sexual sin is the undoing of the holiness of Israel and the Midianites took his advice to entice the Israelites to take the short road from immorality to idolatry. The true holiness of the Land of Israel can be revealed only when the Land is cleansed of sexual immorality and degradation. [Similarly, Jacob went back to Beit El only after vengeance for the rape of Dinah and cleansing his house of idolatry, Genesis ch. 34-5.] It was to bring moral cleansing that 1000 warriors from each of the Twelve Tribes went out against the Midianites, together with Pinchas, who was weighed against all of them. Pinchas was the hero of moral cleansing ever since he killed the Prince of the Tribe of Shimon and his Midianite woman.

The warriors return from this war with war booty, which is documented in detail in our parshah. When we overcome the war against immorality, we can reclaim the lost booty -- the energy that was degraded to the level of the animal, and which can now be elevated and used in pursuit of the holy. However, what Israel takes from the nations must be purified. It was necessary to kill the Midianite males -- the concept of the active ***mashpia*** (source of influence) -- for the active immoral influence had to be destroyed. However, those women who had not "known" a male could be saved: that which is receptive to the Israelite influence can be reclaimed. The material wealth taken from the Midianites also had to be purified. A percentage had to be dedicated to the Temple, and even that which could be released for personal use had to be purified.

Our parshah is thus an important source for the laws of purification of vessels of metal, wood or other materials that had previously been in the possession of and used by non-Israelites (Numbers 31:21-4). "Every thing (literally, word) that can come into fire you must pass through the fire and it will be pure, but it must be purified with the waters of ***Niddah***, while all that cannot come into fire you must pass through the water." From this are derived the laws of kashering utensils that have absorbed forbidden substances, and the laws of immersing vessels in a kosher mikveh. Rabbi Nachman of Breslov (Likutey Moharan I:4) points to the esoteric meaning of these laws, which teach how to repent for our sins. If we sinfully took our holy powers and energies and burned them up in the fires of animal lust, we must take "what came into fire" and "pass it through the fire". We must repent by confessing our sins with words of fire, burning them up with holy intensity, the fire of our passion to now rectify and elevate our energies. And so too, the pure waters of the Torah, the mikveh, purify the vessel, the body.

* * *

THE SONS OF REUVEN AND GAD'S CONDITION

Following the war with Midian, the account of the request of the tribes of Reuven and Gad to take their share of the Land in the conquered territories ***east*** of the River Jordan and Moses' response is written Torah proof of the Children of Israel's possession of these territories in the true "final settlement".

Were the Sons of Reuven and Gad really more interested in pasture-lands for their cattle than having a share in the Promised Land? The Aramaic Targum of Onkelos reveals what is concealed beneath the Torah verse detailing the locations east of the Jordan upon which the Sons of Reuven and Gad had set their eyes. These include ***Mount Nevo***, which the Targum informs us is the burial-place of Moses (Numbers 32:3). That was what the sons of Reuven and Gad had set their eyes on. They already knew what Breslovers know about the grave of Rabbi Nachman, what Lubavitchers have learned about the Ohel of the Rebbe, what those who frequent Rabbi Shimon bar Yochai's gravesite in Meiron or the resting place of the Avot (Patriarchs) in the holy city of Chevron know. The greatest true wealth is our connection with the Tzaddikim who are the true Foundations of the Universe. The graves of the true Tzaddikim are points where the physical interconnects with the spiritual, and where we can make a connection with G-d's truth.

Even so, Moses scolded the Sons of Reuven and Gad for wanting to stay out of the Land, suggesting that they were like the Spies whose perverted use of language led the hearts of the Israelites astray. Coming after the laws of purified language -- vows and oaths -- at the beginning of our parshah, Moses' binding of the Sons of Reuven and Gad with a detailed set of conditions is another lesson in the precision with which we must use language. We have to make commitments, and we have to keep them. We must take care with the way we formulate our commitments, and care to carry them out.

The Sons of Reuven and Gad were committed to supporting their brother Israelites in conquering the Land. This should serve as a model for those who reside outside the Land, whose share in the Land is strengthened by giving support to those who live in it and fight the war there every day.

Parshat ***Matot*** concludes with a detailed account of the territories given by Moses to the tribes of Reuven, Gad and half of Menasheh east of the River Jordan. These include all of the mountain and valley areas from north of the River Arnon, which flows into Yam HaMelach (the "Dead" Sea) up to Chavot Yair, which are the lands south east of the Kinneret (Sea of Galilee).

* * *

PARSHAT MAS'EY

Already in ***Matot*** when Moses castigated the Sons of Reuven and Gad with being like the Ten Spies, the theme of Moses' reproof enters the Torah, and it continues in ***Mas'ey*** and in the book of Deuteronomy. After the events of the forty years wandering, which we have studied in Exodus, Leviticus and Numbers, the time has come to begin to review the lessons and reduce them to their essentials.

Mas'ey begins with a review of the forty years wandering. On the surface, the list of encampments and journeyings seems prosaic. However, the second Targum on the Torah, that of Rabbi Yonatan ben

Uziel, disciple of Hillel, fills in much of the moral significance of the different staging posts in those difficult years, showing that the list itself is a form of reproof. It teaches us that there are times when we must look back, review and draw conclusions and lessons from the past. This is particularly necessary when we stand on the brink of new challenges, as in the case of the Children of Israel, who stood poised to conquer the Land.

Included in the account of the wanderings is a reference to the death of Aaron the High Priest, specifying the date of his ascent to the mountain to die -- the first day of the fifth month, which is the month of Av. This is a reminder to us that the present year is beginning to draw to a close, with only two months to go before the Day of Judgment, Rosh HaShanah, the New Year. As we proceed in the period of Repentance (the Three Weeks, followed by Elul and Tishri) we should take time to review our lives and reflect on where we are trying to go. This way we will be prepared for the challenges of the coming year -- the Conquest of the Land.

* * *

THE BOUNDARIES OF THE LAND AND ITS CONQUEST

Parshat ***Mas'ey*** provides the detailed topography of the boundaries of the Land of Israel, prefixed by G-d's commandment to the Children of Israel to destroy all the evil influences in the Land to make it a place fit for the exalted mission instituted by the Fathers of the World, Abraham, Isaac and Jacob. For Israel, with Jerusalem at its center and its eternal capital, is to be the source of Torah and Light for all the nations. "For the Torah will go forth from Zion and the Word of HaShem from Yerushalayim". The Torah warns clearly that unless all the evil influences are removed from the Land, they will be "like pins in your eyes and thorns in your sides, and they will persecute you over the land in which you are dwelling" (Numbers 33:55).

The Boundaries of the Land are given as a ***commandment*** (Numbers 34:2). While nobody doubts that the true Land of Israel includes all the territories west of the River Jordan, few are aware of where the southern and northern border of the biblical Promised Land actually are.

The final settlement of Israel as prophesied by Ezekiel is shown in Atlas Da'at Mikra published by Mossad HaRav Kook in Jerusalem (p.325). Ezekiel's vision completely defies all present-day conceptions in the mass media of the settlement Israel should accept, showing that the true boundaries of the Land stretch from the eastern arm of the Nile delta up to the Turkish city of Antakya (Antioch) north of 36 degrees Lat. N. The mountain spur above Antakya is ***Hor Ha-Har***, Mount Hor mentioned in Numbers 34:8 as the northern point of Israel's Mediterranean border. Any "settlement" that does not take this into account is doomed to failure, for "G-d's counsel is what will stand" (Proverbs 19:21).

Of course the Land will only become Israel's without contest when Israel will fulfill its part of the Conditions of G-d's Covenant to give them the Land. (The section in ***Matot*** about the Conditions with which Moses bound the Sons of Reuven and Gad is also a lesson about Conditions, to which Moses returns again and again in his discourses in Deuteronomy: "If you will do this, and if you will not.")

* * *

THE LEVITICAL CITIES AND THE CITIES OF REFUGE

Since the Levites did not have a share in the Land, they were given forty-two cities of their own up and down the Land together with all the necessary surrounding areas. The Levitical Cities indicate the distinctive nature of the Land of Israel in contrast to all other lands. Its social geography is centered upon a network of cities where people are free from the immediate requirement to make a living (the Levites received tithes) in order to devote themselves to the study and teaching of G-d's Law. Thus everyone in the Land is always near a center of study and near to someone they can ask for guidance.

The Torah's abhorrence for killing and murder is expressed in the portion that gives the laws of unintentional manslaughter and deliberate murder (Numbers 35:9ff). Not only has our world become desensitized to language, as discussed above. It has also been desensitized to the evil of killing and murder, which are openly celebrated be terrorists as "religious acts", while the TV and movies provide an endless diet of violence to the population.

The spilling of blood is a crime against the Land, and the holiness of the Land of Israel will only shine again when we can cleanse ourselves of this terrible scourge and re-establish the Law of the Torah, which outshines and transcends all manmade laws. The Torah not only teaches the evil of killing and murder but has no compunction about imposing all necessary sanctions in order to eliminate them, including the death penalty. Even one who had committed an unintentional manslaughter had to hide himself away from the rest of society in a city of refuge, unlike today, where killers with blood on their hands are released from jail and celebrated as heroes.

"And you shall not pollute the Land in which you dwell that I dwell in its midst, for I am HaShem dwelling among the Children of Israel" (Numbers 35:34). Speedily in our days. Amen.

CHAZAK! CHAZAK! VE-NIT'CHAZEK!

“Be strong! Be strong – and we will be strong!”

דברים

DEUTERONOMY

DEVARIM

Torah Reading: Deuteronomy 1:1-3:22

Haftarah: Isaiah 1:1-27.

THE BOTTOM LINE

*A*s always, we commence the reading of the Book of ***Devarim*** (Deuteronomy), the last of the Five Books of Moses, on the Shabbat preceding the fast of Tisha Be'Av (the 9th of Av) commemorating the destruction of the Holy Temple. Tisha Be'Av is a call to Teshuvah (repentance), setting us on course for the season of Teshuvah during the months of Av and especially Elul, in preparation for the coming New Year and the Days of Awe. Our study of ***Devarim*** will continue for the whole of this period, until we conclude the annual cycle of the Torah reading at the end of the festival of Succot, on Simchat Torah.

The themes of ***Devarim*** are appropriate for this period. The Book of ***Devarim*** is the Torah's "mouth", summarizing all that has gone before in the "main body" of the Torah. ***Devarim*** calls to the inner ear of the soul of Israel to hear the essential message of the Torah. Each of the twelve months of the year is integrally connected with one of the twelve tribes and one of the twelve basic human faculties (Sefer Yetzirah). The month of Av corresponds to the Tribe of Shimon and the faculty of hearing (see Genesis 29:33). It is significant that the phrase "***Shema Yisrael***! Hear, O Israel" recurs in four key passages in the book of ***Devarim***. The message is that we must "Hear the words of the wise!" (Proverbs 22:17). "These are the words (***Devarim***) which Moses spoke." (Deut. 1:1) -- "***Sof davar***, the last word, after everything has been heard: fear G-d" (Kohelet 12:13).

We find in the opening verses of our parshah that Moses began the concluding discourses of his career "in the fortieth year, in the eleventh month on the first of the month" (Deut. 1:3). This was on the first day of the month of Shevat (Jan.-Feb.), thirty-seven days before Moses ascended Mount Nevo to gaze over the Land of Israel and leave the world on the 7th of Adar. Each of the six winter months is thematically connected with its corresponding summer month. Just as Shevat, fifth of the winter months, is the eleventh month of the year counting from Nissan, so the month of Av, fifth of the summer months, is the eleventh month of the year counting from Tishrei. The months of Shevat and Av are particularly propitious for deeper understanding of the Torah, and it is therefore fitting that Moses' concluding discourses, delivered in the month of Shevat, are the focus of our Torah study during the month of Av.

Moses' concluding discourses constitute a Covenant which he struck between G-d and Israel in the Plains of Moab, just as he had struck a Covenant between G-d and Israel at Sinai forty years earlier (see Deut. 28:69). At the end of the forty years wandering in the wilderness, Moses was now the undisputed leader of Israel. The rebellious generation of the Exodus had all died in the wilderness, to be replaced by the new generation that stood before him now, poised to enter the land under Joshua. All the challenges to Moses leadership -- the Golden Calf, the sin of the Ten Spies, the rebellion of Korach, the sin of Baal Pe'or, etc. -- had been overcome and were now part of history. In ***Devarim***, Moses again and again returns to this history, in order to draw out its lessons for the future.

Thus the opening verse of our parshah of ***Devarim*** appears on the surface to give the location in which Moses delivered his discourse. However, since the various locations mentioned in the verse are all somewhat different, they are construed by the Aramaic Targum and biblical commentators as being a series of allusions to the various sins of the past and the lessons that were to be learned from them (see Rashi on Deut. 1:1). It is with this veiled reproof to the nation that Moses began his final task as leader: to forge the thousands and thousands of Israel -- who were "like the stars of the heavens for a multitude" (Deut. 1:10) -- into a single, unified, purposeful nation that would be worthy of entering the land promised to Abraham and inheriting it for eternity. Thus it is that the book of Deuteronomy begins with reproof but ends with blessing -- "And this is the blessing which Moses, man of G-d, blessed the Children of Israel before his death. Happy are you, Israel! Who is like you, a people saved by HaShem? ...Your enemies will waste away for you, and you will tread upon their high places" (Deut. ch. 33 v. 1 & v. 29).

Throughout Deuteronomy, Moses repeatedly addresses the people by the name of Israel. Not only does the name Israel carry the connotation of victory, "...for you have struggled with G-d and with men, and you have prevailed" (Gen. 32:28). The letters of the name Israel also include the word ***yashar***, "straight", "upright". This is even more explicit in the other biblical name for the Hosts of Israel - ***Yeshurun*** (Deut. 32:15; 33:26). The names Israel and Yeshurun indicate that when the people are united and purposeful under the sole, unchallenged leadership of Moses, the archetypal Tzaddik, they are the epitome of order and rectification. (Kabbalistically, ***Yosher***, the "upright" scheme of the Sefirot, indicates order and repair, as opposed to ***Igulim***, the "circular" scheme, indicating repeated cycles of disrepair and chaos.)

Since the issue of leadership is so crucial, it is the first raised by Moses in his discourses, after recounting how G-d had told him to leave Mount Sinai and begin the journey to the Land of Israel. It was far from easy to lead a people as fractious and argumentative as this. In order for Moses' leadership to permeate to all levels of the people, it was necessary to establish a hierarchical system of "captains of thousands and captains of hundreds, captains of fifties and captains of tens, and police". The verses in our parshah defining the necessary qualities of the people's leaders and judges and explaining how they are to adjudicate (Deut. 1:13-17) constitute the main foundation of the Torah laws of judges and judicial procedure. These deserve particular attention today, when the absence of leadership of true integrity and caliber is the bane of all our lives.

* * *

HISTORY AND PREHISTORY

Moses' discourse in Parshat ***Devarim*** covers some of the key events in the forty years wandering in the Wilderness and the lessons to be derived from them. These include the Sin of the Ten Spies, which is of particular relevance to us this week as we approach Tisha Be'Av, since this is not only the anniversary of the destruction of the Temple but also of the evil report given by the spies in the Wilderness, the ultimate cause of the destruction of the Temple. Similarly, the rectification of ***lashon hara***, evil speech, is one of the main preconditions for the rebuilding of the Temple.

Moses' historical survey retraces the final stages of the journey of the Children of Israel to the Land, including their circuiting of the lands of the Edomites, the Moabites and the Ammonites and their conquest of Sichon king of the Emorites and Og king of Bashan. The original narrative of these journeys and conquests was given in the later parshiyot of the book of ***Bamidbar*** (Numbers) -- ***Chukat***, ***Matot*** and ***Mas'ey***.

The Children of Israel were forbidden to try to conquer the territories of the Edomites, the Moabites and the Ammonites. These three territories were among the ten promised to Abraham (together with those of the seven Canaanite nations), but they were forbidden to the Children of Israel (until in time to come) because they were already in the hands of Abraham's descendants or associates. The Edomites were the children of Esau, Abraham's grandson, while the Moabites and Ammonites were the descendants of the daughters of Lot. Lot had been rewarded with these territories because of his loyalty to Abraham in Egypt by not revealing that Sarah was Abraham's wife (Genesis ch. 12).

Moses introduces some prehistory into his historical account by explaining how the Edomites, Moabites and Ammonites conquered their respective territories from the frightening prehistoric giants who inhabited them previously. For: " 'He explains the power of His works to His people give them the inheritance of the nations' (Psalm 111:6) -- for if the nations of the world say to Israel, 'You are robbers because you have conquered the lands of seven peoples,' they can reply to them: 'All the earth belongs to the Holy One, blessed be He; He created it and gave it to whom he saw fit. When he wanted, He gave it to them, and when he wanted, he took it from them and gave it to us' " (Rashi on Genesis 1:1).

Kabbalistically, the Seven Canaanite Nations correspond to the broken vessels of the seven lower Sefirot (from ***Chessed*** down to ***Malchut***). The conquest of the Land of the Canaanites and its transformation into the Land of Israel parallels the rectification of these seven broken vessels (***Igulim***) and their reconstitution in "upright" form, ***Yosher*** = Israel. The territories of Seir, Moab and Ammon correspond respectively to the three upper Sefirot of Keter, Chochmah and Binah. These will become the inheritance of the true heirs of Abraham in time to come, when the cycle is complete and the world attains perfect rectification.

The Land of Israel was given to Abraham as part of the Covenant. The sign of the Covenant is ***Brit Milah***, the circumcision, in which the foreskin is cut off and the membrane over the organ peeled away, signifying the peeling off and removal of the husks of evil that conceal holiness. In order to conquer the Land of Israel, it was first necessary to conquer the two giant kings who were the main bulwarks of the Canaanites: Sichon king of the Emorites and Og king of Bashan. Sichon corresponds to the foreskin, while Og corresponds to the membrane (Ari). The removal of these "gigantic" evil husks could be accomplished only by Moses, King of Israel: "And there was a king in Yeshurun, when the heads of the people gathered, the tribes of Israel together" (Deut. 33:5).

"All that HaShem your God did to these two kings, so HaShem will do to all the kingdoms to which you are passing over. Do not fear them, for HaShem your G-d, He will fight for you!" (Deut. 3:21-2).

May we see the rebuilding of the Temple quickly in our times!

VA'ETCHANAN

Torah Reading: Deuteronomy 3:23-7:11.

Haftarah: Isaiah 40:1-26.

"AND I TRIED TO INGRATIATE MYSELF."

*I*n the opening word of our parshah of ***Va'etchanan***, Moses tells how "I tried to ingratiate myself" with G-d -- elicit His favor -- praying repeatedly to be allowed to enter the land of Israel, "Eretz HaTzvi", the "Land of Beauty, the graceful gazelle", and come to the place of the Holy Temple. The Midrash teaches that in order to try to revoke the decree against his entry to the land, Moses prayed no less than 515 prayers -- corresponding to the gematria (numerical value) of the word ***Va'etchanan***. The root of this word is ***chein***, meaning the "grace" that is bestowed by G-d as a gift of pure love and kindness. The grammatical form of the word is ***hitpa'el*** - reflexive: the person praying must ***work*** on himself or herself in order to become open to that gift. The parshah is a call to us to the inner work that must be combined with our Torah study: the work in our heart and soul to open ourselves to G-d's grace -- through meditation, contemplation, prayer and refinement of our traits. We must try and try again and again!!!

Parshat ***Va'etchanan***, is always read on this, the Shabbat of comfort after the fast of Tisha Be'Av – ***Shabbat Nachamu*** (so-called after the opening words of the Haftarah). Having mourned past destruction and ruin on Tisha Be'Av, it is now time to put the past behind us. We must bind up our wounds and embark on the work of rebuilding and reconstruction during the coming days of Teshuvah in the months of Av and Elul, leading up to the New Year and Days of Awe. To initiate this period, many Bnei Torah have the custom of taking trips away from the city in order to able to broaden their horizons, gaze at the sky, the hills, the sea and G-d's other wonders for the sake of physical and spiritual reinvigoration.

Parshat ***Va'etchanan*** provides us with spiritual sustenance for this reinvigoration process, giving us the very foundations of our faith in the One, Unified, Incorporeal G-d. In some of the most sublime passages in the Bible, Moses evokes the awesome greatness of G-d, the greatness of Israel, His chosen people, the preciousness of the Land of Israel, and the love and fear of G-d. Moses takes us again through the fearsomeness of the Giving of the Torah, and teaches us our basic declaration of faith, repeated twice daily: ***Shema Yisrael***, ***HaShem Elokenu HaShem Echad***. Many other phrases from our present parshah are also incorporated into the regular set prayers in the Siddur.

* * *

REPAIR AND RECONSTRUCTION

At the center of the parshah are the second telling of the Giving of the Torah at Sinai and the Ten Commandments. In the annual cycle of the Torah reading, we read about the Giving of the Torah once in Parshat ***Yitro*** close to the 15th of Shevat (January-February), and a second time, half a year later in ***Va'etchanan***, which is always read close to the 15th of Av. The account in ***Yitro*** is also read on the anniversary of the Giving of the Torah, on the festival of Shavuot. In this way, we return at regular intervals to the birth experience of the soul of Israel. The mid-point of the months of Shevat and Av are times when our souls begin to ready themselves for actual rebirth forty-five days later in Nissan (Pesach, physical rebirth) and Tishri (High Holidays, Succot, spiritual rebirth).

The difference between the accounts of the Giving of the Torah in ***Yitro*** and ***Va'etchanan*** is the difference between "before the sin" and "after the sin". The account in ***Yitro*** comes in the days of innocent exuberance after the Exodus from Egypt, before the fall -- the worship of the Golden Calf. The account in ***Va'etchanan*** comes long after sin of the Golden Calf, after the deaths of Nadav and Avihu (***Shemini***, Leviticus ch. 10), after the "Graves of Lust", the sin of the spies, the rebellion of Korach and the other sins and rebellions recounted in the Book of Numbers. We are older in more ways than one. With the passage of time, we may have fallen into bad ways. In ***Va'etchanan*** we come back to basics again, the Giving of the Torah and the Ten Commandments -- this time with the purpose of learning how to ***re-*** build and ***re***-construct, even after destruction and ruin.

* * *

STAY YOUNG

We cannot avoid getting older physically, but spiritually we must try to stay young -- for the wiser and more advanced we are spiritually, the closer we should be to G-d's endless, never-exhausted fountain of vitality and grace. "It is not good to be old," cried Rabbi Nachman. "There are pious and righteous elders, but to be old is not good. You must remain young, renewing yourself each day and making a fresh start" (Rabbi Nachman's Wisdom #51).

The journey back to the basics and retelling of the Giving of the Torah in ***Va'etchanan*** come to rectify the sin of becoming old spiritually, which is the main cause of destruction and exile. This sin is so serious that the analysis of its roots, given in our parshah (Deut. 4:25-40), forms the Torah reading of reproof in the synagogue on Tisha Be'Av. "When you give birth to children and children's children and ***you grow old in the land*** and you ***corrupt***."

New converts and returnees who have come to the Torah from far away, with all the excitement and enthusiasm of spiritual discovery, are often shocked and deeply disturbed to find old and seemingly tired communities whose observance of the commandments looks habitual, stale and devoid of inner meaning. Similarly, newcomers to present-day Israel who came in search of the Holy Land are often shocked by the rampant unholiness and corruption they encounter.

The Torah indeed gives us to understand that one of the main hazards of a tradition handed down from generation to generation is that the enthusiasm of the pioneers becomes ossified and encrusted in forms that often alienate people and drive them away. Corruption sets in, leading to the idolatry and evil that are the very opposite of the Torah.

This is the root cause of the exile, leading to the scattering of Israel among the nations.

And yet -- "***even from there, if you seek out HaShem your G-d, you will find Him, if you search Him out with all your heart and all your soul***. In your time of trouble, when all these things find you at the end of days. And you will return to HaShem your G-d and listen to His voice" (Deuteronomy 4:29-30).

The voice we must listen to is the authentic voice of revival and regeneration emitting from outstanding Tzaddikim like the Baal Shem Tov and Rabbi Nachman, who broke free of the encrusted obfuscation of spiritual old-age in order to bring us back to the basics -- the love and awe of G-d that must fire our service.

New enthusiasts should try to judge long-time practitioners favorably. It is far from easy to maintain consistent, energetic service of G-d for years on end, day after day praying the set prayers and practicing the rituals while facing the endless pressures of making a living, bringing up families, etc. in a troubled world where we seem to see no clear sign of Redemption.

Precisely because it is so easy to fall, Moses exhorts us again and again not to allow ourselves to grow old, not to forget, not to go astray. The regular return to the basics -- reading a second time about the Giving of the Torah from a new angle, re-reading the Ten Commandments -- comes to teach us that we must constantly strive to renew ourselves and keep things fresh. "And let these things that I am commanding you ***today*** be on your heart" -- "They should not be in your eyes like an old edict that nobody minds, but like a new one that everyone runs to read" (Deut. 6:6 and Rashi ad loc.).

* * *

TEACH THEM TO YOUR CHILDREN

The greatest challenge for Israel is to hand on not only the outer forms of the Torah but its inner fire to the coming generations. Each of the three founding fathers, Abraham, Isaac and Jacob, strove to inculcate the knowledge of G-d in his children. ***Va'etchanan*** returns repeatedly to the importance of teaching children and inculcating genuine faith in them -- another task that is far from easy. "And you shall teach them diligently to your children." (Deut. 6:7). "When your son asks you in the future, saying 'What are the testimonies, the statutes and the laws that HaShem our G-d has commanded you?' And you shall say to him." (Deut. 6:20).

The Torah's answer to the new generation, given in the ensuing verses, forms the foundation of the Haggadah recited at the Pesach Seder table. In essence, the answer is that there is such a thing as slavery, and that only G-d has the power to release us from it -- for our good -- through the observance of His unique commandments.

Slavery may not be only physical. Today, the most prevalent form of slavery is the mental slavery of those enmeshed and ensnared in secular "culture" which encourages the pursuit of everything except G-d and His truth. At the end of Parshat ***Va'etchanan***, the Torah warns strongly that we must recognize idols for what they are and destroy them. (When we are powerless to destroy the idols of the outside world, we can at least destroy them in our own minds.) The Torah teaches the maintenance of strict separation from idol-worshippers. "For you are a holy people to HaShem your G-d, He chose ***you*** to be a treasured people from all the peoples on the face of the earth… And you shall know that HaShem your G-d is the G-d, the faithful Power, guarding the Covenant and kindness to those who love Him and observe His commandments to the thousandth generation." (Deut. 7:6 & 9).

EIKEV

Torah Reading: Deuteronomy 7:12-11:25.

Haftarah: Isaiah 49:14-51:3.

THE BOOK AND THE SWORD; THE LOAF AND THE STICK

The Midrash on Parshat ***Eikev*** teaches: "The Book and the Sword descended from heaven entwined together; the Loaf and the Rod descended from heaven entwined together" (Sifri). The Book -- the Torah -- brings blessing to the world if we observe it; but if not, a Sword is attached that wreaks the vengeance of the Covenant. The Loaf of Bread, the "staff of life", is given as G-d's blessing when we keep the Torah, but if we stray, the struggles of making a living can turn into a painful rod of punishment.

This Midrash expresses the conditional nature of G-d's Covenant with Israel, a central theme in Eikev and one that appears with increasing emphasis as we advance through Deuteronomy. Eikev begins with the rich blessings and benefits that are the reward for keeping the laws of the Torah. Yet in the course of the parshah, Moses brings out in numerous different ways that these blessings and benefits may not be taken for granted: long-term possession of the Land of Israel and enjoyment of its blessings are strictly contingent upon proper observance of the Covenant on our part. This is clearly stated at the climax of the parshah (Deuteronomy 11:13-21), recited every day, night and morning, as the second paragraph of the ***Shema***. "If you will surely listen. I will give the rain of your land in its time. and you will eat and be satisfied. But if you go astray. you will quickly be lost from the good land that HaShem is giving you."

G-d wants that the benefits and blessings should truly be ours -- that we should have them not as a free gift which the recipient does not appreciate and which embarrasses him, but rather as something we have earned through our own efforts in the face of challenges and difficulties. G-d therefore sends many trials in life, and sometimes takes us through the very wilderness "in order to chastise you, to test you, to know what is in your heart and whether you will observe His commandments or not" (Deut. 8:2). We are here to learn a deep lesson that we have to know not just in our minds but within our very hearts. The lesson is, "that just as a man chastises his son [out of love] so HaShem your G-d chastises you" (ibid. 4:5). We have to learn and know in our hearts that any suffering we endure and all the obstacles in our path are sent not because G-d wants to throw us down but rather because He wants us to strive harder to get up, in order to come to greater good.

* * *

THE BLESSED LAND

The ultimate state of benefit and goodness is expressed in the Torah as Israel living securely in their own land "from the river to the sea" (Deut. 11:24), observing the Torah and enjoying all the blessings of the land. The rectified Land of Israel of this world is to be the earthly replica of the essential Land of Israel, which is the Land of the Living inherited forever by the meek and righteous in the World to Come.

Nowhere in the Torah is there greater praise of the holy Land of Israel than throughout our parshah of Eikev. It is "a good land, a land of streams of water, springs and deep sources emerging in the valleys and in the mountains. A land of wheat and barley and vines and fig trees and pomegranates, a land of oily olives and date-honey. A land in which you will eat bread not in poverty -- you will not lack anything in it: it is a land whose stones are iron and from whose mountains you will hew copper. And you will eat and be satisfied and bless HaShem your G-d over the good land He has given you" (Deut. 8:7-10).

"For the land to which you are coming in order to inherit it is not like the land of Egypt which you left, where you sow your seed and water the land on foot like a vegetable garden. But the land that you are passing over to inherit is a land of mountains and valleys; it drinks water according to the rain of the heavens. It is a land that HaShem your G-d seeks; the eyes of HaShem your G-d are always on it from the beginning of the year to the end of the year" (Deut. 11:10-12).

The actual country of Israel is one of exquisite beauty and grace, with its ever-changing landscape of mountains, hills and valleys and plains. The entire country is a tiny part of the entire earth, yet nothing is lacking, from the ski slopes of Mount Hermon to the arid Negev desert. The seven fruits for which Israel is particularly praised are all of exceptional nutritional value as well as providing numerous other benefits. Almost every other conceivable variety of fruits, vegetables and spices also grows somewhere in Israel. Why so many different species all grow so well in this tiny land is explained in the Midrash, which teaches that subterranean energy channels emanate from the "Foundation Stone" on the Temple Mount, the source of all creation, spreading throughout Israel, and fanning out from there to all parts of the world. Each channel has the power to stimulate a particular species. If people knew the exact location of these subterranean channels, they would be able to grow any kind of tree or plant they wanted (Kohelet Rabbah 2:7; see Rabbi Nachman's Wisdom p. 167).

The key difference between Israel and Egypt, which represents all other lands, lies in the water economy, which is the key to agriculture and therefore to the whole economy. In Egypt, the main source of water is the Nile, whose annual rise is one of the fixed regularities of nature. For the farmer in Egypt, making a living is less of a trial of faith. He knows when the river can be expected to rise, and he knows it is up to him to put in the "foot-work", carrying water from field to field to irrigate his crops so as to produce food. It is easy for him to come to believe that everything works according to the laws of nature, and that his own "foot-work" (operating the natural causes) is what "produces" his food and livelihood.

Israel's precarious dependence on rain from heaven for its water supply makes it harder to fall into the error of believing that we single-handedly "produce" our own livelihood through our own material efforts. We depend on G-d. No matter how efficiently we till our fields, if the rains don't come from heaven, we will not be able to produce anything. The rainfall in the Land of Israel is temperamental! Whether the rains fall sparsely or in abundance does not depend on anything we can do on the material plane. Rather, it represents G-d's response to our efforts on the moral and spiritual planes of our lives. The rainfall and everything else in Israel are subject to G-d's direct supervision in every detail, and thus, "the eyes of HaShem your G-d are always on it from the beginning of the year to the end of the year".

The purpose of being in the Land of Israel is to live in a state of closeness and interactivity with G-d, understanding that in everything we do in this world we are "partners" with Him. We are here to earn the goodness we enjoy through our own efforts, but we must understand that our efforts can only succeed when they are in alignment with His will as expressed in the Torah. It is a dangerous sin to believe that "my power and the strength of my hand have made for me all this prosperity" (Deut. 8:17). On the contrary, it is necessary to remember always that "It is He who gives you the power to produce prosperity" (ibid. v.18).

* * *

WHAT DOES G-D ASK OF YOU?

In Parshat Eikev one of the main focuses of Moses' reproof is the sin of the Golden Calf. This represents the exact opposite of the relationship with wealth and prosperity that G-d wants in the rectified Land of Israel. The sin of the Golden Calf represents the pursuit of material prosperity and pleasure for their own sake. Putting their own strength, power and pleasure at the center of the world drives men into forgetfulness: man forgets G-d.

G-d wants man to be blessed with material wealth not for its own sake, but because when his needs are provided he can better devote himself to the pursuit of the knowledge of G-d and His Torah. In the rectified Land of Israel, prosperity leads to... "And you shall eat and be satisfied and bless HaShem your G-d" (Deut. 8:10).

This verse contains the commandment to bless G-d after eating, from which the sages also derived the obligation to bless Him before eating or partaking of other material pleasures. The blessing before and after eating elevates it from the level of a mere physical function to an act of service that brings us closer to G-d by enhancing our awareness of His hand in providing our livelihood.

The essence of what G-d asks of us, as expressed in our parshah, is to seek awareness and knowledge of G-d in all the different aspects of our lives. "And now, Israel, what (***mah***) does HaShem your G-d ask of you except to revere HaShem your G-d, to go in all His ways, to love Him and to serve HaShem your G-d with all your heart and with all your soul" (Deut. 10:12).

The Rabbis taught that what G-d asks of us -- ***mah*** -- is actually ***me'ah***, "one hundred", alluding to the one hundred blessings that make up the daily order of our prayers (the morning blessings, the blessings before and after food and the thrice-repeated 18 blessings of the Amidah standing prayer). By regularly blessing G-d throughout the day and praying to Him for all the different specifics in our lives, we heighten our consciousness of His active involvement in every area of our lives. This is how we overcome "forgetfulness".

RE'EH

Torah Reading: Deuteronomy 11:26-16:17.

Haftarah: Isaiah 54:11-55:5.

AND YOU SHALL CHOOSE LIFE

"*S*ee: I am setting before you today a blessing and a curse." (Deut. 11:26). Moses asks us to see and understand the most important fact about our existential condition: that we are free. Each of us is placed within a unique matrix of circumstances that set the overall parameters of our lives. Yet within those parameters, we are constantly faced with options and divergent pathways, and our task is to choose between them. Our freedom is a trial because while we may see (or imagine we see) where we want a given pathway to take us in the short-term, as time-bound humans we can never know the long-term consequences of our choices at the moment we actually make those choices.

Only G-d has perfect knowledge of all the short-term and long-term consequences of the options that face us. While He gives us the freedom to make our own choices, He offers us guidance based upon His knowledge. Thus the Zohar calls the commandments of the Torah "advice". Each commandment is advice about which turn to take at each juncture in the road of life. Nothing compels us to follow the commandments: if there were any compulsion, we would not be free. G-d wants us to have the merit of choosing our destiny for ourselves -- He wants us to see and understand for ourselves, and to make wise choices. "***See***: I am setting before you a blessing and a curse". "...And you shall choose ***life***". (Deut. 30:19).

Moses was addressing the Children of Israel in the plains of Moab, where they were poised to enter the Promised Land under Joshua. Moses instructed them to perform a powerfully striking ceremony on entry into the Land. This was designed to imprint deeply in the consciousness of the nation the terms on which they would possess the

Land. Six of the twelve tribes were to stand on Mount Gerizim and six on Mount Eival, while the Priests and Levites were to stand in the valley between them chanting a list of fundamental Torah prohibitions, blessing those who observe them and cursing those who violate them. (The actual performance of the ceremony is described in Joshua chapter 8.)

Our parshah of ***Re'eh*** opens with the beginning of Moses' instructions about this ceremony (Deut. 11:26-32). Further instructions and the text of the chant are given four parshiyot later in ***Ki Tavo*** (Deut. 27:11-26. Thus we find that the main body of the book of Deuteronomy is "sandwiched" between the beginning of Moses' instructions for the ceremony of blessings and curses at the start of ***Re'eh*** and his further instructions for the ceremony given in the middle of ***Ki Tavo***. The main body of Deuteronomy is made up of the detailed commandments in many different areas of life contained in the parshiyot we read on this Shabbat and for the next three weeks.

The remainder of Parshat ***Re'eh***, the whole of Parshiyot ***Shoftim*** and ***Ki Teitzei*** and the first part of ***Ki Tavo*** thus constitute the "repetition of the law" that gives the book of Deuteronomy its name. In Torah literature, this book is called ***Mishneh Torah***, "the repetition of the law", while the Greek words that make up the name Deuteronomy mean exactly the same -- the repetition of, or second law. It is not that this law is any different from the code of Exodus (as set forth in Parshat ***Mishpatim***) or that of Leviticus (set forth in Parshat ***Kedoshim***). Rabbinic exegesis of Torah law in the Midrash and Talmud shows that all the different passages supplement one another and constitute a single, unified code. The law is "repeated" because it is only through ***mishnah*** -- constant repetition and review -- that we bring the Torah deep into our hearts and make it rule our lives.

The sandwiching of the code of Deuteronomy, the ***Mishneh Torah***, between the beginning and end of the instructions for the ceremony of blessings and curses on entry into the Land comes to emphasize that keeping the Torah is the essential condition for Israel's possession of the Land. The opening parshiyot of Deuteronomy set forth the fundamentals of faith and trust in G-d, love and awe and the other basic traits we are asked to cultivate. Now we come to the detailed laws of the Torah, as set forth in this and the ensuing parshahs. It was over this complete code, with its foundations and all its details, that Moses struck a Covenant with Israel in the plains of Moab, as recounted in ***Ki Tavo***, which we will read shortly before the New Year and Days of Awe.

The most striking feature of the Code as set forth in Deuteronomy compared to the laws in Exodus, Leviticus and Numbers is the constant return to the centrality of Jerusalem and the Temple in the life of the nation. "To the place that Hashem your G-d will choose from all your tribes to place His name there to dwell -- search it out and come there!" (Deut. 12:5). On conquest of the land, the Israelites were charged with totally uprooting and destroying all vestiges of Canaanite and any other kind of idolatry in order to ensure the success of the pure monotheistic order they were to establish in their place. The unity of G-d could not be revealed through the multiple shrines of the heathens "on the high mountains and on the hills and under every leafy tree". G-d's unity is revealed only when the consciousness of all Israel and of the entire world is focussed on the House of HaShem on Mount Moriah, the "Mountain of Teaching". For "...the Torah will go forth from Zion and the word of HaShem from Yerushalayim" (Isaiah 2:3)).

Later in the Code of Deuteronomy (***Shoftim***, Deut. 17:8ff, etc.) we will encounter Mount Moriah as the seat of the sages and elders of the Sanhedrin, Israel's true Supreme Court, whose proper place is in the Hewn Chamber on the Temple Mount. However, in our present parshah of ***Re'eh***, the focus is on Jerusalem and the Temple as the center of the nation's religious life, which itself is inextricably bound up with agriculture and the economy. Blessing reigns in Israel when the first-born animals and animal tithes are offered on the Temple Altar; when meat is consumed not purely out of lust, but in order to partake of peace and thanksgiving offerings; when the first-fruits are presented in the Temple; when Terumah is given to the priests and the tithe to the Levites, while the Israelites take up their second tithe to eat in holiness and purity within the boundaries of Jerusalem. "Three times in the year, all your males shall appear before the Lord your G-d." (Deut. 16:16).

Complete blessing can dwell only when the law is scrupulously observed. "***All*** the word that I am commanding you, you shall guard to do: ***you must not add to it and not subtract from it***" (Deut. 13:1). Some of the severest sanctions in the Torah are reserved for those who encourage others to deviate from the law, such as the false prophet, those who lead whole towns astray, and notably the ***Meisit*** ("inciter to idolatry" -- Deut. 13:2-19). The Torah insists that sanctions may be imposed only through due legal procedure -- "And you shall search out and investigate and question thoroughly" (Deut. 13:16). Nothing could be further from the Torah law on the eradication of idolatry than the practice of those who "burn their sons and daughters in fire to their gods" -- those who send young male and female suicide-terrorists to indiscriminately kill innocent men, women and children and babes in arms in the name of religion. The severity of the law of the Torah is directed not at innocents but at smooth-tongued, malicious, evil and dangerous inciters who whip up entire nations to madness.

But "You are children to HaShem your G-d": our best protection against the smooth-tongued incitement to stray from the Torah to which we are exposed every day is our own personal holiness and sanctity. Thus the laws in our parshah against incitement are followed immediately by the laws of holiness and abstention from the consumption of forbidden species of animals, which causes spiritual degradation. We are to regulate our physical appetites. We are to tithe our crops, and instead of simply eating the fruits immediately at home in order satisfy our bodily needs, we are to take a tithe (Ma'aser Sheini) to eat in Jerusalem "in order that you will learn to revere HaShem your G-d all the days". Self-restraint applies not only to farmers but to those involved in the money economy as well. Thus our parshah contains the laws of restraining our appetite for wealth through giving charity and loans to the needy, and remitting debts in the Sabbatical year. Again and again we are charged to remember the poor and needy, the Levite, the widow and the orphan.

Through our compassion, we will arouse the compassion of the Almighty as we prepare to enter the month of ***Elul***, the time of Teshuvah, love and compassion. The letters of the name of Elul are the initial letters of ***Ani Ledodi Vedodi Li***: "I am my Beloved's and my Beloved is mine" (Song of Songs 6:3).

SHOFTIM

Torah Reading: Deuteronomy 16:18-21:9

Haftarah: Isaiah 51:12-52:12

*T*he annual cycle of Torah readings is so arranged that Parshat ***Shoftim***, "Judges", is always read on the first Shabbat of the month of Elul, season of compassion and repentance, when all hearts yearn to come back to the Source. The opening words of the parshah -- "Appoint judges and police for yourselves in all your gates" -- contain a personal message for all of us. The key step in coming back to G-d is when we "appoint judges and police" for ***ourselves*** -- in the gates of our own minds and souls. We must examine our traits, activities and behavior and consider carefully whether they accord with G-d's Torah and how they could be improved. Then we must find ways to "police" ourselves so as to enforce our good resolutions and carry them out, taking the next steps forward to greater holiness in all the different areas of our lives.

Together with its personal spiritual advice for each one of us, Parshat ***Shoftim*** contains the blueprint for a Torah state in Israel ordered under its judges, its supreme court, its king, priests and prophets. Parshat ***Shoftim*** is at the center of the "trilogy" of parshiyot in which Moses sets forth the intricate details of the Mitzvot making up the "Mishneh Torah", his repetition of Torah law prior to his departure from the world. Following the opening parshiyot of Deuteronomy, which brought us the basics of faith, love and fear of G-d, last week's parshah, ***Re'eh***, set forth the blueprint for a blessed country cleansed of idolatry, where people's minds are constantly focussed on the service of G-d in the Temple. The blueprint in ***Re'eh*** is for a nation cultivating the land, giving tithes to the priests and Levites, caring for widows, orphans and proselytes, giving loans and charity to those in need... The annual cycle revolves around the three pilgrim festivals when everyone comes up to Jerusalem to "appear before G-d", experiencing the awe of the Temple, partaking of sacrifices and the second tithe in holiness and purity, and learning to revere G-d.

Next week's parshah, ***Ki Teitzei***, the third in this "trilogy", focuses more upon the commandments that relate to the particulars of our daily lives in the world -- family, property, how we build our houses (with a parapet), our clothes (Tzitzit), personal morality, who we admit into our communities and many others. Thereafter, Parshat ***Ki Tavo*** will complete the "repetition of the law", concluding with the blessings and curses over which Moses struck the Covenant with the Children of Israel in the Plains of Moab prior to their entry into the Land.

Our present parshah of ***Shoftim***, which is at the very center of this "trilogy" of parshiyot containing Moses' "repetition of the law", sets forth the necessary order of leadership and government through which the Torah nation can thrive in the Land of Israel. The parshah gives us the commandments relating to those who are the key to living successfully in the Holy Land: the judges and police, the Supreme Court (Sanhedrin), the king, the priests and the true prophets. It is these leaders and officers who are to lead and guide the nation in following the path of the Torah. ***Shoftim*** also sets forth the laws of murder and manslaughter, whose purpose is to ensure personal security within the country, and the laws of warfare, whose purpose is to bring security from external enemies.

* * *

JUDGES AND POLICE

"Justice! You must pursue Justice -- in order that you may live and inherit the Land." (Deut. 16:20). According to the Midrash, "This teaches that the appointment of judges is to give life to Israel and to let them dwell on their land and not to cause them to fall by the sword" (Sifri, Shoftim 144). A Torah judiciary with police to enforce Torah law is the very key to life and security in the land.

According to the blueprint, the true judges of Israel are not to be an aloof elite with responsibility to no-one. The legal system is not to be a tangled jungle rife with corruption and special protection for the rich and powerful.

The entire judicial system of the Torah nation is predicated upon universal study and knowledge of the Torah, making regular working citizens capable of serving as members of a Beit Din -- a "house of law" ("court") of three judges (for non-capital) or twenty-three (for capital) cases. A true Torah Israel is one so blessed that those earning their living through the labor of their hands are able to complete their work in less time, so as to be able to study the Torah assiduously as well, as in the case of many of the outstanding sages of the Talmud. According to the blueprint, the minimum town of one hundred and twenty male residents must contain a Beit Din of 23 together with an additional three rows of twenty-three students listening to and learning from their elders (Sanhedrin 17b). In this way, justice is at hand and quickly available every day, without the aggrieved parties having to submit themselves to a protracted, expensive, grueling struggle with slick lawyers and a heaving, endlessly complex legal system.

"If there are police, there are judges; if there are no police, there are no judges" (Sifri). If there are no police to enforce the law, the judges may judge all they like, but to no effect. In addition to study, the effective rule of Torah law is also predicated upon police who are subject to the authority of the Torah judges. Some may smile at the above suggestion that the first resort for justice should be the local Beit Din of Torah scholars, wondering how many of today's yeshivah alumni would be capable of acting as judges, let alone having police under them. It should be remembered that one of the reasons why the study of Talmudic law often appears detached from life in the rough and tumble of the actual world is because during most of the past two thousand years, rabbinical courts everywhere have been stripped of all meaningful sanctions with which to impose and enforce Torah law. The result is that the Torah has authority only over those who give it authority in their lives. Indeed, contemporary "political correctness" is appalled at the idea of rabbis "interfering" in areas that are considered in the realm of personal conscience, such as whether a person worships before a statue or image or violates the Shabbat, or what he or she does with another consenting adult. Yet under Torah law all of these may involve capital punishment, as we find in the case of idolatry in our parshah (Deut. 17:5). Many other sins that the wider society does not consider "criminal" can render a person liable to 39 lashes, such as wearing a forbidden mixture of wool and linen or eating meat cooked with milk.

The wider society obviously has some way to go in order to accept the law of the Torah. Those who yearn for the rule of Torah law and the blessing that it will bring can learn from our present parshah of ***Shoftim*** that constant study of study of the law is the foundation of the entire system.

While every layman is expected to be versed in the law, the commandment to "pursue Justice! Justice!" is interpreted to mean you should go to a "beautiful" Beit Din and seek out the best judges: the true sages and guardians of the Torah.

Our parshah instructs us that "when a matter of law is too wondrous for you, you shall rise up and go up to the place which HaShem your G-d will choose." (Deut. 17:8). If the local scholars and mavens do not know the correct answer, we are instructed to search out the wisest and most profoundly learned. It is evident from our parshah that the spiritual source of the wisdom of the Torah lies on Mount Moriah, "the Mountain of Teaching" -- the Temple Mount. In Temple times, there was a hierarchy of three courts that were in constant session on the Temple Mount: one at the very entrance and one inside, while the Supreme Court, the Sanhedrin, sat immediately adjacent to the inner Temple courtyard (Azarah), in the Lishkat HaGazit, ("Hewn Chamber").

The teachings of the sages of the Sanhedrin in Temple times constitute the oral Torah tradition handed down from teacher to student going back to Moses and Joshua. This is incorporated in the Mishnah and Talmud, which are the core of the study of Torah law today. Obedience to the oral law as handed down by the true sages is itself one of the commandments of the Torah in our parshah: "According to the Torah that they will teach you and the law that they will tell you shall you do: you shall not depart from the word that they tell you right or left." (Deut. 17:11). Even an outstanding sage who deviates from the majority opinion of the sages of the Sanhedrin is liable to the death penalty as a "rebellious elder" (ibid. v. 12-13). It is noteworthy that the punishment of the rebellious elder is one of those cases (like that of false witnesses) that is to be loudly publicized among the people. Here is another respect in which the blueprint for a Torah state differs widely from the present-day reality, in which media controlled by narrow interests can put anyone they like on public "trial", while the quest for true justice is like trying to grasp a phantom. In the Torah state, it is from the Temple that the announcement goes forth about who is truly evil, "and all the people will hear and be afraid, and will not act in insolent defiance any more" (ibid. v. 13).

* * *

THE KING

For some people the very word king is associated with images of contemporary "royalty" that render it somewhat misleading as a translation of the Hebrew word ***melech***. The Hebrew word refers to the ruler who has power over a sovereign political entity. Our parshah teaches that such a ruler is part of the Torah blueprint for the successful state (Deut. 17:14-20). Yet the Torah conception of the ***melech*** could not be further away from the kinds of rulers who have power in states throughout the world today including those who still bear royal titles.

As exemplified by David Melech Yisrael, the Torah ***melech*** is first and foremost a saintly student and lover of the Torah. While every Israelite is commanded to write his own Torah scroll, the king is commanded to copy another scroll from the authoritative Temple text and to take it everywhere he goes. He is to read from it constantly -- this is what gives him his life and power (see Likutey Moharan I:56). King David testified that he would nightly rise before midnight in order to meditate on the Torah (Psalms 119:148). Yet he did not flinch from getting involved in the rough and tumble of the actual world. "My hands are filthy from blood and aborted tissue in order to purify a woman to permit her to her husband" (Berachot 4a).

The Talmud instructs us even to go to see the kings of the nations -- in order to understand the difference between them and the true kings of Israel (Berachot 9b). Surviving non-Israelite monarchies have, with the complicity of the media, fostered a fairy-tale image of royalty whose vanity and emptiness have become starkly visible through an endless succession of scandals.

This is the precise opposite of ***Melech Yisrael***, who is the uncompromising Defender and Champion of the Torah of Truth. The true kings of Israel today are the humble sages and Tzaddikim who live modestly, without limousines, mansions and villas, artwork, jewelry and the other trappings of "royalty". Their wealth is the true, enduring wealth of their Torah wisdom and holiness, and the merits they have accumulated through their strenuous efforts and exertion on behalf of the community.

In the Torah state, the king himself must subject himself to the authority of the Sanhedrin and the prophets. While the king has responsibility for the internal and external security of the state, he must submit weighty matters of state, such as whether to go to war, to the sources of holy spirit: the priests and the prophets. Thus Parshat ***Shoftim*** presents commandments relating to the status and privileges of the priests in the Torah state, and to the qualifications of the prophet and how true prophecy is to be distinguished from false prophesy and divination.

* * *

SECURITY

The greatest scourge of contemporary society has become the cheapness of human blood, which is being shed daily without scruples in the rampant criminality and terror that have spread all over the world. The abhorrence of the Torah for bloodshed appears in many places and is prominent in our parshah, which contains the laws of murder and manslaughter and the cities of refuge for unintentional killers. We have already encountered some of these laws in precious parshiyot (***Mishpatim***, Exodus ch. 21, ***Mas'ey***, Numbers ch. 35, etc.)

Some are under the impression that the Torah requirements for valid testimony to convict a killer are so demanding that in practice it would be impossible to bring criminals to justice. For example, in a Beit Din, the witnesses must be Torah-observant, and their testimony must withstand rigorous investigation, while circumstantial evidence is inadmissible. It is true that the Torah requirements for valid testimony are very stringent, yet Torah law also provides the ***melech*** with sanctions with which to make sure that Torah leniency does not lead to social chaos. Thus the lawful ***melech*** of the Torah state can impose prison sentences and even capital punishment where necessary even in cases where a Beit Din could not impose such sentences.

The laws of warfare contained in Parshat ***Shoftim*** show that from the Torah standpoint, the critical factor in the wars we face are not our numbers, arms and equipment as against those of our enemies. The critical factor is our faith in HaShem and the courage with which we are ready and willing to fight for our convictions. The "pep talk" to the troops is given by the priest. His opening words are: "***Shema Yisrael***" (Deut. 20:3) -- alluding to the words with which we declare our faith twice daily.

The Torah commands us not to lose our sensitivities even in time of war. Even when fighting our enemies, we are not allowed to wantonly destroy property. It is in the context of the laws of warfare that the Torah gives us the law of "***Bal Tashchit***" ("Do not wantonly destroy." Deut. 20:20). If this law applies to our enemies' property even in time of war, how much more does it applies to our own property and to public property in time of peace. We are to value that which has value, and not to needlessly waste and destroy. This applies to the natural wealth and resources of the earth, which are being mindlessly exploited and destroyed for the sake of immediate gain without a thought for the long-term.

The closing mitzvah of Parshat ***Shoftim*** is that of the heifer whose neck is broken in a ceremony that comes to atone for an unsolved homicide - a case in which a body is found in the open but the killer is unknown. It is noteworthy that the judges of the town nearest to where the body is found require atonement. It is their responsibility to see that their town is properly organized to take care of visitors and the needy, so that no-one is forced to take to the road in search of hospitality, thereby exposing himself to the attendant dangers from roaming killers.

"Atone for Your people Israel, whom You have redeemed, Hashem, and do not put innocent blood among Your people Israel, and let the blood be atoned for them" (Deut. 21:8).

KI TEITZEI

Torah Reading: Deuteronomy 21:10-25:19.

Haftarah: Isaiah 54:1-10.

WINNING THE PEACE

*O*n first examination, our parshah, ***Ki Teitzei***, may appear to be a collection of many apparently unrelated commandments in a wide variety of different areas. It is not immediately clear in what way the opening words of the parshah -- "When you go out to ***war***" (Deut. 21:10) -- set the theme for the whole of the rest of the parshah. The question is sharpened by the fact that in the previous parshah, ***Shoftim***, we already had a Torah section beginning with precisely the same words: "When you go out to war against your enemy" (Deut. 20:1). As discussed in the commentary on ***Shoftim***, it is in that section that the Torah sets forth the main laws relating to the conduct of actual war. Our present parshah of ***Ki Teitzei*** begins with a mitzvah that applies after the battle is already over -- what to do with a beautiful captive. Yet five verses later, the Torah turns to the laws of inheritance, education of children, lost property and other areas that have little apparent connection with war.

There are indeed a few more references to actual war later on in our parshah. The Israelite camp must be pure (Deut. 23:10); a newly married man is exempt from military service (Deut. 24:5); and at the end of the parshah, we are commanded to remember the first war against Israel, that of Amalek. However, the greater part of the parshah deals with laws that relate not so much to war on the actual battlefield as to life on the home front. In the home itself, in social life and in business, out and about in the town, out in the field and out in the wilds of our own hearts, we confront a different enemy: the Evil Inclination. It is against this enemy that we must learn the stratagems of warfare and battle. "The Torah speaks against none other than the Evil Inclination" (Rashi on Deut. 21:11).

Many of the situations we face every day confront us with choices. These include difficult choices between what reason, intuition and conscience may be telling us to do, and what our more impulsive side is pushing us to do. In Parshat ***Ki Teitzei***, the Torah provides us with guidance in making the right and good choices when fighting the battles of daily life in the home, at work, in business and in many other contexts.

The opening mitzvah of the parshah, that of the beautiful captive, addresses a fundamental issue facing all who seek to observe the Torah in the fullest way possible. Since the Torah regulates our interactions with the outside world down to the very food we take into our mouths and the clothes we wear, what, if anything, are we allowed to take from the alien cultures around us? The beautiful captive embodies all that is most alluring and enticing in the alien culture. The Torah tells us to "let her hair grow long and her nails grow like claws": instead of allowing ourselves to jump at surface attractiveness, we must take a little time to discover how quickly this fades and turns ugly. The Torah teaches us not to fall for immediate surface appeal but to consider the longer term consequences and ramifications of the choices and decisions we make. The beautiful captive may turn into a hated wife who bears a glutton, drunkard son. The Torah sees to the end of the matter.

One bad choice can lead to a lot of evil and suffering. On the other hand, a single good choice, even over something tiny, can lead to amazing goodness -- in this world and the next. What could be more insignificant than walking on a road somewhere and happening to find a bird's nest with a mother and eggs or fledglings? How can it be that sending away the mother bird before taking the eggs or fledglings (it costs you nothing) guarantees long life in this world and the next? (Deut. 22:6-7). Only the One who is above time and Who sees from the beginning of a thing to the end knows what are the long-term consequences of our actions in this world, for good or for bad. It is precisely because we do not see the long-term consequences of our actions that we need true guidance in making our choices. The commandments contained in ***Ki Teitzei*** give us practical guidance in our home and family life, in making a livelihood and doing business, in how we talk and many other areas "in order that He may bestow good on you and you will lengthen your days" (Deut. 22:7).

Each of the commandments in the parshah must be taken on the level of ***p'shat*** -- the simple meaning -- and each one involves detailed binding laws, as discussed in the relevant sections of the Talmud and Codes. At the same time, each word of each verse contains the deepest levels of ***sod*** -- secret meaning -- so that when we fulfil these laws in practice, we even unknowingly create configurations of G-dliness and goodness in the world around us and in our own hearts and souls. In the following discussion of the commandments contained in our parshah, they are discussed not in the sequence in which they appear in the parshah but under themes.

THE HOME AND THE FAMILY

The opening mitzvah of the parshah, that of the beautiful captive, takes us directly inside the home, which is where the captive is taken to "grow her hair and nails". Life in the home and in the family is a central theme throughout the parshah. Immediately following the law of the beautiful captive comes a hint of marital discord (the hated wife), followed by the Torah law of family inheritance and the birthright. This is followed by the law of the gluttonous son, whose penalty is to be stoned to death. The requisite amounts of meat and wine the gluttonous son would have to imbibe were so gigantic that in practice no one would ever fulfill all the conditions that would make them liable to the death penalty. The Torah does not want to kill the son, but rather to teach the essence of good parenting, from childhood onwards and especially during puberty and adolescence. Children need not be given everything they want. They must be taught to listen to the voice of mother and father, wisdom and understanding.

The education of girls for the life of Torah and the holiness of Israel is no less important than that of boys. The stoning of the girl whose new husband found her to have been unfaithful after their betrothal is not only a terrible punishment for the girl. It is a bitter lesson for her father, outside whose house the execution takes place. "See the offspring you have raised" (Rashi on Deut. 22:21). The holiness of the

Israelite home and family is based upon ***kiddushin***, the act of betrothal whereby husband and wife sanctify and dedicate themselves to one another. In bringing up a new generation, the parental duty is to ensure that girls understand the holiness and seriousness of marriage and of marital fidelity. They must understand what is happening to their pubescent bodies and the attendant dangers in the outside world and from the lurking Evil Urge. This education is particularly important today, when the world is flooded with a culture that encourages teenagers to think of nothing but sexual attraction and romance all day every day. The laws of rape and seduction in our parshah underline how carefully parents must protect their daughters (and sons). Protection must start by lovingly teaching our children about the uniqueness and holiness of Israel and the special level of conduct required of ***b'ney melachim***, children of kings -- "for you are children of HaShem".

Our parshah contains the laws of marriage and divorce that make up most of ***Seder Nashim***, the Order of the Mishnah relating to these areas. These include the laws of ***yibum***, the Levirate marriage, and ***chalitzah***, the ceremony for nullifying it, with all their many secrets. Many of the basic laws of ***kiddushin*** and ***nisu'im***, betrothal and marriage, are learned from verses in our parshah, as are the laws of the ***get***, "bill of divorce". The prohibition against a divorced woman who married another man from subsequently remarrying her first husband sets Israel apart from the alien culture that licenses switching back and forth from one partner to another. The holiness of the bond between husband and wife is founded on its exclusiveness. In the realities of life in the world we live in, divorce is sometimes necessary and must be carried out with the proper procedure. However, there is no doubt that the Torah prefers not to license divorce (which "makes the altar-stones weep") but rather that man and wife should joyously build their home together to fulfil "and your camp shall be holy" (Deut. 23:15) for many long, good years. The first year of marriage sets the foundation for all that follows. In that year the groom is commanded that "he make joyous his wife that he took" (Deut. 24:5). The surest foundation for joy in the home is the study and practice of the Torah.

Bound up with the laws of marriage are the laws relating to personal status and those entitled to enter the community of Israel. The community excludes male Ammonites and Moabites (though King David himself was descended from a Moabitess), and Egyptians and Edomites to the third generation. A different status is that of the ***mamzer***, who as the child of an incestuous relationship of Israelites is also inherently flawed and may not marry into the community. The purpose of these laws is to protect the purity of the Israelite family.

The home is a private domain -- so much so that even a creditor may not enter to take a pledge but must wait outside for the debtor to bring it out. But while the home is private, it must be a place of dignity so that G-d's holy Presence may dwell there. Dignity begins with personal hygiene and cleanliness, which is why the Torah commands us to attend to our physical needs "outside the camp" and properly cover the waste. Within our homes, we are free to do all that the Torah permits, but we must keep our eyes open and take precautions against potential dangers. "Make a parapet for your roof". The law to make a parapet to prevent someone falling off the roof is the foundation of the general Torah law that potential hazards of all kinds should be removed (Shulchan Aruch, Choshen Mishpat #427). Not only does the Torah govern how we build our homes. It even governs the clothes we wear: we may not wear mixtures of wool and linen, and men must wear Tzitztit. The Tzitzit are the first line of defense against immorality (which is why the commandment of wearing Tzitzit immediately precedes the laws of the betrothed maiden). A man must not wear women's clothes or ornaments and vice versa.

MAKING A LIVING: BETWEEN MAN AND HIS FELLOW

Commandments relating to making a living -- from plowing the land to loans and the money economy -- also take up major parts of Parshat ***Ki Teitzei***. Just as the separation between Israel and the nations is part of G-d's order, so is the separation between different species of animals and vegetables. One must not drive the plow with an ox and a donkey together. One may not plant one field with diverse species. What distinguishes Israel is the trait of kindness and compassion, which must be carefully cultivated. When harvesting the crops, gifts must be left for the unfortunate and the needy: the proselyte, the widow, the orphan and the poor. The farmer must even be sensitive to the feelings of his ox: while threshing, he may not muzzle the ox to prevent it munching on some of the produce while at work.

Relevant to all are the laws governing the respective rights and obligations of employers and employees. The employee must work industriously and may not abuse the privileges the Torah gives him. Having completed his work, he is entitled to prompt payment: now the mitzvah is on the employer. The laws in our parshah relating to the money economy include those of giving interest-free loans to fellow Israelites and the strict prohibition of taking interest (***ribit***). Business activity is to be governed by the laws of fair weights and measures.

Not only are we bound to conduct our business dealings with integrity. We are responsible for the property of others if they lose it -- our parshah contains the laws of lost property. And if our friend gets into trouble -- if his donkey can't carry the load -- we must help him rearrange the load.

* * *

DOUBLE STANDARDS -- AND AMALEK

The detailed laws in our parshah culminate in what on one level is a business law -- the prohibition of keeping a big and a small weight: a big weight to use in weighing what one buys, and a small weight in weighing what one sells. We are to use one standard in our business dealings, and likewise, one standard in all of our judgments and evaluations: the Torah standard. We may not judge ourselves and those we like favorably while judging those outside our preferred circle unfavorably. We are to examine ourselves and others and everything in our lives with sobriety, carefully examining to see how things measure up according to the Torah standard. It is this that protects us from Amalek.

From the proximity of the prohibition of double standards to the law of remembering and wiping out Amalek, we learn that having double standards is what brings the scourge of Amalek. The war against Amalek is a theme during this month of Elul, just as it is in the month of Adar, which is six months earlier and diagonally opposite/facing Elul in the circle of the months. Just as fighting Amalek is necessary in Adar in preparation for Nissan, the month of redemption, so it is necessary as part of the Teshuvah process during Elul as we approach Rosh HaShanah and the Days of Awe.

Amalek "encountered you [***karcha***] on the way" (Deut. 25:18). The Rabbis stated that Amalek "cooled [***kar***] you" -- When the Israelites were flushed with joy and innocent fervor immediately after the Exodus, Amalek attacked with demoralization and despair. Amalek attacked with ***mikreh***, "chance" -- the philosophy that there is no order in the universe and that therefore everything is permitted. Amalek attacked with ***keri***, the wasteful emission of seed through sexual permissiveness and immorality. These are the very opposite of the holiness that is the foundation of Israel.

The alien culture around us is now reaching its climax in the espousal of the unholy. The Torah states that a man shall not wear the clothes and ornaments of a woman, and vice versa. Yet the alien culture is obsessed with gender and cross gender issues, and has legitimized homosexual relationships -- an abomination in the eyes of the Torah -- to the point that the countries which consider themselves most advanced are those that have legislated to give homosexual couples the same rights and benefits as husbands and wives. The Midrash clearly states that giving sanction to homosexual marriages brings ***androlomusia*** -- chaos in which the innocent suffer with the guilty. We can see with our own eyes how the very world that has sanctioned this mockery of marriage is reeling from the fires of war and terror, crime, violence, economic recession, disease...

The foundation of the holiness of Israel has nothing to do with this mockery of marriage, this vain emission of seed. The foundation of the holiness of Israel is ***kiddushin***, the sacred bond of marriage and fidelity between man and his wife. This is the foundation of family, continuity, the education of children, refinement, modesty, compassion and all other good traits.

KI TAVO

Torah Reading: Deuteronomy 26:1-29:8.

Haftarah: Isaiah 60:1-22.

*O*ur parshah, ***Ki Tavo***, puts the seal on Moses' detailed exposition of the commandments in the Mishneh Torah (=Deuteronomy) -- the "Second" or repeated Torah -- and recounts the Covenant that G-d struck with Israel in the plains of Moab prior to their entry into the Land. ***Ki Tavo*** thus brings us into the closing sections of the Five Books of Moses, the very climax of the Torah. This is fitting reading as we approach the coming Day of Judgment -- Rosh Hashanah -- and the Days of Awe.

The commandments contained in our parshah are almost the last commandments written in the Torah -- except for the two commandments contained in next week's reading, the double parshah of ***Nitzavim-Vayelech***. (Those relate to the teaching of the Torah -- its public reading at the ***Hakhel*** assembly in the Temple following the Sabbatical year -- and to the accurate transmission of the Torah through writing a Torah scroll).

THE FUTURE MODE – THANK YOU

The commandments contained in our present parshah, ***Ki Tavo***, relate to the longed-for, glorious future: "And it shall be when you come to the Land". The opening Hebrew word of the parshah is a permutation of the holy Name of HaShem. This seals His eternal promise that the time will indeed arrive when ***you will come to the land***. The time will come when you will be able to present your first fruits with gratitude in the Holy Temple, separate your priestly tithes and other gifts, and eat the fruits of your labor within the walls of the Holy City.

The opening section of ***Ki Tavo*** gives the commandment to present the first fruits in a basket by the altar in the Temple as a gift for the Kohen-priest, including the declaration of thanks made on presentation of the fruits. The text of this declaration, "The Aramean (=Laban) tried to destroy my father (Jacob)." (Deut. 26:5-9), is so fundamental to the identity of Israel that it forms the basis of the Pesach Haggadah with which we retell our national story every year on the night celebrating the birth of the nation through the Exodus. The main body of the Haggadah consists of a word-by-word homiletic commentary on these verses.

The mitzvah of the first fruits is immediately followed by the commandments relating to tithes, which also involve a declaration. Periodically all accumulated gifts of agricultural produce to the Levite and poor etc. that have not yet been distributed must be cleared out of the house. This is done after the end of the first three years of the Sabbatical cycle, on the eve of Pesach of the fourth year. Following the distribution of the remaining gifts, the householder declares that he has fulfilled each one of the various commandments relating to agricultural produce in their proper order -- therefore, "Look down from the dwelling place of Your holiness from the heavens and bless Your people." (Deut. 26:13-15). This is known as ***vidui ma'asrot***, the "confession" over the tithes. This declaration is the opposite of a confession of sin. It is an enumeration of the merits gained by faithful adherence to the commandments of the Torah, like a laborer listing what he has done for his master before inviting his blessing.

With the mitzvah of the first fruits and the commandments relating to the tithes, gifts and consumption of the produce of the Land, the Torah has come the full circle. At the beginning of Genesis, we learned of man's basic sin, which was bound up with the eating of fruit: the forbidden fruit of the Tree of Knowledge of Good and Evil. Man took without asking -- he stole, with all the consequences. The serpent tricked Adam into taking the fruit, and thereby brought death upon him and robbed him of his blessings. Jacob had to use trickery against Esau and Laban to retrieve the blessings back from the serpent. Jacob's children had to go down into Egypt in order to rectify all that fell through the eating of the forbidden fruit. They had to endure slavery in order to learn the meaning of freedom and its obligations. Only after much toil and tribulation did they come to the Land, wrest it from and cleanse it of the accursed Canaanites, seed of the serpent, till it, plant and tend it until they saw their first-fruits.

A person inspecting the long-awaited luscious fruits gradually ripening on his tree of figs or pomegranates would tie a thread to mark out the choicest first fruits. Instead of marking them out for his own self-gratification, he would set them aside to present as a gift to the priest at the side of the Temple altar. The first fruits -- ***bikurim*** -- relate to the ***bechorah***, the birth-right, which alludes to ***Chochmah***, "wisdom". It was wisdom that Adam defiled in taking the forbidden fruit. Esau, embodiment of the serpent, rejected the birth-right of wisdom, but Jacob took it back -- and vowed at the site of Adam's creation to dedicate the choice first tithe to G-d.

The rectification of the trickery of the serpent, which tempts man to make self-gratification his only altar, is through the steady application of the Torah commandments that regulate how and what we take from the world around us, including the very food we put into our mouths. Before we enjoy the fruits of our labors, we must think of the priest, the Levite and the poor, and separate all the obligatory gifts and tithes. The fulfillment of all the relevant commandments elevates and puts blessing into the fruits that remain for our own enjoyment.

In the declarations over the presentation of the first fruits in the Temple and over the separation of gifts and tithes, man uses the unique faculty G-d has given him -- speech -- as a means of deepening his connection with G-d through heightened consciousness of his identity as an Israelite and as G-d's servant fulfilling His commandments. Saying "Thank You" to G-d out loud is very important.

Presentation of the first fruits in the Temple is the very first of the agricultural commandments fulfilled by the farmer: he thinks about it while the fruit is still ripening on the tree, before he even begins harvesting. The declaration about tithes comes after an entire cycle of three years of harvests and steady fulfillment of all the intricate details of the commandments applying to the fruits in different years. First comes Terumah, the gift to the priest, and then the First Tithe (Ma'aser) for the Levite. In the first and second years, the Second

Tithe (Ma'aser Sheini) is to be eaten in purity in Jerusalem by its owner, but in the third year, the owner cannot eat the Second Tithe himself. He must give it to the poor (Ma'aser Oni). If a person has fulfilled all these commandments in all their details, he is entitled to stand up after all this work and list what he has accomplished.

There is a practical lesson for us here as we stand now in the middle of the month of Elul, the period of ***teshuvah***, repentance, self-examination and inner work. Teshuvah is not only a matter of confessing sins. We have all sinned, but we have all done a lot of good too. In looking at ourselves and weighing our lives and behavior, we must give due consideration to all the good things that we do. When we weigh their true worth and importance as acts of loving obedience to the King, it will inspire us to go forward with greater confidence, in the knowledge that if we strive to do His will, He will surely bless us.

* * *

AND TO GO IN HIS WAYS

The last commandment contained in ***Ki Tavo***, based on the words "and to go in His ways" (Deut. 26:17) is to model our personal traits on the traits and attributes of G-d. "Just as He is merciful and gracious, so you should be merciful and gracious..." The refinement of our traits is the inner work in the heart that G-d asks of the Israelites, an essential part of the spiritual work of the month of Elul. The repetition of the Thirteen Attributes of Mercy in the Selichot (penitential prayers) recited in this season comes to arouse us to follow these attributes in our daily lives.

It is indeed the traits of kindness and compassion that are the marks of the true Israelite and the distinctive attributes of ***am segulah***, the "treasured nation" (Deut. 26:18) whom G-d has chosen to observe His Torah and enjoy its blessings. The very exaltedness of this calling gives Israel a weighty responsibility. Thus the Covenant entails not only privileges and blessings but also heavy sanctions for its infringement. Our parshah impresses upon us the seriousness of the

Covenant with its account of the solemn ceremony that was to accompany the people's entry into the Land. The Torah was to be written on stone, and the twelve tribes were to stand on two mountains adjacent to Shechem, six on each mountain, while the priests and Levites standing in the middle recited a litany of blessings and curses.

The first reference to this ceremony was made at the beginning of Parshat ***Re'eh***, which we read four weeks ago, before Moses entered into the details of the law code of the Covenant in the trilogy of ***Re'eh***, ***Shoftim*** and ***Ki Teitzei***. Now, in ***Ki Tavo***, after completion of the law code, the Torah depicts this striking ceremony to impress upon us that Israel's presence in the Land is not for the sake of having mere territory. The Land is given as the place in which to fulfill the Torah. It is when Israel dwells in the land in order to observe the commandments that they are "for praise and for a name and for glory... a holy nation" (Deut. 26:19).

On entry into the land, they were to set up great stones washed with lime and write the Torah on them "with clear explanation" (Deut. 27:8) -- "in the seventy languages" (Rashi ad loc.). The fact that the Torah had to be written in all the languages of the world shows that the presence of Israel in the land is not merely of particular interest to Israel alone but of universal significance for the whole of mankind.

For this reason, this commentary is entitled ***Universal Torah*** even though many sections of the Torah deal with commandments that apply exclusively to Israel and not to the other Children of Noah. Nevertheless, numerous commandments and teachings in the Torah apply to all humanity. Moreover, Israel's observance of the Torah and their possession of the Land of Israel as the place designed for this are in the interests of the whole of humanity. As expressed in the words of the rabbis, "If the nations understood the value to them of the Holy Temple, they would have surrounded it with armed guards". All those whose actions and policies obstruct the building of the Temple are doing a terrible disservice to the entire world.

Israel and its people and Jews everywhere are the focus of interest for everyone in the world precisely because of our exalted mission as the

Treasured Nation. The history of Israel and the Jews, with its great heights and terrible lows and degradation, is a lesson writ large for all humanity on the righteousness of G-d. He gave a Covenant with blessings and curses, and the infringement of the Covenant has brought all the curses listed in the parshah in all their terrible details.

If so, fulfillment of the Covenant will certainly bring all the amazing blessings listed in our parshah. Our obligation in this generation is to return to the Covenant with all our hearts so that we will rapidly witness the complete redemption, peace for Israel and the spread of the light of the Torah from Zion to the whole world.

NITZAVIM-VAYELECH

Torah Reading: NITZAVIM: Deuteronomy 29:9-30:20
VAYELECH: Deuteronomy 31:1-30.

Haftarah: Isaiah 61:10-63:9

DECLARING THE END FROM THE BEGINNING

"***D***eclaring the end from the beginning and from ancient times things that are not yet done, saying 'My counsel shall stand and all My pleasure I shall do' " (Isaiah 46:10).

Parshat ***Nitzavim*** is always read on the last Shabbat before Rosh HaShanah (New Year) and is often (though not always) coupled with its sister parshah of ***Vayelech***, with which it shares the same theme. According to tradition, these and all the remaining parshahs of the Torah were delivered by Moses to the assembled Children of Israel on the very last day of his life (Rashi on Deut. 29:9). As the climax and summing up of the whole Torah, the stark reproof and sublime poetry of these parshahs make them appropriate reading prior to and during the coming Days of Awe. In this period, we must make a very honest reckoning about time past and take the necessary lessons to heart in order to fortify ourselves for the New Year. We stand poised to face its challenges, just as Israel stood in the Plains of Moab, poised to enter the Land.

Atem nitzavim -- "You are standing". The Hebrew word ***nitzavim***, translated as "standing", has the connotation of firmly founded stability. This is the stability and fortitude that come from the knowledge of the Torah that we internalize in our hearts. Here, as we stand at the end of the Torah, we ought to be much wiser than we were at the beginning. Shortly, we will be "entering the Land", starting all over again from the beginning, ***Bereishit***. Just before we "enter the Land", the New Year, Moses tells us to stand and reflect on the lessons we have learned so far, in order to be able to start over again on a better footing.

Moses explicitly addressed this section of the Torah to all Israel in all the generations: "those who are here with us standing this day before G-d, and those that are not here with us today" -- the unborn souls of all the later generations. The Torah's lessons were not only addressed to the time of Moses, the ancient world, the Middle Ages or only the generations preceding the "Enlightenment" and the birth of modern science and technology. Our parshah is explicitly addressed to "the last generation, your children who will arise after you" (Deut. 29:21). This is the generation that faces the consequences of the mass abandonment of the Covenant, the anger and concealment of G-d, the many evils and troubles. This is the generation that will say, "Is it not because my G-d is not within me that these evils have found me?" (Deut. 31:17). Those standing at the end of time are in a position to look over the entire span of history all the way back to the beginning. Then they can testify that everything foretold thousands of years ago in these parshahs, including the loss of the Land, the tribulations of exile, the "hiding" of G-d from the world, the return to the Land and today's Teshuvah movement, have all come to pass.

These lessons are addressed not only to Israel, on whose very flesh they have been taught again and again. The stark lesson of G-d's righteousness is addressed to "the stranger who will come from a distant land" (ibid.) and to the entire world. "... And they will see the wounds of that Land and the illnesses with which G-d has afflicted it. Sulfur and salt, conflagration. And all the nations will say, Why has G-d done this to this Land, what is this great burning anger? And they will say, Because they abandoned the Covenant."

As we daily witness the fires that have been ravaging Israel and its people in front of our very eyes, Moses tells us bluntly to be in no doubt whatever about one thing: "Lest there be among you a man or woman or family or tribe whose heart is turning away today from HaShem our G-d to go to serve the gods of the nations. And when he hears the words of this curse, he will bless himself in his heart saying I will have ***Shalom*** even though I go in the stubbornness of my heart.

G-d will not desire to forgive him" (Deut. 29:17-19). We are to have no doubt whatever that it is impossible for Israel to enjoy ***Shalom*** in the Land of Israel except through embracing G-d's Covenant and His Torah.

We may ask what we can do if we ourselves want to keep the Torah but others do not. Why should the righteous and innocent suffer collective punishment because of the sins of those who have abandoned the Covenant? Moses addresses this question in the deep, deep teaching that says: "The things that are concealed belong to HaShem our G-d, but the things that are revealed belong to us and to our children forever to carry out all the words of this Torah" (Deut. 29:28). Only G-d knows what is in the heart of each person, and G-d's dealings with the entire world contain mysteries that we cannot understand because we do not possess His perfect knowledge of all things, past, present and future. These mysteries do not belong to us -- we cannot understand the way G-d deals with each one of His creatures in accordance with His perfect knowledge. Our province is what has been revealed to us in the Torah. The Torah teaches us what G-d asks ***us*** to get up and do in this world, without looking at what others may or may not be doing.

In the words of Rashi (ad loc.): "If you say, ‘What is in our hands to do?’ You punish the many because of the wicked thoughts of the individual. Surely no man knows what is in the hidden depths of his friend? G-d answers: I do not punish you over what is concealed, which 'belong to HaShem our G-d', and He will exact payment from that individual. It is what is revealed that belongs to us and our children -- to eradicate the evil from within us, and if justice is not carried out on them (for known wrong-doing) the many will suffer."

Immediately following this comes what is known as ***Parshat HaTeshuvah***, the "Chapter on Repentance" (Deut. 30:1-10), which some people have the custom of reciting daily in order to keep it constantly in mind. Lest we be disheartened by the harsh words and dire threats contained in the preceding and following sections, Moses here emphasizes G-d's unstinting compassion and kindness as he calls on us to return to Him with all our hearts. Moses promises us that G-d

will definitely turn around the captivity and exile and gather in the exiles from all the nations, even those outcast to the furthest reaches of the heavens. Moses promises that "G-d will bring you to the land of your fathers and you will inherit it, and He will benefit you and multiply you even more than your fathers! And G-d will circumcise your heart and the heart of your seed to love HaShem your G-d with all your heart and all your soul in order that you should have life!" (Deut. 30:5-6). The first four initial letters of the Hebrew words for "your heart and the heart of your seed..." (***E***t ***L***evav'cha ***V***'et ***L***evav...) spell out the name of the present month, ***Elul*** (Baal HaTurim). For this self-circumcision of our hearts is the essence of the work we must do this month.

The Torah is not in the heavens or over the seas. It is right here: "For the matter is very close to you, in your mouth and in your heart to ***do it***" (ibid. v. 14). Moses wants us never to forget our existential situation in this world as agents possessing free will. In order to win the battle of free will, our work here in this world is first and foremost with our mouths and in our hearts. Again and again Moses reminds us that we are faced with a blessing and a curse -- the blessing if we follow the ways of the Torah and the curse if we do not. Our task is to use our mouths in prayer and self-empowerment in order to fortify our hearts in the path of Torah and service of G-d. "Life and death I have put before you, the blessing and the curse. And you shall choose life in order that you should ***live***, you and your seed" (ibid. v. 19).

* * *

VAYELECH - THE TRANSMISSON OF THE TORAH

With the Torah almost complete except for the concluding Song (***Ha'azinu***) and Moses' Blessings (***Ve'Zot HaBrachah***), it was necessary to ensure the transmission of authority from Moses to his divinely-appointed successor, Joshua and the transmission of the Torah to the nation as a whole and to all the later generations.

Parshat ***Vayelech*** describes how the leadership of Israel was transferred to Joshua in the eyes of all Israel in order to give him perfect legitimacy after Moses would be gone. Having instructed Joshua to be strong and courageous in leading the people into the Land, Moses wrote the Torah and gave it to the Cohen-Priests and the Elders of Israel. (According to tradition, on the last day of his life, Moses wrote the Torah scroll that was to be kept in the Sanctuary as well as a Torah scroll for each of the Twelve Tribes, a total of thirteen scrolls.)

Moses then gave the commandment known as ***Hakhel*** after the first Hebrew word of Deut. 31:12. "***Assemble*** the people, the men, the women and the children and the proselyte that is in your gates, in order that they should hear and in order that they should learn and revere HaShem your G-d and take care to perform all the words of this Torah." This mass assembly is to take place in the Temple once every seven years during the festival of Succot of the year immediately following the Shemittah (Sabbatical) year. Everyone is to assemble in the "Women's Courtyard", where the king is to read publicly extensive sections of the book of Deuteronomy setting forth G-d's Covenant with Israel and the blessings and curses (Sotah 41a). The ***Hakhel*** Assembly was undoubtedly a formidably powerful experience for all who took part, and so it will be when it is restored. The effects of the public reading of Deuteronomy are described in the Book of Kings (II Kings, chs. 22-23), which tells how in a time of deep crisis in Eretz Israel, King Josiah solemnly renewed the Covenant and brought the people to rededicate themselves to the Torah and its commandments.

* * *

AND NOW, WRITE FOR YOURSELVES THIS SONG

"And now, write for yourselves this song and teach it to the Children of Israel, put it in their mouths." (Deut. 31:1).

This verse is the source of the very last mitzvah contained in the Torah: that each Israelite should write his own Torah scroll. One who is unable to write a scroll himself can appoint a scribe as his agent. When a person contributes money for the writing of a Torah scroll, it is attributed to him as if he fulfilled this mitzvah. The Codes state that in our generations, the mitzvah is also fulfilled through the acquisition of printed Torah literature for use in Torah study.

In the words of Rabbi Nachman: "The Talmud teaches us that 'The day will come when the Torah will be forgotten' (Shabbat 138a). Therefore many books are printed and bought, with people building up their own libraries. Since even the simplest tailor has books, the Torah is not forgotten. As each book is published, people rush to buy it, building up respectable collections. In this manner, the Torah does not fall into oblivion.

What people do not realize is that these books are of no help unless people look into them and study their teachings. How can books prevent the Torah from being forgotten if nobody studies them?" (Rabbi Nachman's Wisdom #18).

HA'AZINU

Torah Reading: Deuteronomy 32:1-52

Haftarah: II Samuel 22:1-51

THE SONG OF G-D'S JUSTICE

Some songs are happy, some are sad. Some are for entertainment. Some come to tell a story or teach a lesson. Some express the inner heart and soul. Unique among all songs is the song of Moses in our parshah, ***Ha'azinu*** is the song of G-d's perfect Justice -- the ultimate reproof to man.

The Hebrew word for song, ***shirah***, is related to the word ***sher***, which means a chain or necklace. A song is a chain, thread or structure that connects various particulars together in order to make a meaningful order. As the very climax of the Torah, Moses' song of ***Ha'azinu*** gives order and meaning to the history of the people of Israel with its great highs and terrible lows. Everything comes to show the faultless, inexorable justice of G-d. "The Rock -- His work is perfect, for all His ways are Justice, the G-d of faithfulness in Whom there is no wrong, He is righteous and straight!" (Deut. 32:4).

This may be easy to say, but it is very hard to actually know and believe in our heart of hearts. Nevertheless, Moses challenges us to join him in this song of testimony, so that we too will know and declare G-d's justice. The song is "interactive": Moses chants, calling upon us to respond. "For I will call upon the Name of HaShem -- ascribe greatness to our G-d" (ibid. v. 3). This verse is the Torah source for the prayer leader's call to prayer and the congregational response, both in the synagogue – ***Bar'chu*** -- and at the table introducing the blessings after eating bread -- ***Nevorech*** (Berachot 45a). ***Ha'azinu*** challenges us to respond: to wake up, see and acknowledge G-d's truth and justice, and to respond in the proper way, by repenting. ***Ha'azinu*** is such an important expression of the essence of Israel's faith and destiny that some communities had the custom of reciting it daily in the morning prayers together with ***Shirat HaYam*** ("Song of the Sea") (Rambam, Laws of Prayer 7:13). In the Temple, successive portions of ***Ha'azinu*** were read every Shabbat in a six-week cycle as part of the service accompanying the Shabbat additional offering (Rambam, Temidim U'Musafim 6:9).

"Listen, O heavens, and I will speak. Hear, O earth, the words of my mouth" (Deut. 32:1). Moses calls upon the heavens and earth, G-d's impassive, unwaveringly obedient servants, as his witnesses. For mortal man is too devious and full of ploys to be a valid witness -- he has a vested interest: he wants to justify himself. "Why did this happen to me? It isn't fair." Moses confronts us -- the latter generation that he is addressing -- with independent testimony that cannot be denied: the actual history of the people of Israel from the very beginning to the very end, for it is all encapsulated in ***Ha'azinu***. "Remember the days of the universe, understand the years of generation after generation; ask your father and he will inform you, your grandfather and they will tell you..." (v. 7). What has happened in the past and what is happening now to Israel is of significance to the entire world. For Israel is at the very center. "When the Supreme gave the peoples their inheritance, when He spread out the children of.man, He established the boundaries of the nations according to the number of the Children of Israel..." (v. 8).

The history of Israel is the history of Adam writ large. Adam was created out of dust and nothingness and placed in G-d's sublime garden, but he quickly rebelled and sinned, causing G-d to punish and chasten him, in order to make him repent and to cleanse him. Similarly, G-d "found" the Children of Israel in a wild, desolate land and built them into a nation, giving them to ride on the high places of the earth -- the land of Israel and Jerusalem. But their very good fortune and prosperity became their undoing. "And Yeshurun became fat and he kicked" -- causing G-d to let loose all the evils and terrors of persecution and oppression that have plagued the people of Israel for thousands of years. Only when we internalize the message that rebellion leads to nothing but pain in the end, and that we have no recourse except in G-d -- only then will G-d relent and swing everything around to goodness and blessing – ***Ve'Zot HaBrachah*** (the closing parshah of the Torah).

* * *

G-D ALWAYS HAS THE UPPER HAND

We cannot escape from G-d and His Covenant, with its privileges, responsibilities and its terrible sanctions. The stark severity of the message of ***Ha'azinu*** may cause discomfort among those in today's obese, irreverent world who seek a sweet, undemanding spirituality that complements and enhances contemporary lifestyle without causing any radical upsets. People are bewildered by the war, terror, crime, disease and other scourges afflicting us, but would like to see them as mere aberrations that should be able to be eliminated if only we could apply sufficient human ingenuity. ***Ha'azinu*** teaches the futility of trying to overcome these G-d-sent scourges without confronting the rebelliousness and deviousness in our own hearts. For G-d always has the upper hand. "For I am He, and there is no god with Me: I kill and make alive, I struck the blow and I will heal, and none can save from My hand" (v. 39).

"If only they would be wise and apply their intelligence to this, and understand their latter end. How could one chase after a thousand and two put ten thousand to flight if not because their Rock sold them and HaShem delivered them?" (vv. 29-30). How could it be that small groups of Nazis were able to uproot thousands from their homes and towns and lead them literally like lambs to the slaughter? How could it be that today a people that is not a people have the whole world dancing to their tune, while small cells of terrorists torment and demoralize the entire population? How can this be if not that it is G-d's doing?

If it is true that our sins as a nation have brought us great suffering, it must also be true that the stirrings of Teshuvah in our hearts will also prove to be the channel for abundant blessing and peace. Rabbi Nachman of Breslov taught that when Israel accepted the Torah, their essential wisdom lay in their willingness to throw away their own sophisticated wisdom and humbly submit themselves completely to G-d's superior wisdom. Rabbi Nachman brings proof from Onkelos' Aramaic translation of the verse in ***Ha'azinu***: "O foolish people and not wise" (Deut. 32:6) -- "O nation that received the Torah and were not sophisticated" (see Likutey Moharan I:123).

We cannot redeem ourselves with sophisticated ploys but only through taking the ancient, unglamorous path of Teshuvah -- honest self-scrutiny, remorse, contrition, owning up to the foolishness and evil in our own hearts and taking ourselves in hand in order to better fulfill G-d's commandments. ***Ha'azinu*** calls us to repent with all our hearts and come home to G-d as we stand before Him in prayer during these Days of Awe. Repentance -- Teshuvah -- is the hallmark of the true savior, Melech Mashiach, as personified in David, the messianic king of Israel. David came to complete the work of Moses in rectifying the original sin of Adam. The striking fact about David is that he sinned. His greatness lay in the fact that he had the courage to acknowledge it, and to repent. The true messiah is not a flawless, superhuman saint who rides on clouds of glory. He is one who -- on his level -- knows sin and knows the devices of man's heart. And he knows that only G-d can rectify.

"Cleanse me of my sin and purify me from my transgression... O G-d, create in me a pure heart and renew within me a proper spirit... I will teach sinners Your ways and transgressors will return to You" (Psalm 51).

As soon as we learn that there is no other way but to repent, we will be redeemed. And then: "Sing aloud -- O you nations -- of His people, For He does avenge the blood of His servants and render vengeance to His adversaries, and will make atonement for the land of His people."

VE'ZOT HA-BRACHAH

Torah Reading for Simchat Torah: Deuteronomy 33:1-34:12
Additional reading: Genesis 1:1-2:3
Maftir: Numbers 29:35-30:1

Haftarah: Joshua 1:1-18 (Sephardi ritual) Joshua 1:1-9

AND THIS IS THE BLESSING

*A*fter the succession of stern rebukes to Israel in the preceding parshahs, we finally come to the conclusion of the Torah, which is all goodness and blessing. Ve'Zot Ha-Brachah: "And this is the blessing with which Moses, man of G-d, blessed the Children of Israel before his death" (Deut. 33:1).

The last of the Torah's fifty-three parshahs thus completes the circle to make the perfect garden: 53 is the gematria of the Hebrew word ***gan*** = "garden". The Torah began with the creation of Adam, recounting how he was placed in the Garden of Eden, only to fall and be driven out. Similarly Abraham, Isaac and Jacob planted themselves in the Land of Israel, which is intended to be a garden of a land. But their children fell into exile in Egypt, and the glorious redemption and the Giving of the Torah at Sinai were followed by the making of the Golden Calf and the other sins in the wilderness. The purpose of all Moses' labors instilling G-d's law into the hearts of the people of Israel was to bring about the complete rectification of Adam's sin in order to enable his children to come back into the garden and enjoy goodness and blessing in their land forever.

The Kabbalah explains that G-d brought about the Creation through the concealment of His infinite light and perfect unity, leaving a seemingly separate, finite realm of lack and imperfection. This provides man with an arena of challenge where he can earn higher levels of connection with G-d through his own efforts. The flaw in the Creation is man's rebellious streak. When he succumbs to it, he intensifies the darkness and evil in himself and the surrounding world. But he is also vested with the power to repent and to overcome the evil. In tracing how man became separated from G-d and teaching him the pathways he must follow in order to reconnect, the Torah provides the complete remedy for the whole of Creation.

Having recounted man's sins and the resulting tribulations -- imperfection and disunity -- and having set forth the code of law through which man repairs himself and the world, the Torah ends with rectification and unity. "And this is the blessing. And there was a King in Yeshurun when the heads of the people were ***gathered***, the tribes of Israel ***together***" (Deut. 33 v. 1 & v. 5). All the different pieces finally come together again and everything returns to unity. The name Yeshurun refers to Israel in the aspect of Yosher, straightness and rectification. ***Ve'Zot Ha-Brachah*** speaks of the greatness of Israel and their destiny -- each tribe individually and all together collectively. "Happy are you, O Israel! Who is like you? O nation saved through HaShem" (ibid. v. 29). Nothing in the world can stand between G-d and Israel. Not only was He revealed to them at Sinai. He is even revealed to them out of Se'ir and Paran -- Edom, Ishmael and the other forces of concealment: "HaShem came from Sinai, from Seir He shone to them." (v. 2). Through the power of the Torah, even that which seems furthest from G-d can be brought back and reconnected with Him.

Although the twelve tribes of Israel are all unique, each with their different qualities -- multiplicity -- they all share a common destiny: to lead the world back to G-d -- unity. Thus, it says of Zevulun and Issachar, "They will call nations to the Mountain [= the Temple Mount], they will slaughter offerings of righteousness." (v. 19). Of Joseph it says, "He will gore the nations, ***together*** even the ends of the earth" (v. 18). Finally, all the scattered sparks will be gathered back together again. In the end, after all their struggles and suffering -- "And Israel will dwell securely, the fountain of Jacob alone, in a land of corn and wine. Indeed, his heavens will drop down dew" (v. 28).

Everything is in its proper place. Everything has been rectified. Moses' mission has been fulfilled, and as a mortal man, he too must die. We cry when we read of the death of Moses -- we cry over our own mortality. Yet we must know that eventually we have to die, for only through the death of the self can we be merged with the All-encompassing One. There are no exceptions to G-d's immutable law, not even in the case of Moses, who was the greatest of all the prophets. For failing to sanctify G-d one time in the wilderness (Numbers 20: 1-13), Moses was not allowed to enter the Promised Land. Yet selflessly, he brought the Children of Israel -- his children -- to the borders of the land, and all that was left for them to do was to enter and make their conquest.

Moses comes to the end, yet it is not the end, because life continues, and where the older generation leave off, the new generation pick up and carry on. After the death of the old comes the birth of the new. It is never the end, because as soon as we reach the end of the Torah, we immediately go back to the beginning and start all over again! This very continuity is the Joy of the Torah, ***Simchat Torah***, the day on which we complete the annual cycle of the Torah and begin again. Just as G-d is Eyn Sof – No End -- so, the Torah has no end. When you reach the end of the cycle, the circle is complete and you start again from the beginning. For the end is seamlessly attached to the beginning, and the circle goes around and around.

Thus on ***Simchat Torah*** the Children of Israel take all the Torah scrolls out of the ark and dance around and around the reader's desk in circle after circle, to indicate the endlessness of the Torah. You might have thought it would be impossible for finite man to have any connection with the Infinite G-d. Yet in His compassion, G-d has given us a way to connect with Him: through cycle after cycle of Torah study. Through each circle and each cycle, we expand the horizons of our knowledge of G-d, drawing down His all-encompassing light around and inside ourselves, becoming steadily more and more suffused with His unity, love and peace.

May we have the merit of studying the entire Torah time after time, cycle after cycle, until "the earth will be full of the knowledge of HaShem as the waters cover the seas" (Isaiah 11:9).

Made in the USA
Middletown, DE
30 December 2020

30418335R00186